Medical Negligence Litigation:

A practitioner's guide

STEPHEN IRWIN is a barrister practising from Doughty Street Chambers in London. He is a specialist in medical negligence cases and has written and lectured on the topic for some years. He also practises in the fields of personal injury, legal professional negligence and related public law.

CLAIRE FAZAN is a solicitor and partner in charge of the personal injury and medical negligence department of Bindman and Partners in London. She specialises in medical negligence litigation on behalf of plaintiffs.

RICHARD ALLFREY is a barrister and member of Doughty Street Chambers, specialising in medical negligence, personal injury, education, welfare law and other public law cases. He is a part-time chairman of social security, disability, child support and special educational needs tribunals.

Medical Negligence Litigation

A practitioner's guide

Stephen Irwin
Claire Fazan
Richard Allfrey

LAG Legal Action Group
1995

This edition published in Great Britain 1995
by LAG Education and Service Trust Limited
242 Pentonville Road, London N1 9UN

Reprinted 1996

British Library Cataloguing in Publication Data
A CIP catalogue record for this book is available from the British Library.

ISBN 0 905099 55 9

Phototypeset by J&L Composition Ltd, Filey, North Yorkshire
Printed in Great Britain by BPC Wheatons Ltd, Exeter

I don't want to be a doctor, and live by men's diseases; nor a minister to live by their sins; nor a lawyer to live by their quarrels. So I don't see there's anything left for me to do but be an author.
Nathaniel Hawthorne to his mother

Acknowledgements

In writing this book we have been given invaluable help and support from many colleagues who work in different ways in the field of medical negligence litigation. We would like particularly to thank the following for help, ideas and information:

David Body, solicitor, of Irwin Mitchell
Peter Bright, solicitor, of Geoffrey Stevens
John Hare, obstetrician and gynaecologist
John Holmes, solicitor, of Beachcroft Stanleys
Robin Oppenheim, barrister, of Doughty Street Chambers
Paul Rees, barrister, of 1 Crown Office Row
Rosamund Rhodes-Kemp, solicitor, of Russell Jones &
   Walker
Lewis Rosenbloom, paediatric neurologist
Arnold Simanowitz of AVMA
Gareth Thomas, obstetrician and gynaecologist
Oliver Thorold, barrister, of Doughty Street Chambers
Adrian Whitfield QC, of 3 Serjeants Inn

Special thanks are due to Marina Jacovou who has spent a considerable amount of time helping us with gathering together information and in typing and improving our word processor skills.

We must also acknowledge the enormous support and understanding we have received from our spouses and children, who must have felt there would never come a day when the words '. . . but I need to work on the book' would not be uttered.

SI
CF
RA

Foreword

BY THE RT HON LORD JUSTICE KENNEDY

When I was appointed to the bench more than a decade ago, one case in which I had advised years earlier, but which had not yet reached trial, was a medical negligence case involving injuries to a very young child. The real reason for the slow progress was that the solicitor instructed had, I am sure, never previously conducted a medical negligence case, certainly not one of any substance, and was understandably afraid of getting it wrong. This excellent work will, I hope, help to ensure that such cases are better handled in the future.

As the authors point out, lawyers should not embark upon medical negligence litigation without a sound grasp of ordinary personal injuries litigation, and if the case is of any complexity, it is bound to be of assistance if at least some of the legal team have experience in this specialist field. But even the experienced will find this book valuable. It sets out the basic principles of the law which has to be applied, and shows how to build up the case, from the moment when a solicitor is first instructed right through to the recovery of costs and the handling of an award after judgment has been obtained. There is also a chapter dealing with the medical inquest, and a look at the future, with some valuable appendices, including a checklist of records, a glossary of medical terms and case papers in *Brown v Barchester Health Authority,* which show how the principles set out in the text can be applied in practice. I look forward to the argument when the case gets to the Court of Appeal!

Meanwhile this book will surely be a valuable addition to the library of anyone practising in this field.

Paul Kennedy

Contents

Table of cases

Table of statutes

Table of statutory instruments

CHAPTER 1

Introduction

Now for my life, it is a miracle of thirty years, which to relate, were not a History, but a piece of Poetry, and would sound to common ears like a Fable. For the World, I count it not an Inn, but an Hospital; and a place not to live, but to dye in. The world that I regard is my self; it is the Microcosm of my own frame that I cast my eye on; for the other, I use it but like my Globe and turn it round sometimes for my recreation.

Sir Thomas Browne, *Religio Medici*

The nature of medical litigation

Medical accident litigation is both demanding and exciting. As with other professional negligence cases, the lawyer must understand two sets of professional expertise. He or she must grasp the essentials of the narrow corner of medicine involved in a given case and marry that received medical knowledge with legal concepts and language. That lends a complexity and interest to the medical case not always found in the conventional accident case.

Even compared with other professional negligence cases, the medical case offers more stimulation – at least to the taste of the authors. The subject-matter is inherently of interest to everyone. Not everyone employs an architect or requires advice on their investment portfolio, but everyone possesses a body and visits the doctor. What is more, almost everyone will need more medical treatment in the future than they have in the past. We love and fear doctors, and particularly surgeons. Despite our era of tatty hospital corridors, technology and Trusts, a faint air of 1 necromancy hangs around them still; there is a touch of the White Knight and there is a touch of the Magus.

These vague feelings translate into specifics when dealing with medical cases. We have written this book for those who act or who want to act for plaintiffs. The clients are patients, meaning by definition that they have been the passive recipients of the blows of fate and disease and of the interventions of doctors. Only rarely does a question of contributory fault on the part of the client arise, in contrast to almost any other field of litigation. The medical practitioners have been the agents, and whatever the event, must usually accept responsibility for it. Their position today in relation to their patients is, in reality, as powerful as ever it was. To adopt a phrase from another area of law, the relative bargaining power between the parties is usually very clear.

Other fields of professional negligence litigation are all about money. While legal or engineering negligence can carry great intellectual interest, such cases do not often carry the emotional charge and personal impact of the medical case, where the consequences of professional failure are often so swift, un-expected, personal in the extreme and devastating to the patient and to the family of the patient. While the medical lawyer will spend much of his or her practice thinking about money and quantifying claims, there is usually a sense that the financial aspect of the case is a necessary but secondary consequence of the litigation, not the heart of the matter.

Judgments about professional action are less certain in medicine than in most other fields. If a limitation date is missed, it is missed. If the loading calculation of a bridge is wrong, it is wrong. Such things may be very complicated, but in the end they are black and white. If, however, a surgeon decides to organise a scan of an insensible patient to see if there is a haemorrhage in the brain and where it is, rather than take him or her straight to theatre to bore a hole in the skull, the correctness of that decision is not black and white.

The primary facts are not usually in dispute, or if they are, the dispute is usually relatively confined. The medical lawyer will be fairly free of the wrangles about who said what to whom, and whether they meant it. In this regard the medical profession acts neither as knight nor magus, but recording angel, noting down their own sins, later to be cast up against them. This is very convenient for the lawyer.

In the end, whether a lawyer takes to this field of practice or hates it is a matter of personal inclination and capacity. The authors have found in it the fascination which brought Sir Thomas Browne, that great physician and writer, firstly to practise as a doctor and then to record his wonder at what was around him and inside him.

Entering the field

We have assumed that the legal practitioner reader of this book has experience of conducting conventional personal injury actions. Partly that is because this book has a sister volume, *Personal Injury Practice* by Hendy, Day and Buchan, which deals with personal injury actions, and there would be duplication if that subject-matter were to be covered again. Perhaps more importantly, we do not believe that anyone should attempt to run a medical negligence action, at least without close supervision, until he or she is a moderately experienced personal injury practitioner. To do so is to invite disaster. There are pitfalls enough for the lawyer learning to handle medical cases, without also having to learn at the same time the basics of personal injury practice.

When that experience has been gained, there are certain obvious further steps to take. The practitioner needs a small library, the contents of which we touch on in chapter 5. The less experienced practitioner should try to ensure that there is an experienced medical lawyer willing to be consulted when problems arise: if there is one within the same chambers or within the same firm, that will be easy. If there is no such resource 'in-house', then it is worth trying to make contact with someone in other chambers or another firm who will be prepared to help. Action for the Victims of Medical Accidents (AVMA) offers a lawyer's service and will be a very useful source of help, information and education. The plaintiff's lawyer should certainly join AVMA, and it is also suggested that the beginner joins the Association of Personal Injury Lawyers (APIL), if not already a member. APIL has a special interest group concerned with medical negligence. Between them, these organisations provide an enormous resource for lawyers in the field.

For barristers, the Professional Negligence Bar Association (PNBA) will also provide access to a very high level of expertise amongst the membership and a growing programme of continuing education. There is an annual weekend course, evening sessions during the year and, at the time of writing, consideration is being given to special help for those working in chambers without senior or experienced medical counsel.

Although many doctors will regard this panoply of organisations as a threat, the authors believe that the growing level of organisation within this specialist branch of the legal profession is wholly good. As people become more specialist and more educated within their specialism, they provide better representation for clients, they take fewer hopeless cases, they waste less time and they command more easily the respect of their opponents and the courts. In the end, better quality representation for patients is good for doctors too.

When equipped with the necessary books and in touch with existing experienced practitioners, the lawyer entering the field needs application and patience. The medical case is very time-consuming, particularly at the beginning. The first cases should not be rushed. If they are, then there is a high risk of mistakes. For this reason, the first cases will probably not be profitable. Thus it is suggested there is probably little point in taking on a few cases, unless the hope is to build a substantial practice. The authors hope they have made it plain how rewarding such a practice can be, once developed.

This book

This book has been written with a very specific readership in mind: solicitors and barristers who practise or wish to practise in the field, acting on behalf of plaintiffs. If lawyers who act for the defence in medical cases, interested lay people, or forensically minded doctors find the book of interest, the authors will be very glad. However, the primary aim in writing the book has been to attend to the concerns of the plaintiff's lawyers. They hope this has avoided the different levels of content and the different assumed levels of knowledge which might otherwise confuse the approach. For the reasons set out above, they have assumed knowledge and experience of the conventional personal injury action.

Even as it is, many lawyers turning to the book will be told things they already know very well. The authors hope this is not too exasperating: they know from experience as readers of other legal books that they would rather be told things they know than worry that things are left out, because it is assumed they are too obvious to mention. Again, readers can be reminded of things forgotten, and put right about solecisms which should never have entered their minds. And so, the book plays safe and makes the basic points, as well as the more sophisticated ones, without, it is hoped, being too didactic in tone.

The very highly specialised field of group actions is not dealt with, nor is there an attempt fully to cover structured settlements. It is indicated when and how structured settlements should be considered, and precedents are given that will 'hold the fort' while an investigation is mounted into the virtues of such a settlement in the given case; if a particular structure needs to be evaluated, more specialist texts exist to guide the practitioner through the process.

The contents and structure of the book are simply organised. It begins with the substantive law of medical negligence. There are much longer books dealing with the topic in a more academic or theoretical way, some of them covering the topic extremely well: this book tries to give a more concise but reliable account. Thereafter the chapters follow as closely as possible the steps in a case as it develops. Sometimes a topic, for example, interlocutory applications, can arise repeatedly during the development of the case – in such a case the subject is dealt with systematically in one chapter, but there may be references to the topic elsewhere in the text.

The chapter on handling the medical inquest is placed towards the end of the book, as it forms a separate element. Where a fatal accident claim follows a 'medical' inquest, the inquest will naturally come first, but it would be a distraction to place it early in the book. Nevertheless, the reader faced with a fatal medical case should not overlook the chapter because of its position.

Also at the end of the book, there are a number of appendices. Most of them speak for themselves and need no introduction here. We have avoided a multiplication of precedents for pleadings, since the authors have found them distracting and bewildering when encountered elsewhere, and since they are not particularly helpful in this field. There is no room for 'standard' medical pleadings.

The authors have tried to breathe life into the subject by creating the fictional case of *Brown v Barchester Health Authority.* The reader will find the case papers in Appendix 3. These papers, scrutinised and approved by doctors, represent a compressed trial bundle for trial on liability, and contain statements, a digest of medical notes, a cardiotocograph (CTG) trace, letters, applications, full pleadings, an initial schedule of damages, interrogatories and answers, and final medical reports ready for trial. The authors record again their immense debt to those people who helped with the creation of these case papers – they are named in the Acknowledgements. The judgment in the case of *Brown* is not included. The case is still undecided. On balance, the authors feel it is likely that the case will be lost on causation. The plaintiff's solicitors would certainly consider any reasonable offer.

Finally, for interest, there is included in the postscript the daily newspaper reports of the case of *Bolam v Friern Hospital Management Committee.* It is felt that this usefully supplements the official report in [1957] 1 WLR 582.

It is intended that the law should be stated as at 31 December 1994.

CHAPTER 2
The substantive law of medical negligence

There is a wisdom in this beyond the rules of physic.
Francis Bacon, *Of Regimen of Health*

Introduction

The aim of this chapter is to give a brief but clear summary of the substantive law of medical negligence. One of the themes is that it is rare that precedent will be decisive in whether a case has prospects of success. The legal principles which govern the medical case are relatively few; it is their application which is complex. The chapter indicates the areas where there is legal complexity or where the seeds of change in the law may be found.

History

The law of negligence is not new in its application to medical practitioners. For example, in *Everard v Hopkins* (1615) 2 Bulst 332, Lord Chief Justice Coke found that the plaintiff could bring an action for the negligent application of unwholesome medicines. In *Hancke v Hooper* (1835) 7 C&P 81, Lord Chief Justice Tindal found that the defendant, who was a surgeon, was:

> responsible for the act of his apprentice; therefore the question is whether you [the jury] think the injury which the Plaintiff has sustained is attributable to a want of proper skill on the part of the young man, or to some accident. A surgeon does not become an actual insurer; he is only bound to display sufficient skill and knowledge of his profession.

The modern law: the test of negligence

In 1957, the benchmark test of the English law of medical negligence was laid down by McNair J in *Bolam v Friern Hospital Management Committee* [1957] 1 WLR 582. (Extracts from the *Times* report of the case appear in the Postscript, p. 240.) His directions drew heavily on the decision of Lord President Clyde in *Hunter v Hanley* [1955] SLT 213, a Scottish case of the previous year. McNair J told the jury:

> . . . where you get a situation which involves the use of some special skill or competence, then the test as to whether there has been negligence or not is not the test of the man on the top of a Clapham omnibus, because he has not got this special skill. The test is the standard of the ordinary skilled man exercising and professing to have that special skill. A man need not possess the highest expert skill; it is well established law that it is sufficient if he exercises the ordinary skill of an ordinary competent man exercising that particular art.
>
> A doctor is not guilty of negligence if he has acted in accordance with a practice accepted as proper by a responsible body of medical men skilled in that particular art. . . . Putting it the other way round, a doctor is not negligent, if he is acting in accordance with such a practice, merely because there is a body of opinion that takes a contrary view. . . .

This test of law was given specific House of Lords approval in *Maynard v West Midlands Regional Health Authority* [1984] 1 WLR 634, *Whitehouse v Jordan* [1981] 1 WLR 246 and a number of subsequent authorities.

A good rule of thumb, followed by many lawyers in the field, is that if 10% of properly qualified practitioners in a given field would accept what was done as being reasonable, then it was not negligent, whatever the other 90% would say. Equally, if the deviation from the normal practice can be justified by reference to uncommon special expertise or scientific advance which has not yet been widely disseminated or understood, then it is unlikely such practice would be thought negligent. The matter is very well put in *Medical Negligence* by Nathan and Barrowclough (1957):

> . . . [the] medical man cannot be permitted to experiment on his patient: he ought not in general to resort to a new practice or remedy until its efficacy and safety had been sufficiently tested by experience (*Slater v Baker and Stapleton* (1767) 95 ER 860). On the

other hand the courts will not press this proposition to a point where it stifles initiative and discourages advances in techniques . . . a line must be drawn between the reckless experimentation with a new and comparatively untried remedy or technique, and the utilisation of a new advance which carries with it wholly unforeseen dangers and difficulties.

The 10% rule is nothing more than a rule of thumb. One must always consider the particular facts of the case. Indeed, it should be underlined that the *Bolam* test was a direction to the jury, and the decision as to whether the treatment fell within acceptable practice is a decision of fact. It is for this reason that it is necessary to stress that previous decisions are not precedent, decisive of the issue of negligence in any subsequent case. Each case turns wholly upon its own facts.

Some practitioners treat the *Bolam* test as if it meant that when two or more experts who are ostensibly qualified and responsible can be found to give evidence in support of the defence, that is conclusive of the issue in the case. That is clearly not the law, nor is it the way cases are decided in practice. In *Chapman v Rix* (1959) 103 SJ 940, Lord Goddard observed:

> . . . But I desire to add that if Lord Justice Romer meant that if a doctor charged with negligence could find two other doctors to say they would have acted as he did that of itself entitled him to a verdict, I could not agree with him if there was evidence the other way. . . If there are two recognised schools of thought on a subject, to follow one cannot be negligent, and this is what I prefer to think Lord Justice Romer really meant.

The speech of Lord Scarman in *Maynard v West Midlands Regional Health Authority* (above) carries the same meaning – the court must examine the evidence and evaluate the experts, and the weight of their evidence. If at the end of that evaluation, the defendant's actions conform with the practice of a *responsible* body of opinion, the courts will not find negligence.

A useful case to cite in this context is *Edward Wong Finance Co Ltd v Johnson Stokes & Master (a Firm)* [1984] AC 297. In that case the Privy Council found that the practice of the *majority* of Hong Kong solicitors was negligent. *Bolam* was not cited in argument or in the judgment, and the case is not a medical one. However, it would be difficult and inconsistent if the effect of *Bolam* were an absolute rule, as a matter of law, that practice supported by *any* substantial group of doctors *cannot* be negligent, when the practice adopted by the majority of the solicitors' profession in a relatively populous jurisdiction *can* be negligent.

There are some reported cases which appear to set express limits on the *Bolam* test. In *Hucks v Cole* (1968) 118 NLJ 469, the Court of Appeal warned that the practice must be inherently reasonable, however many doctors were doing it. This Court of Appeal consisted of Lord Denning, Lord Diplock and Lord Sachs, who all concurred in the judgment. In the course of his judgment Lord Sachs said:

> When the evidence shows that a lacuna in professional practice exists by which risks of grave danger are knowingly taken, then however small the risks, the courts must anxiously examine that lacuna – particularly if the risks can be easily and inexpensively avoided. If the court finds on an analysis of the reasons given for not taking those precautions that, in the light of current professional knowledge, there is no proper basis for the lacuna, and that it is definitely not reasonable that those risks should have been taken, its function is to state that fact and where necessary to state that it constitutes negligence. . . . On such occasions the fact that other practitioners would have done the same thing as the defendant practitioner is a very weighty matter to be put in the scales on his behalf, but it is not . . . conclusive.

In a much more recent case, the Court of Appeal has approached the matter in a similar way, albeit in obiter dicta, and in a curious way. In *Bolitho v City and Hackney HA* (1992) 3 BMLR 111 at 119 Farquharson LJ stated:

> There is no inconsistency between the decisions in *Hucks v Cole* and Maynard's case. It is not enough for a defendant to call a number of doctors to say that what he had done or not done was in accordance with accepted clinical practice. It is necessary for the judge to decide that evidence and decide whether that clinical practice puts the patient unnecessarily at risk.

Dillon LJ at p132 further complicated matters by saying that the court could adopt the reasoning of Sachs LJ in *Hucks v Cole*, but only if 'clearly satisfied that the views of that group of doctors were *Wednesbury* unreasonable, ie, views such as no reasonable body of doctors could have held.' At the time of writing, leave has been granted to allow *Bolitho* to be heard in the House of Lords.

It is difficult to make sense of this reasoning. It is easy to grasp that if a practice is condoned by a responsible body of practitioners in the relevant field, it cannot be negligent. It is also easy to accept the theory that if the defendant in a given case has done something wholly unreasonable, then it would be negligent, even though a responsible body of doctors would condone it. It is more difficult to think of a practical example of an unreasonable act which would nevertheless be condoned by a responsible body of doctors. It is more difficult still to reconcile the way the test is put in *Bolitho*; what is implied by the additional requirement that the judge should decide 'whether that clinical practice puts the patient unnecessarily at risk'? Does it mean that the judge decides that for himself, having listened to all the experts? If that is so, the *Bolam* test is a dead letter and negligence in this field falls to be decided as it would be decided in any other professional field.

In the meantime, the only approach which the practitioner can adopt with any confidence is to follow the mainstream of cases wholly in line with the conventional application of the *Bolam* test. The application of the *Bolam* principle has been reported in far too many cases to sumarise them here. Indeed, for the reasons set out above, the wisdom of even the most erudite attempt to summarise the application of the *Bolam* standard to each field of medical, surgical or dental practice is questionable. It is a great mistake for the lawyer to consider that he knows what the *Bolam* standard is in any case until he is confident he has been advised thoroughly and carefully by proper experts in full knowledge of the precise facts of the case under consideration.

The significance of the authorities where *Bolam* has been affirmed is to underscore its general acceptance and broad application, and to give some guidance as to how it may properly be applied and understood. In that light (in addition to *Maynard v West Midlands Regional Health Authority* [1984] 1 WLR 634), *Sidaway v Board of Governors of the Bethlem Royal Hospital and the Maudsley Hospital* [1985] AC 871, *Wilsher v Essex Area Health Authority* [1987] QB 730, *Gold v Haringey Health Authority* [1988] QB 481, *Knight v Home Office* [1990] 3 All ER 237 and other recent English authorities reported in the specialist reports and journals may properly be understood as illustrative of the vigour of the *Bolam* test, but no more than generally informative as to its particular application.

Contractual duty of care

The contract which arises between the private patient and doctor or surgeon certainly implies the *Bolam* duty of care. In most cases, there will be no distinction, or no significant distinction, between the duty owed under the contract and that which may arise in tort at common law.

However, depending on the evidence in the case, it may be possible to claim that there was a higher duty of care owed to the private patient. If, for example, a patient has been drawn to use an expensive private clinic, and to be treated by surgeons nominated by the clinic, by reason of advertising which suggests that the clinic only uses surgeons of the highest possible expertise, then it is at least arguable that the duty of care is much higher than the minimalist *Bolam* standard. This proposition appears to be supported by dicta of Lord Donaldson MR in *Hotson v East Berkshire Health Authority* [1987] 1 All ER 210 at 216. The case of *McLeish v Amoo-Gottfried* (1993) *Times* 13 October should be borne in mind if pleading any case with an alleged special duty, and perhaps in any private case. This case is analysed at p 149 in chapter 14 on damages.

Who owes the duty of care?

It is axiomatic that the doctor, surgeon, dentist, nurse or paramedic owes a duty of care when treating a patient. However, there are situations of contact with the patient when the duty is not or may not be owed. In *M v Newham LBC* [1994] 2 WLR 534, the Court of Appeal (Sir Thomas Bingham MR dissenting) held that the duty of a doctor examining a child in connection with an investigation into alleged sexual abuse was limited to (a) respecting the confidences of the child and (b) 'not to cause harm in the course of the examination or treatment'. A similar situation may arise when a doctor is examining a patient on behalf of an insurance company. The doctor is certainly under no duty to treat the examinee, and certainly is under a duty not to harm him or her positively. But is the doctor under a legal duty to warn the examinee of some sinister sign which needs urgent investigation? It would be interesting to see if the courts would apply a *Bolam* test to the ambit of duty as well as the standard of care, if such a case arose.

It is established now that a health authority carries vicarious liability for all medical, surgical, nursing or paramedical staff of whatever grade. This was in doubt in the early period of the existence of the National Health Service, but such liability was stated to exist by Lord Denning in *Cassidy v Ministry of Health*

[1951] 2 KB 343, and is never now challenged in NHS cases. It is presumed that such liability applies also to NHS trusts.

There is a debate, which is probably academic, as to whether a health authority or trust carries a non-delegable duty of care to ensure that care is taken by its staff. The proposition is untested in the English courts, but such a duty has been established in Australia; see *Ellis v Wallsend District Hospital* [1990] 2 Med LR 103.

It seems likely that there is some direct liability on the part of a hospital authority which fails to provide adequate standards of staff for the service undertaken; see *Wilsher v Essex AHA* [1986] 3 All ER 801, per Browne-Wilkinson VC at page 833. Clearly a hospital authority can be liable directly, as any corporate body may be, if the system of work damages employees or if the general conditions damage visitors such as patients.

The situation as to vicarious liability is different in the context of private medicine. Put simply, the patient enters into a contract with the surgeon or the physician who is engaged to treat the patient. No vicarious liability arises on the part of the hospital, unless the surgeon or doctor is provided by the hospital in pursuance of a contract with the hospital. There probably is vicarious liability, for example, where it is alleged that a junior doctor in residence in the hospital was negligent. Equally, the nursing and paramedical staff are provided by the hospital for the care of the patient, and the hospital is paid by the patient or on behalf of the patient, for the services of the nurses. In such circumstances, vicarious liability will arise.

As is stressed in chapter 11 on pleading, it is essential to take a cautious approach in cases of private medicine. Where vicarious liability may be in doubt, it is essential to sue any doctor by name, even if it is thought there *is* vicarious liability.

There is one other circumstance where the hospital or health authority or trust should be sued on the basis of direct duty. This should be done if there is any question of a 'resources' defence, ie, that the failure of care arose from a lack of money or resources to provide the necessary service. This point is dealt with below.

The principles of causation and damage

These principles will be familiar to any civil lawyer. However negligent the doctor, no action can be successful unless the negligence causes damage or injury. If the negligence made no difference to the outcome of the disease, there is no cause of action. The standard to which all points need to be proved is that of natural probability.

The conventional doctrine of causation in medical cases is that there is no recovery for the loss of a prospect of recovery if the chance of that recovery was less than probable. In *Hotson v East Berkshire Health Authority* [1987] AC 750, the House of Lords restated that once it is established, on a balance of probabilities, that the damage was caused by the negligence, then the plaintiff recovers in full even if his natural chances of regaining full health, setting aside the effects of the negligence, would be far less than 100%. The corollary is that if, given proper treatment, the plaintiff's chances of avoiding the damage complained of were less than 50%, then he has no action because those chances were reduced to nil by negligence. This approach was supported by the House of Lords in *Wilsher v Essex Area Health Authority* [1988] AC 1074, to which we return below.

In the light of that test, it will be obvious how the estimation of prospects of recovery or the prospects of avoiding death or injury takes on predominating importance in many cases. This exercise has to be gone through firstly on the assumption that the allegedly negligent acts did happen and then on the assumption that they did not. If the prospects of injury or recovery lie on the same side of probability whichever assumption is made, then there is no action. The medicine of such calculations is often of forbidding difficulty. Would the baby probably have survived without brain injury if delivered by Caesarean section by a given time instead of allowed to proceed to assisted vaginal delivery by some later time? The obstetric experts will often differ as to when and how the *Bolam* line was crossed, even where they agree there was negligence. Thus, the situation is evidentially complicated even where there is only one cause of the damage, and the question is whether treatment of an acceptable standard would have prevented the damage.

The situation can be even more problematic where there are alternative or compound causes of the damage. Let us suppose that the paediatric experts, thinking of a brain-damaged child, consider that there is a probability, but not a certainty, that the brain damage arose from hypoxic damage around the time of birth. The alternatives to perinatal hypoxic damage are some unknown genetic cause or some unknown incident during earlier pregnancy. They will always be reluctant to quantify the relative probabilities in terms of percentage chance. In the same case, let us suppose the obstetric experts vary as to whether the baby should have been delivered 20 minutes or 45 minutes earlier than in fact he was.

Considering causation on such facts is quite common in medical cases. It can be an almost impossible task, in which the search for probability is quite artificial. Yet if the case is to be presented as being within the conventional test, the practitioner must try to establish that 'probably but for' the negligence the damage would not have happened.

On our example, that requires

a) a mathematical estimate of the relative likelihood of this damage arising from perinatal asphyxia as opposed to any other cause,
b) a decision as to when the last acceptable time was at which the baby should have been born, and
c) a mathematical estimate of the relative likelihood that birth by that time would have prevented the damage if it was caused by perinatal asphyxia.

However difficult and unpalatable it may be to the experts, logic dictates that only by a quantification of chances can probability be established in any case. In the last analysis, an opinion that X was the probable cause of Y is a mathematical proposition, albeit a simple one.

In practice, experts will be most reluctant to conduct this kind of exercise. Almost always the medical reaction is to condemn estimating any precise percentages of likelihood as spurious. They will commonly be brought to a conclusion ('I think the baby would have been undamaged if delivered by noon'), but they will commonly refuse to analyse their conclusion mathematically ('There is a 20% chance of the damage being caused before delivery and a 10% chance that perinatal asphyxia would have damaged the baby even if delivered by noon, and therefore a 70% chance that the baby would have been undamaged if delivered by noon').

It is important to recognise that the probability test *can* operate relatively simply in cases of compound or alternative causes of damage. If a given outcome for a patient depends on *both* (a) a disease and (b) a failure to treat a disease adequately, then the failure to treat the disease was causative of damage if the consequences of the disease could probably have been arrested or mitigated by the treatment. It is usually more helpful to experts, when discussing the law of probable cause in such a case, to use the negative formulation – 'but for the inadequate treatment, would any damage probably have resulted and if so, what damage?'

The phrase 'made a material contribution' to the damage arises in *Hotson v East Berkshire Health Authority* [1987] AC 750, HL and in all the other leading cases, and is a great cause of confusion, by reason of its potential or actual ambiguity. It is used as a secondary formulation to the term 'caused', which understandably encourages the bold to think it means something different from 'caused'. The authors believe that, within mainstream judicial thinking, it does not avoid the need to prove that the negligence was the probable cause of the damage. It is usually a convenient way of dealing with negligence which was one of the compound causes of damage, without in any way weakening the requirement that the damage would probably not have resulted but for the negligence.

It is useful to illustrate the point by considering the facts of *Hotson*. The plaintiff was a boy who fell out of a tree and fractured the top end of his thigh. Such a fracture usually grossly disrupts the blood supply to the top of the thigh bone. It is that part of the bone which is responsible for growth, and if the relevant part of the bone dies through lack of blood supply, that leg will grow no more. Surgery is essential in such a case, within a very short time, in order to try and improve the blood supply so as to maximise the chances of avoiding bone death.

The surgeons were negligent and delayed surgery until four days after the fall. The experts were driven to quantify the relative chances of avoiding bone death (a) if the surgery had been done as quickly as it should, and (b) given the actual delay. The judge found that the relative chances were (a) a 25% prospect of avoiding bone death if surgery was done quickly, and (b) a nil prospect of avoiding bone death by surgery carried out after four days. He awarded the plaintiff 25% of the damages appropriate to compensate him fully. The defendants appealed.

It is important in understanding the case to record that the plaintiff's counsel advanced their case by stating they accepted the 'probability' test. They said that they had proved negligence, and that they had proved probability of damage – the damage being that the plaintiff had lost a 25% prospect of avoiding bone death. While admiring their conceptual clarity, the authors believe this was a distinction without a difference. We return to the point below.

The defendants' appeal was successful. The plaintiff received no damages in respect of his lost chances of avoiding bone death, *because they were less than 50%*. Yet the House of Lords continued to employ and approve the phrase 'made a material contribution to' the damage as being an appropriate foundation for causation. If the phrase could mean that surgical negligence 'made a material contribution' to the damage, by extinguishing the chance of 25% recovery, the House of Lords should have decided the case in favour of the plaintiff.

There are some authorities which swim against the tide of the 'but for' test of causation. The best known case is *McGhee v National Coal Board* [1973] 1 WLR 1. The facts are well known, and if any argument turns upon the case it needs to be read in full. In the very briefest summary, the plaintiff contracted dermatitis from exposure to brick dust. There was no argument that the dust caused the disease, and that he got the dust from work. The only negligence proved against his employers was that they failed to provide him with washing facilities so that he could wash off the dust before travelling home. Thus his exposure during the working day was not the consequence of negligence, but the continued presence of dust on his skin on his way home was negligently caused.

The experts were unable to quantify the relative contributions of exposure during the working day and the continued contact on the way home. They could not say whether the prolonged contact at the end of the day was the straw that broke the camel's back. The House of Lords held that in such circumstances, it was for the employer to show that the negligently caused exposure was not the probable cause and/or did not make 'a material contribution'.

It is the authors' view, with great respect to the many distinguished commentators on *McGhee*, that it cannot really be reconciled with the majority of authorities on personal injury causation. Other courts (notably the House of Lords in *Wilsher v Essex Area Health Authority* [1988] AC 1074) have tried to explain away *McGhee* in various ways, but in the end Lord Reid can only be taken to mean what he said, which was that where the proportional contribution to damage could not be established, and defendant employers were responsible for all the possible causes of damage, tortious and non-tortious, then it is for the defendants to show that the damage would not have occurred apart from their fault.

So far as the authors are aware, *McGhee* has never been followed in a medical case. However, there are some interesting authorities which are inconsistent with the pure 'but for' test promulgated in *Hotson*. In *Clark v MacLennan* [1983] 1 All ER 416, the court reduced personal injury damages to reflect the background risk, which amounted to less than probability, that the plaintiff might have suffered the damage in question without the tort.

The authors are not convinced that there will be any change from the 'but for' test, despite the difficulties which it produces in practice. Such change might be even more confusing. If a plaintiff could succeed in obtaining 30% of the damages where s/he could show that the negligence probably caused him or her to lose a 30% chances of avoiding the damage complained of, then what would be the corollary? Could a defendant restrict the damages to 70% where a plaintiff could only show that the negligence converted a 70% chance that the damage could be avoided to nil? What if the negligence converted a 70% chance of avoiding the damage into a 40% chance, and the plaintiff suffered the damage – should the plaintiff get 70% compensation or 30% compensation? In those circumstances 30% would seem to be logical, once the courts move away from an all-or-nothing approach. If that were the law, plaintiffs would only be fully compensated where they could prove that the negligence converted a 100% chance of recovery to nil. Where would be the threshold below which no action was possible? Could a plaintiff sue for 1% of the damage where a 1% chance of cure was negligently lost?

Is there any justification for distinguishing between the plaintiff who, through negligence, has probably lost a chance of 25% of escaping damage, and the plaintiff who can demonstrate a 25% chance that he was negligently treated, where the treatment actually deprived him of a probable prospect of escaping damage? The probable outcome for each plaintiff was exactly the same.

It should be noted that where 'primary' damage is established, the plaintiff can recover for 'secondary' consequences which have not yet occurred and are less than probable. Damages are regularly recovered for a risk less than probability that the plaintiff will develop osteoarthritis in the future. Conceptually, there is a conflict with the application of the probability test to primary damage. In practical terms, compensation for the loss of chances of avoiding secondary damage or loss makes good sense and is usually the just outcome.

As was indicated at the outset, causation is very troublesome in the field of medical litigation, and part of that difficulty arises from the law. Thus the law of causation has received fairly extensive treatment in this chapter. In the end, however, the authors believe that the *Hotson* test will survive. No more complex approach is likely to gain favour with the judges. The probability test should be the touchstone for the practitioner thinking about any medical negligence case.

Res ipsa loquitur: system and resources

It sometimes emerges in a case that the experts cannot say precisely what went wrong, but that something must have gone wrong, and negligently wrong, to explain the outcome. It can also emerge that the real problem, on close examination of the facts, is that the defendants (usually a hospital) were under-resourced. These are separate points, but may often arise in the same case. It is therefore convenient to treat them together.

The maxim 'res ipsa loquitur' is classically defined to mean that a prima facie case has been proved which is such as to shift the onus of proof onto the defendant, to some degree; see *Woods v Duncan and Others* [1946] AC 401. Essentially, it is an evidential principle, whereby the court is invited to infer that the result could not have been achieved without (for our purposes) negligence. This principle has been applied in medical cases, despite judicial dicta that it should not 'save in an extreme case'; see *Hucks v Cole* (1968) 112 SJ 483. Two examples of the application of the principle are its adoption by the Court of Appeal in *Cassidy v Ministry of Health* [1951] 2 KB 343, and also by the Court of Appeal in *Bull and Another v Devon Area Health Authority* (1993) 4 Med LR 117, although Stuart-Smith LJ remarked in *Delaney v Southmead Health Authority* (1992) 9 June, CA that 'For my part I am doubtful whether [the maxim] is of much assistance in a case of medical negligence, at any rate when all the evidence in the case has been adduced.'

The principle must not be relied on or pleaded as a substitute for proper analysis of the case. However, where there are a number of possibilities, all, or almost all, of which involve negligence, but the plaintiff cannot prove the probability of any one of the various possibilities, then the use of the maxim is appropriate.

The common usage of the word 'negligence' implies that some individual or individuals have failed through lack of effort. We have already seen that in this field, a lack of effort or attention is not necessary to establish *Bolam* negligence. The individual may be energetic and attentive in the care of his patient, but lack the requisite skill. Equally, there is no need in law to establish that individual A or individuals B and C were negligent. If it can be established that the system failed, even though no individual can be identified who is personally responsible for the failure, then the action may still succeed.

A more difficult point is whether a failure which is regarded as unacceptable by all, in that the care provided was demonstrably below the standard of treatment which could be thought acceptable, can be defended on the basis that the defendants lacked the resources to do their job. It is remarkable how seldom this has surfaced in the reported cases. Perhaps that is a function of the history of the National Health service, which has been one of expanding resources. It may be that this will change.

There is a difficult complex of public law which touches on this point. The effect of *R v Secretary of State for the Environment ex p Notts County Council* [1986] AC 240 is that a health authority cannot challenge the governmental allocation of money by saying there is not enough money to do the job adequately. In *R v Secretary of State for Health and Social Security ex p Walker* (1992) 3 BMLR 32, the court refused to intervene to adjust the surgical waiting lists. It similarly refused in *Collier v Birmingham Area Health Authority* (1987) unreported, even though in that case the surgeon wished to carry out life-saving cardiac surgery on the boy patient concerned, and was prevented by a lack of sufficient ITU nurses, which led to repeated cancellations of the surgery. The boy died. Another public law case with similar judicial debate is *R v Secretary of State for Health and Social Security ex p Hincks* (1990) 1 BMLR 93.

In *Knight v Home Office* [1990] 3 All ER 237, Pill J essentially relied on a resources argument to find that medical standards in the Brixton prison hospital could not be expected to be the same as in an ordinary hospital. The *Bull v Devon AHA* case (above) contains considerable judicial discussion of this point, and the case is essential reading for any practitioner faced with this problem. The authors do not pretend to know how the courts will handle this problem when it arises in a case where it is unavoidably the crux of the case and cannot be sidestepped.

Warning and consent to treatment

This question is perhaps the most difficult in the field. On this topic, the courts have given bolder signals about themselves setting limits to what is acceptable medical practice, but have not done so in a clear and decisive way. The leading case is *Sidaway v Board of Governors of the Bethlem Royal Hospital and Maudsley Hospital* [1985] AC 871, HL. The five Law Lords who decided the case appear to have split three ways in their approach to the issue. Since the issue is so vital in assessing the prospects of other cases, the authors propose to try and summarise the three strands of thinking.

Lord Diplock took the purest *Bolam* line on the point. He found that the question whether an omission spontaneously to warn a patient of inherent risks in a proposed treatment constituted a breach of his duty of care towards that patient, fell to be decided by the *Bolam* test, without any qualification. If a substantial body of professional opinion in the relevant specialism and of suitable qualification believes that a given warning can responsibly be omitted, then it is not negligent to omit the warning.

Lord Keith of Kinkel, Lord Bridge of Harwich and Lord Templeman also regarded the matter as principally to be determined by the *Bolam* principle, but with a proviso. The proviso was that there might be circumstances where the proposed treatment involved a substantial risk of grave consequences in which a judge could conclude that, notwithstanding any practice to the contrary accepted as proper by a responsible body of medical opinion, a patient's right to decide whether to consent to the treatment was so obvious that no prudent medical man could fail to warn of the risk save in emergency or some other sound clinical reason for non-disclosure.

Lord Scarman dissented from the *Bolam* line taken by the others. He supported a moderate doctrine of 'informed consent' to medical treatment. In his view, English law should recognise a duty of a doctor to warn his patient of material risk inherent in the treatment he is proposing.

Lord Bridge delivered some *obiter* remarks with which the others appeared to assent, and which are important. He stated that when questioned specifically by a patient of apparently sound mind about risks involved in a particular treatment proposed, the doctor's duty must be to answer both truthfully and as fully as the questioner requires.

It follows that on this topic, the majority in the House of Lords placed two important limitations upon the application of the *Bolam* test. Firstly, save in special circumstances, there must be a duty on the doctor to warn of very serious possible consequences of treatment. It is important to note that the risk in *Sidaway* was a very small risk of very serious consequences. It is clear that the majority in the House meant that the law imposes a duty to warn of very serious consequences, even where the risk is very small. Secondly, if a patient questions specifically about the risk, then full and honest answers must be given, even if that may lead to a frustration of the clinical objective of the treatment proposed. There can be no *Bolam* defence to a failure to give a 'full and honest' description of the risks of a procedure to a patient who asks directly.

Naturally, good practice as defined by *Bolam* will also very often require warnings to be given before treatment is commenced. Indeed it is worthy of note that medical practice is changing very rapidly on this topic. More and more doctors and surgeons are warning more and more fully about the relative risks and advantages of surgical procedures and medical treatment. This is partly a matter of style and of generation. The cumulation of the obligations imposed by the law and of those imposed by *Bolam* acceptable practice will determine what warning must be given before treatment.

It has been emphasised how important it is to approach each medical negligence case on its facts. Principles of general application are of doubtful use in this field. However, since here the law intrudes and sets some of the standards, it is helpful to try and define some general principles.

The following formulations are cautiously suggested.

(a) No 'informed consent'
There is no doctrine of 'informed consent' in English law, as there is in some of the North American jurisdictions. For the most

part, what is said in warning patients, or advising them before obtaining consent to treatment, falls to be judged by the *Bolam* test: what is good practice? The courts do recognise that the warnings given have clinical implications: if every risk was described every time, far too many patients would decline suitable treatment.

(b) Patients' questions must be answered

If asked directly by the patient about risks or side-effects, a doctor must answer fully and truthfully, even if that puts the patient off. The patient who asks for information before giving consent must be given it and must not be fobbed off.

(c) Possible side-effects should be mentioned

If there is a common risk or side-effect, however minor, then good practice normally will mean that the patient should be warned of that side-effect or risk. There is a balance between the desirability of the treatment on the one hand and the risk of frightening the patient and the need to warn on the other. If the treatment is essential for the patient's health, then it may be acceptable clinically not to warn of minor side-effects. If the treatment is entirely elective (such as, for example, most plastic surgery), then good practice will normally expect full warnings before consent to surgery is taken.

(d) Slight risk of serious consequences should be mentioned

If there is even a very slight risk of very serious consequences, then a warning is required, save in special circumstances.

Assault, battery and trespass to the person

Administration of treatment, and particularly surgery, in the absence of consent, constitutes assault, battery or trespass to the person. In practice these terms are used at least as overlapping terms, although technically, assault is a putting of the subject in fear of battery, while falling short of battery. Trespass to the person is a generic term including both battery and assault. There are extensive discussions of these alternative causes of action in a number of authorities. See:

— *Chatterton v Gerson* [1981] QB 432, QB

— *Sidaway v Boards of Governors of the Bethlem Royal Hospital and Maudsley Hospital* [1985] AC 871, HL
— *Devi v West Midlands Regional Health Authority* (1980) 7 May (unreported), CA
— *F v West Berkshire Health Authority* [1990] 2 AC 1, HL

However, it seems clear that there will often be a defence to such an action that the doctor or surgeon was acting within *Bolam* principles in treating the patient, or alternatively within the proper limits derived from the judicial dicta in *Sidaway* outlined above. If such were established, then consent to the interference with the body would be established.

It is suggested that nothing is gained, in the ordinary 'consent' or 'warning' case, by alleging such additional grounds of action. There are judicial dicta which may be invoked to suggest that such pleading is excessive.

The situation is different where a non-medical motive may be inferred. For example, if there was a sexual motive for unnecessary 'treatment', the case for including this ground of action would be strong. There might of course be a balance to be struck between the advantage of placing the action on that kind of footing, where damages are at large, and the risk that the doctor's employer may choose to say that a sexual assault cannot have been in the course of the doctor's duty, thereby avoiding vicarious liability.

Damage to the unborn child

In chapter 14 on damages are set out the differing bases of compensation, between the claim for damage to a child which occurred before its birth, and damages in respect of a child who 'should never have been born'.

The legal basis for action by the parents of a child who should never have been born is straightforward. The medical failure complained of, whether of abortion, contraception or sterilisation, is a failure of treatment to the live adult, resulting in loss. However complex and indeed circular the computation of loss may be, the primary legal footing is conventional.

There is greater conceptual complication in an action by a child based on events before birth. Before birth, there is no legal person in existence to suffer injury or to sue. A foetus which is stillborn as a consequence of negligence can never sue. How then can the child sue? In respect of children born alive after 22 July 1976, a statutory basis for action is provided by the Congenital Disabilities (Civil Liabilities) Act 1976. The basis of the right to take action is clearly defined in that short Act. The test for action is a *Bolam*-type formulation, and it is interesting to see how the parliamentary draftsman rendered the common-law test into statutory language. Although there are limitations on this right of action, it is difficult to imagine circumstances where a medical tort causing injury to a foetus before birth would not give rise to a right to sue after the birth.

The common law has reached a parallel position as a consequence of *Burton v Islington Health Authority* [1993] QB 204. This is of academic interest save where the child in question was born before the commencement of the Act in 1976. For practical purposes, there is no distinction to be made between the statutory and common law actions.

Summary

In an avowedly practical book, it is appropriate to keep an account of the substantive law as concise as possible. For practical purposes at present, the *Bolam* principle underpins every case of medical negligence, and authority can rarely contribute to the decision whether or not actionable negligence exists in a given case. The issue of consent requires the most careful legal consideration, since it is the one area where expert advice may not tell the practitioner the whole story. The law of causation and its application can be very difficult.

There is one caveat. As observed above, the authority of *Hucks v Cole* and *Bolitho* could be used to suggest that if an action by a doctor is inherently unreasonable, then it may be negligent, even if it could be supported on a *Bolam* basis, although imagining many circumstances where a responsible body of opinion would support something that was unreasonable is not easy.

However, the *Bolam* test is coming under increased academic scrutiny and has been the subject of considerable adverse comment from very senior counsel in cases concerning compulsory treatment of minors and others under disability, and concerning the cessation of parenteral feeding of patients in a persistent vegetative state. The test is applied in England with greater deference to doctors' views and standard-setting than in other common law jurisdictions. It is possible that we shall see a change in the ambit and interpretation of the *Bolam* test.

CHAPTER 3
Legal aid and funding the action

> The man in the street is invariably afraid of the expense of professional advice on matters of law. He has a wholesome dread of the Table of Fees, and a firm conviction that lawyers' bills are 'ill to pey'. For him this book has been prepared.

The People's Journal Lawyer, *The People's Law Book*

It will be essential for both the client and the solicitor to know from the outset how the case will be funded. This chapter discusses the funding of the action and, in particular looks at legal aid and how the lawyer maximises cashflow during the duration of the legal aid certificate.

Legal aid

There are two types of legal aid cover which may be available to the client in a medical negligence action. These are green form cover for initial advice and civil legal aid for the main part of the investigation and the proceedings.

The green form scheme

The green form scheme enables those who qualify on financial grounds to get up to two hours' initial help and advice from a solicitor. To qualify the client's disposable income and disposable capital must both be within the eligibility limits at the time the green form is signed. In 1994 a client with no dependents must have had no more than £1,000 disposable capital and no more than £70 weekly disposable income to qualify.

If cover for more than two hours' work is required, the solicitor must seek an extension from the Legal Aid Board before the two hours expire. Those firms with a legal aid franchise will be entitled to grant their own extensions.

The green form scheme is not available for the taking of any step in proceedings, nor will authority usually be granted for cover to obtain counsel's opinion. It can, however, cover disbursements such as the cost of obtaining medical records.

Civil legal aid

In order to be granted civil legal aid an applicant will have to satisfy both the legal merits test and the financial eligibility limits.

Under the provisions of the Legal Aid Act 1988 s15(2) the rule is that a person shall not be granted civil legal aid for the purpose of any proceedings unless he satisfies the area office that he has reasonable grounds for taking, defending or being a party to the proceedings. The notes for guidance in the *Legal Aid Handbook* (published annually for the Legal Aid Board by Sweet & Maxwell) state that there are reasonable grounds to proceed if:

a) there is an isssue of fact or law which should be submitted to the court for a decision;
b) the solicitor would advise the applicant to take or defend proceedings privately, ie, if he had means which were adequate to meet the likely costs of the case or would make payment of the likely costs possible although something of a sacrifice; and
c) the applicant shows that, as a matter of law, he has reasonable grounds for taking or defending proceedings, ie, that there is a case or defence which has reasonable prospects of success, assuming the facts are proved.

Even if the legal merits test is met, legal aid may be refused if the benefit to be achieved would be outweighed by the likely level of costs.

As with other types of personal injury litigation, the applicant in a medical negligence case is allowed a higher maximum level of disposable capital than in other cases. Currently the maximum is £7,780 income (as compared with £7,060) and £8,560 capital (as compared with £6,750) (Civil Legal Aid (Assessment of Resources) Regulations 1989 reg 4).

A substantial amount of medical negligence litigation is and will continue to be legally aided. Throughout this book the authors have assumed that the reader either has a working knowledge of the legal aid system or will have access to the current *Legal Aid Handbook*. There are, however, a number of general points relating to legal aid which are worth highlighting and which should help the efficient conduct of a case and help to maximise income and cash flow for the legal aid practitioner. Where a particular point relating to a specific stage of a case arises, it is addressed in the relevant chapter.

The application

The application for civil legal aid is made by submitting the standard legal aid application form (currently form CLA1) and the financial application forms appropriate to the client's circumstances (there are different forms for those in employment, those in receipt of benefit, those who live abroad and children).

As with all applications for legal aid, the client's interests are best protected by a detailed and clear application, highlighting:

a) why it is believed that care may have been negligent;
b) why it is necessary to investigate the quality of care; and
c) how the client has been injured and suffered financial loss.

The application form should refer the Legal Aid Board to the appropriate sections of the applicant's statement, which highlight (a) why it is believed that medical care was negligent and (b) what the consequences have been. It is not safe to assume that the person dealing with the application will actually read through a statement which runs to several pages or will achieve any understanding of the complexities of the case.

If applications are prepared in this way, the risk of legal aid being refused in a meritorious case should be low.

If documents already exist which might lead the Legal Aid Board to conclude that there is no reasonable prospect of succeeding on a claim, the application should comment on these. For example, a post mortem report may recite that death arose from 'natural causes'. The fact that this does not preclude the death being negligently caused needs to be spelt out.

Particular points on financial eligibility

There are four points relating to financial eligibility particularly relevant to medical negligence claims which warrant mention here. These are:

— the maximum level of disposable income and capital
— claims for children
— claims for pensioners
— claims for clients whose capital or income has resulted from the condition which is the subject of the allegation.

Disposable income and capital

As has been indicated above, the applicant in a personal injury action is allowed a slightly higher level of disposable income and capital than other legal aid applicants.

Children

Children (including applicants over 16 but in full-time education or undergoing vocational training) are assessed for eligibility for legal aid in their own right and not on their parents' financial position (Civil Legal Aid (Assessment of Resources) Regulations 1989 regs 4 and 8). However, this is not the case for green form advice and it will, therefore, be the adults' resources which will be assessed to determine green form eligibility.

It must be remembered that where the claim relates to what is known as a wrongful birth case (see chapters 1 and 14 on law and damages), the claim is for the parent and not the child. Therefore it is the parent who is the applicant and it is his or her resources which are to be assessed in order to determine eligibility.

Pensioners

Where the applicant is of pensionable age and his or her annual disposable income (excluding any net income derived from capital) is less than the figure prescribed by the regulations, a specified amount of capital is disregarded in computing disposable capital (Civil Legal Aid (Assessment of Resources) Regulations 1989 Sch 3 para 14A). The consequence of this is that some pensioners are eligible for legal aid despite the fact that their capital exceeds the current maximum limit of £8,560.

Income or capital which has arisen as a consequence of the alleged negligence

In computing the income or capital of the person concerned, the value of the subject-matter of the dispute in respect of which the legal aid application has been made must be excluded. (Civil Legal Aid (Assessment of Resources) Regulations 1989 reg 5). Thus, in the case of *R v Legal Aid Board ex p Clark* (1992) *Times* 25 November it was held that money received by a litigant in connection with the incident giving rise to the legal dispute in respect of which a legal aid application has been made was not to be taken into account in assessing the litigant's means for computing the amount of her contribution. In that case the money received was a lump sum retirement allowance where retirement was on medical grounds as a result of the injury complained of.

Cashflow and legal aid

Payments on account

As the investigation and conduct of medical negligence claims can continue for several years, it is crucial that the practitioner maximises cashflow during the period of legal aid cover. There are several ways this can be done.

Once a legal aid certificate has been granted the solicitor can claim payments on account of disbursements by submitting a CLA28 form (Civil Legal Aid (General) Regulations 1989 reg 101).

After the certificate has been in existence for 12 months a claim on account of profit costs can be made (Civil Legal Aid (General) Regulations 1989 reg 100). For the financial year 1995/96, 75% of the claim will be paid by the Board, subject to a deduction for any previous payments made under the scheme. Regulation 100(9) of the General Regulations provides that payments on account made under the the regulation shall be made at the prescribed rates under the Legal Aid in Civil Proceedings (Remuneration) Regulations 1994.

It should be noted that counsel can also make a claim on account of fees under the same provision. For this reason it is essential that counsel is sent a clear copy of the original legal aid certificate in every case. An amended certificate is not sufficient, since it will not give the date of original grant. Without that date, no interim claim will be allowed by the computerised system.

When proceedings to which a legal aid certificate relate have (a) been issued for 12 months and (b) it appears unlikely that an order for taxation will be made for a further 12 months, and (c) delay in taxation of those costs or fees will cause hardship to the solicitor or counsel, a sum on account of profit costs or counsel's fees can be claimed. (Civil Legal Aid (General) Regulations 1989 reg 101).

Maximising income and reducing the impact of costs on the client

All practitioners, whether acting for legally aided or privately funded clients, have to have a constant eye on justifying work done. The prudent practitioner will always record time spent on the file as the work is done. It is also very desirable for counsel to prepare a note for reference on taxation, setting out an explanation and justification of the work done. This will maximise the prospects of recovery of those costs against the defendant and thereby reduce the costs to be borne by the client, either directly by way of solicitor client costs or indirectly through the impact of the legal aid statutory charge. Thus, when preparing attendance notes the solicitor should always have in mind the provisions of RSC Order 62 Appendix 2(2), known as the seven pillars of wisdom.

At the time of going to press no one really knows exactly what the impact of the new prescribed rates for legal aid work (Legal Aid in Civil Proceedings (Remuneration) Regulations 1994) will be. Potentially the impact on medical negligence practitioners could be great. A significant percentage of medical claims which are investigated are not proceeded with because it is not possible to prove either negligence or causation. In those cases, if a legal aid certificate has been granted, the costs are paid by the legal aid fund.

Where costs are to be paid by the legal aid fund in this way and where the certificate was granted from February 1994, the prescribed standard rates will be paid, unless the practitioner can show that a piece of work on the case, or the entire case, warrants payment at an enhanced rate in accordance with the new regulations. For this reason detailed attendance notes prepared with the provisions of RSC Order 62 Appendix 2(2) and the basis upon which enhanced rates will be paid under the Legal Aid in Civil Proceedings (Remuneration) Regulations 1994 in mind will be essential both for the preparation of the costs claim or bill and for any subsequent argument on those costs.

Another point for the legal aid practitioner to bear in mind in terms of maximising income is the possibility of seeking prior authority from the Legal Aid Board for expert's fees (Civil Legal Aid (General) Regualtions 1989 reg 60). The benefit to the practitioner of doing this is that if the expert's fee is not recovered at all or only in part against the defendants on taxation, it will be recoverable against the legal aid fund (Civil Legal Aid (General) Regulations 1989 reg 63). This obviously means that it will have an impact on the statutory charge and thus the client's authority to incur the fee must be sought. Indeed, any grant of authority will expressly refer to this requirement.

Some practitioners have experienced difficulty in persuading a legal aid area office to grant prior authority for expert fees because of the level of fee being sought. Where the fees are those of a forensic accountant, for example, it will undoubtedly smooth the course of the application if the solicitor seeks and refers to estimates of fees (including hourly rates) from two or three firms. However, such a process is completely unrealistic where the expert concerned is a medical one and where the opinion is not being sought because the expert gives the cheapest opinion, but because he or she is the best and most appropriate person to advise in the particular case. Where the expert's fee is on the high side the prudent solicitor should ask for an explanation of the calculations behind the quoted fee and should refer to this on the application for authority. Those solicitors who do not seek prior authority will find that an explanation of the calculation of fees is invaluable in justifying fees on taxation.

Limitations on the certificate

When legal aid is granted in a case of medical negligence, the current initial limitation on the certificate used by the Legal Aid Board is 'Limited to obtaining the appropriate medical records (including if necessary an application for pre-action discovery), obtaining independent medical report(s) (one per specialism) and thereafter to the preparation of papers for Counsel and obtaining Counsel's opinion on merits and quantum, to include the settling (but not the issue or service) of proceedings if counsel so advises.'

However, in some cases (particularly those for which legal aid has only been granted following an appeal) the limitation will be different and probably less comprehensive. In other cases where liability is not likely to be in issue, it may be possible to persuade the Board to issue a certificate at the outset covering all stages up to issue of proceedings and exchange of expert evidence.

There are few medical negligence actions in which a decision whether or not to proceed can be made on the basis of the advice of one expert alone. If it is clear at the outset that more than one expert will need to be instructed, it is necessary to specify on the application form (CLA 1) what types of expert will be required in order to ensure that the limitation is worded so that it will be possible to instruct each of them.

The limitation also now generally includes a costs limit, requiring the solicitor to report to the area office if profit costs, disbursements and counsel's opinion exceed the stated figure. The Legal Aid Board warns that a failure to do so may mean that subsequent profit costs will be deferred. An initial costs limit of £2,500 (or possibly of £5,000) is unlikely to cover the cost of obtaining records and the necessary expert opinion. Thus, either an increased limit should be sought immediately or a very careful watch kept on costs and an increase sought before the initial limit is exceeded.

The introduction of a cost limit on certificates means that it is now necessary to estimate the costs of the work to be done very carefully when applying for a limited certificate.

If legal aid is refused, the client must re-consider funding with the solicitor. If legal aid is granted, the next stage of the investigation into the potential claim can begin. This is considered in chapter 5.

Where the client is not eligible for legal aid

Many solicitors will be instructed by clients who are not eligible for advice under the legal aid green form scheme or for civil legal aid on financial grounds. The numbers of people who fall into this category has increased considerably with recent changes to legal aid eligibility.

Furthermore, solicitors will find that many clients who qualify for legal aid, but who are assessed to pay a contribution, regard a monthly instalment towards their legal aid throughout the duration of the certificate (which in a medical negligence claim could well be between three to five years) as too great a financial burden to carry.

These factors mean that solicitors in the field of medical negligence litigation (as with other fields of civil litigation) have to consider carefully whether there are any alternative methods of funding the investigation and action. For example, is the client a member of a trade union which might provide funding or does the client have legal insurance cover? Failing such alternatives, solicitors will have to consider whether or not they are able to offer privately funded clients any degree of flexibility in terms of payment of bills, whilst at the same time bearing in mind recent decisions such as *British Waterways Board v Norman* (1993) *Times* 11 November.

In that case, the Divisional Court reaffirmed the indemnity principle that if the party in whose favour the order for costs is made has not incurred any liability for costs, then nothing is recoverable under an order for costs. Mrs Norman was not eligible for legal aid in a case which her solicitors considered was strong and in which she was, therefore, likely to obtain an order for costs against the defendants. When she was successful, the defendants appealed against the order for costs on the grounds that Mrs Norman had no liability for costs to her solicitors and that consequently they could have no liability to her. The Divisional Court found that the solicitors would only have expected to have been paid if Mrs Norman was successful and obtained an order for costs and that, therefore, there must have been an understanding that they would not look to her for the costs if she was unsuccessful.

By the time of publication of this book it should be possible for solicitors to enter into conditional fee arrangements with clients in personal injury actions. However, it is understood that the insurance to cover opponents' fees if the case is lost will not initially be available for medical negligence litigation. Thus, at the time of publication, it is unlikely that conditional fee arrangements will provide a solution for the plaintiff with no source of funding for the action.

Summary

It is essential for both solicitor and client to know from the outset
how a case is to be funded. In the following chapters we examine
how a claim is prepared and conducted.

CHAPTER 4

The first interview and preparing to investigate a claim

Van Buren looked attentively into Stephen's face, and after a moment he said, '. . . In the meantime, shall we start at the head?'

They worked steadily, with a cool, objective concentration: each had a clear understanding of the matter in hand – the relevant organs, those that might be useful for later comparison and those that might be discarded – and words were rarely necessary. Maturin had been present at many such dissections; he had carried out some hundreds himself, comparative anatomy being one of his chief concerns, but never had he seen such skill, such delicacy in removing the finer processes, such dexterity, boldness and economy of effort in removing superfluous material, such speed; and with this example, he worked faster and more neatly than he had ever done before.

Patrick O'Brian, *The Thirteen-Gun Salute*

Introduction

This chapter will describe the steps to be taken before beginning investigation of a potential claim and, in particular, the preparation necessary for the lawyer before seeing the new client for the first time and the approach to the first appointment.

Identifying and understanding the issues

Establishing what is wrong

In deciding to seek legal advice, the client will usually already have formed the view that unsatisfactory care has been given.   37

This view may have been formed, for example, because the result of treatment has not been as expected or because the client does not understand what has happened and considers that any explanation that has been given has been inadequate. It is unlikely that the client will have any detailed understanding of what it is necessary to prove in order to pursue a claim for compensation in respect of that care.

On the initial contact with the new client it is advisable for the lawyer to find out the answers to the following questions:

a) What type of injury has been suffered?
b) As a result of what medical treatment, drug regimen or procedure was this injury suffered?
c) For the treatment of what condition was he or she undergoing this treatment or procedure?
d) When did the treatment and injury occur?
e) What does the client hope to achieve as a result of consulting a lawyer?
f) How will the case be funded? (Eligibility for legal aid and possible alternative sources of funding are discussed in chapter 3.)

If the client is seeking advice in respect of an inquest, the reader should refer to chapter 19.

Preparing to see the client

The need for preparatory research

Armed with the answers to the questions asked on the initial contact (see above), the lawyer can do some general research into the following in advance of the first detailed discussion of the case with the client:

— the original disease or condition;
— the treatment or surgical procedure;
— the current condition;
— the possible progression or consequences of both the original condition and the treatment or procedure.

The first step in the investigation of the claim is to take a detailed proof from the client. It is obviously advisable that this is done as early as possible in order to guard against the risk of the client forgetting the accurate detail of what has happened. The client's proof will be the basis of the letter requesting records, the instructions to experts and eventually of the witness statement that will be disclosed to the defendants. However, unless some preparatory research is done to ensure that the lawyer knows what questions need to be asked, it is possible that important questions will not be asked, or information which is crucial to the outcome of the case will be forgotten or ignored.

For example, because of embarrassment, ignorance, or cultural background, the terms 'tummy ache' and 'headache' may be used to describe any number of different types and degrees of pain. The first may cover anything from indigestion to acute pain indicative of a medical emergency, while the second can mean anything from a mild, transient headache to the acute headache which can precede a stroke. The solicitor must ensure that any medical terminology used by the client is accurate, otherwise confusion may result. Failing to get the client to give a precise and detailed description of the symptoms may mean that experts are not given information which will be vital to advice on liability or causation.

A failure fully to appreciate what a client has experienced may also prejudice the quantification of the claim, both because the length and severity of symptoms is not recognised by the lawyer and because the lawyer fails to perceive the psychological impact on the client.

Some solicitors find it helpful to send clients a questionnaire to complete and return before the first appointment. A checklist of questions can be helpful as an aid to gathering the background information referred to above. However, a standard questionnaire can never be tailored to the individual case and it is, therefore, never advisable to use it as an alternative to taking a detailed proof.

How to research

The information given about why advice is being sought will enable the lawyer, before seeing the client, to research which parts of the body may have been affected both by the original condition and the current condition. Although this may sound unnecessary, there is good reason for making this effort. For example, in cases involving a possible negligent late diagnosis of a condition such as cancer, the client may be unaware that symptoms complained of some time before the diagnosis were in fact the early signs of the condition developing. Thus before seeing the client it will be helpful to look up any relevant condition and treatment in a medical dictionary. Having done so, a basic medical textbook on the field in question should indicate some accepted treatment of the condition.

Although it will be necessary to refer to more detailed, specialist medical texts at subsequent stages of a case, it is not always essential to do so at this very early stage. There are many books written for the lay reader which can give the lawyer helpful background information. Those solicitors who are members of the AVMA lawyers resource service will be able to seek background material from AVMA. Useful literature may also be available from some of the organisations listed in appendix 13.

Doing this initial research will prove to be invaluable for the rest of the case. In time, the knowledge gained will come to assist with other cases.

The first interview

Remembering what has led the client to seek advice

The lawyer must bear in mind that the client has had an experience that has probably resulted in a partial or complete loss of confidence in the medical profession. As a consequence, the client may very likely be wary of other professionals, including lawyers.

It should also be remembered that many clients will be distressed, angry, grieving the loss of someone close to them or suffering from expectations which have been bitterly disappointed. It is important that the lawyer should appreciate this, since an understanding of the individual client's pain or anger will improve the lawyer–client relationship and the final quantification of general damages. This is not a field for the insensitive practitioner.

Lawyers who specialise in medical negligence litigation quickly discover that a complaint often voiced by clients is that they were not kept informed about what was happening to them or their family. So far as possible, it is vital to try and explain realistically at the outset what advice, action or result can or cannot be given or achieved.

The client will almost certainly expect immediate advice on whether or not there is a claim. The lawyer will need to explain that it is rarely possible to give advice on the merits of any claim until independent medical advice based on the records has been obtained. It is essential that the client understands what has to be proved in order for a claim to be successfully pursued and the steps and potential delays involved in doing so.

It is, however, usually possible to advise the client at the end of the first interview whether there seems to be enough evidence to warrant further investigation. For example, it may be obvious that there has been no significant injury or financial loss and so regardless of whether care was negligent, there can be no feasible basis for a claim.

Liability and causation

The substantive law of liability and causation was discussed in chapter 2. However, when preparing for the first interview with the client, and throughout the subsequent investigation of the claim, it is important to bear in mind what will have to be proved for the claim to succeed.

The separate issues of liability and causation are highlighted in medical negligence litigation perhaps more than in other tort-based claims. By definition, at the outset of the treatment, the plaintiff's condition was such that it warranted medical care or investigation. In order to succeed, a plaintiff must prove not only that the care or treatment received was negligent, but also that the injuries were caused by the identified negligence and not by the disease or accident which called for treatment. This must be borne in mind at all times when considering causation. If the damage could not have been caused by the medical condition, then the problem is easily solved. If the damage was caused by the underlying condition, then would competent treatment have meant that the disease or accident would probably not have caused the damage it did?

The client may be seeking advice because it is believed either that consent was not given for a particular procedure or consent was given without knowledge of all or any of the risks of that procedure. This also is discussed in more detail in chapter 2.

In the case of a client who believes that there was a negligent failure properly to inform of any risks before consent was given for treatment, it will be necessary to ask whether consent would still have been given in the face of full explanation (a) of the risks of having the treatment and (b) of the risks of not having the treatment. The assessment of what decision the client would have made has to be made in the knowledge of whatever pain he or she was suffering at the time and without the benefit of hindsight. In discussing the case and in taking the proof (see below) it is vital to reconstruct *all* the factors which will have influenced the mind at the time, and not merely concentrate on those which have assumed retrospective importance since the treatment is thought to have failed.

The client may be seeking advice because it is believed that a pregnancy could have been avoided or terminated had different care been given. If this is the case, it is what is known as a 'wrongful birth' case and, therefore, the claim is not for the child but, rather, for the parent. Instructions will have to be taken on whether in fact the pregnancy would have been discontinued or avoided and if so what this would have meant physically, practically and financially.

Generally, the proof or proofs should be full rather than compressed. It is always easier to ignore material which is in the end irrelevant than to divine material which is not addressed directly.

Taking the proof

The next task is the essential one of taking a detailed history of what has happened, including any relevant medical history. If the client is seeking advice about a failure to diagnose a particular condition, it is especially important to take a chronological history of symptoms and of every occasion on which the client consulted a doctor or paramedic about any symptom which might have been an indication that the condition was present.

If there is a possibility that the client may not live until the trial, the lawyer must ensure that the proof is signed in its initial form (even if it is handwritten) so that it can be submitted in evidence under the Civil Evidence Act 1968.

In every case it is necessary to know:

a) what the client told the doctor on each consultation, what was said to the client, what was diagnosed and what form of treatment, if any, was given. What response, if any did the client have to the treatment?

b) the identities of the medical staff seen on each consultation if this is known;
c) whether there has been a change of doctor or hospital and, if so, why;
d) the address at which the client was living at the time of each consultation and whether he or she was known to the doctor or hospital under any other name;
e) whether there were any witnesses present at any of the appointments or procedures and, if so, who they were and how they can be contacted. For example, if the claim relates to the management of a baby's delivery, the father may have been present during labour and delivery and may have a much clearer memory of the events than the mother;
f) any relevant medical history. For example, if the case is an obstetric one, it is necessary to know the details of any other pregnancies;
g) the reason the client has sought legal advice, including his or her reason for believing care has been negligent;
h) the ways in which the client believes he or she has suffered physically, psychologically and financially from the medical care provided;
i) whether a formal complaint about the treatment been made through either the NHS or FHSA complaint schemes. If so, what stage has the complaint reached and if completed, what was the outcome?

Warning the client about costs, legal aid and clawback

Clearly, the client must be advised of the risks and consequences of pursuing an action. Such advice must address at least:

a) the likely level of costs for investigating and then pursuing a claim (see below);
b) the risk to the privately funded client of having to fund the defendant's costs in the event of losing;
c) the potential impact to the legally aided client of the Legal Aid Board's statutory charge; and
d) the potential impact of the clawback of benefits on the level of damages recoverable.

On the initial contact and at the first interview with the client the lawyer must establish whether the case is going to be privately funded or legally aided. A legal aid assessment must be made.

Costs

If it is apparent that the client will not qualify for legal aid, he or she should be warned about how costly medical negligence claims are, to investigate and to run. It comes as a shock to lawyers and clients alike to discover that the cost of merely investigating whether or not there is a claim can amount to several thousand pounds and that the costs of running the claim will often far exceed the damages that will be recoverable.

For example, the total costs (including experts' and counsel's fees) of a claim of maximum severity, such as a claim for a child that has suffered brain damage and which settles immediately prior to the commencement of a trial, can easily amount to £90–£100,000 or more, *on each side*. At the other end of the scale, the costs of a county court claim involving two experts which settles immediately before trial can easily reach £15,000 to £20,000 per side.

Legal aid and the statutory charge

If the client is to benefit from legal aid, it is necessary to explain the statutory charge and how costs unrecovered on taxation will be deducted from the damages before the resulting net sum passes to the client. The client also needs to know that legal aid is unlikely to be granted initially to run the claim all the way to trial, but rather only will be granted to cover the initial investigation and will then be extended stage by stage.

Clients should also be advised that a change in financial status may affect legal aid eligibility or the level of contribution. Thus, the client needs to be warned that any change in circumstances should be reported to the Legal Aid Board.

Benefits clawback

It is important to warn clients who have been receiving benefit about the possible effects of the clawback provisions under the Social Security Administration Act 1992 and Social Security (Recoupment) Regulations 1990). This is discussed at length in general personal injury textbooks.

Additional information and support

If it is apparent at any stage of a case that a client could be entitled to and benefit from the support provided by any statutory authorities or voluntary agencies, he or she should be informed of this. For example, the client may not be aware that some form of home help, respite care, equipment or transport provision may be available through social services which may make a substantial difference to the quality of life for the victim and the carers. Similarly, a significant amount of help and support is available through various voluntary agencies whose work centres on particular types of illness or disability.

Set out in appendix 13 is a list of organisations which may be able to provide help and information. In addition to these, AVMA now has a client support service. Information about this is available from AVMA.

If it is apparent that financial benefits such as the disability living allowance are not being claimed by a client who may be entitled, advice should be given in respect of this. (This will be obligatory for those firms with a legal aid franchise.)

Complaints procedures

Systems exist whereby patients can complain about care provided by doctors or medical staff. However, the Wilson Committee is reviewing complaints procedures and its report is expected shortly after publication of this book. For this reason and because the committee's report may lead to broad change, the various complaints procedures which currently apply are not set out in detail.

Many clients may be interested in making a complaint. The possibility of doing so may be of particular importance to those clients who will not qualify for legal aid either on financial grounds or because the money value of the claim is so small.

Although current complaints systems are not designed to determine whether or not care was of a negligent standard, sometimes the complaint will lead to a formal indication that procedures were not followed; alternatively, it may emerge that following the accident the procedures have been changed. For some patients with small claims this will be redress enough.

For those who will not qualify for legal aid, a complaint may provide a useful indication as to the possible strength of a negligence action. For example, it may be indicated that it would have been preferable for treatment in the accident and emergency department to have been provided several hours earlier than in fact it was. Where it is believed that the client suffered a severe and permanent deterioration in condition over that period, such an indication may be sufficient for the client to decide to risk precious funds in investigating the cause of the injury.

Lawyers advising clients should ensure they are familiar with current formal and informal complaints procedures in respect of care provided by doctors and medical staff, whether in GP practice, NHS or private hospital. The client will need to know what redress may be available through the different systems and what the time limit for making a complaint is.

It may be helpful for the lawyer to make contact with the patient's local Community Health Council (CHC). CHC's have considerable experience in advising patients about the complaints procedures and will generally help them to make the complaint.

The lawyer should also be aware of the role of the Health Service Commissioner or Ombudsman in investigating administrative matters relating to health care and of the provisions of the patients' charter.

After the first interview

After the first interview, the history taken from the client should be put into the form of a statement and sent for approval, amendment and signature.

Forms of authority should also be sent to the client for signature. These will be required to authorise:

— release of medical records from doctors and hospitals
— details of employment and income from employers
— details of benefit received from the Department of Social Security.

If legal aid forms were not completed at the appointment, these also need to be sent to any client who is applying for legal aid.

It is always advisable to send a new client a letter confirming the instructions that have been given and what work will be undertaken as a result of those instructions. Rule 15 of Annex 1A of the Solicitors Practice Rules 1990 requires a solicitor to ensure that clients are at all relevant times given any information appropriate to the issues raised and the progress of the matter. Those solicitors with a legal aid franchise are also required to confirm in writing the advice given and send the client a case plan.

Investigating and running a medical negligence claim is lengthy and complex. For this reason, the authors believe that this should be explained in detail in this follow-up letter as well as at the first interview. As well as explaining the procedure, the letter should restate the advice given on costs. In the case of clients who will benefit from legal aid, the letter should repeat the explanation of the potential impact of the statutory charge.

Any time limit for commencing proceedings in each new case needs to be considered. Imminent limitation dates should always be diarised to ensure that they are not missed and some in-house checking system needs to be instituted to ensure that they are not missed in the future. Limitation is discussed in detail in chapter 10.

Thought needs to be given to whether the applicant will need to commence proceedings through a next friend under RSC Order 80 or CCR Order 10. If so, an initial decision has to be taken about who this should be. What is involved has to be discussed with that person and his or her consent obtained. If there is no one apparently suitable, the Official Solicitor may have to be asked to act. The role of the next friend is discussed in more detail in the context of commencing and pursuing proceedings in chapter 11.

Where the case is a death claim, consider on whose behalf the claim should be run. Is the person who has sought advice a potential plaintiff? If not, does he or she have authority to give instructions on the plaintiff's behalf?

CHAPTER 5

Commencing the investigation: pre-action discovery

'Yes,' said the man, 'but I am no longer obliged to hear you now.' – once more the muttering arose, this time unmistakeable in its import, for, silencing the audience with a wave of the hand, the man went on: 'yet I shall make an exception for once on this occasion. But such a delay must not occur again. And now step forward.' Someone jumped down from the platform to make room for K., who climbed onto it. He stood crushed against the table, the crowd behind him was so great that he had to brace himself to keep from knocking the Examining Magistrate's table and perhaps the Examining Magistrate himself off the platform.'

Franz Kafka, The Trial

Obtaining the records

Which records need to be obtained?

It is imperative to obtain *all* those records relating to the condition and treatment that is the subject of the investigation. It will also be necessary to obtain the client's records prior to and since that period, since these may contain information which is integral to the potential claim. For example, there may be a previous medical history which should have alerted treating doctors to this patient having a higher risk of an adverse reaction to the particular treatment under investigation.

Over a period of years some clients will have consulted numerous doctors and been seen at several different hospitals. If the complaint is not in respect of GP care it may be advisable to obtain the GP records before incurring the expense of requesting copies of all of the hospital records. If the GP records are complete, they will indicate not only the ailments for which the

48

GP has been consulted, but also what referrals and admissions have been made to hospitals and what treatment has been given.

Clearly, if what is being investigated is a failure to diagnose torsion of the testicle in a teenage boy, it is unnecessary to obtain the records which relate to an emergency admission to another hospital at the age of six when he broke his leg playing football. On the other hand, if the boy has been referred by his GP to a psychiatrist or child psychologist because he appeared to be depressed or had developed behavioural problems after the failed diagnosis, those records may be crucial in proving that he had suffered psychiatric injury as a result of the alleged negligence.

Many hospitals now institute an investigation into anything which they would describe as an adverse incident, regardless of whether or not there may be grounds for a patient to commence proceedings. Any letter requesting records should ask for confirmation whether such a report has been prepared and, if so, for disclosure of that report. The authors take the view that the documents relating to such internal investigations cannot be privileged, since the dominant purpose for which they will have been prepared will not have been for the purposes of litigation (*Waugh v British Railways Board* [1980] AC 521), but rather in accordance with usual procedure. So far as medical negligence cases are concerned, this principle was upheld in *Lask v Gloucester Health Authority* (1985) *Times* 13 December.

The procedure for requesting GP records is covered below. It is worth bearing in mind that, with certain exceptions, in respect of records generated from 1 November 1991, the client has the right to request access to his or her records under the Access to Health Records Act 1990. It is, therefore, worth checking with the client that no such request has already been made and if it has been whether the records have yet been received.

It is necessary to consider whether this is a case in which occupational health records or the records kept by health visitors may contain useful information. If so, ask for them. If the case involves a child, it may be helpful to ask for school records or assessments to ascertain whether academic performance has been affected by the injury. In the case of children with severe dis-abilities, it may be useful to ask for local authority educational statements if the parent does not have a copy. If the case is about the way in which a prescription was written or made up, it will probably be necessary to obtain a copy of the prescription from the Prescription Pricing Authority, Bridge House, 152 Pilgrim Street, Newcastle-upon-Tyne NE1 6SN.

The right to pre-action discovery

As with any personal injury action, Supreme Court Act 1981 s33 entitles potential parties to a medical negligence action to disclosure of documents likely to be material to the claim from other potential parties, before the action commences.

Those advising the plaintiff must identify what records need to be obtained in order to properly investigate the claim. They then need to identify whether they are in the possession of potential defendants, against whom pre-action discovery can be sought and enforced, or alternatively, whether they are in the possession of those who are unlikely to be parties to any action and so against whom discovery can only be enforced after proceedings have been commenced.

How to obtain records from potential defendants

Voluntary pre-action disclosure

In order to succeed on an application for pre-action discovery of records an applicant has to show that

a) he or she is likely to be a plaintiff in an action for damages for injuries and loss suffered as a result of negligent care, and
b) the person against whom discovery is sought is also likely to be a party to the action, and
c) that person is likely to have or to have had documents relevant to issues likely to arise in the claim.

Generally, health authorities, NHS trusts and doctors (whether consulted on the National Health Service or privately) are prepared to give voluntary pre-action discovery of records to solicitors, so long as a prima facie case for the entitlement to pre-action disclosure is made in writing. Consequently, any letter requesting voluntary pre-action discovery from a potential party should set out all that would need to be included in an affidavit in support of an application for pre-action discovery (see appendix 3B for specimen letter).

If voluntary discovery is not given, an application for pre-action discovery should be made and the refusal to give disclosure voluntarily should be referred to, both in the substantive application and on the question of costs (see section below on costs of the application).

It may still be necessary to make an application for pre-action discovery, even where it has been indicated that voluntary disclosure will be given or where it has been given. For example, there may be a long delay after the indication that voluntary disclosure will be given and it may be necessary to issue a summons in order to speed up the process and to protect the client's position vis-à-vis the limitation period. Similarly, disclosure of vital records may not have been given even though others have been disclosed. If this occurs, a summons should be issued requiring those specific records to be disclosed pre-action.

To whom the request should be made

Where care was provided by NHS or NHS trust As we have seen above, to prove entitlement to pre-action discovery under Supreme Court Act 1981 s33, the applicant has to show that the respondent is both likely to be a party to any action and has or has had documents relevant to issues likely to arise in the claim. The application should, therefore, be directed to the potential named party in whose control the records lie.

If the claim is in respect of care given in an NHS hospital, the letter should be addressed to the district manager of the health authority responsible for the particular hospital. If it is in respect of care at a trust hospital, the request should be made to the chairman or chief executive of the trust.

When requesting records from a trust it is always advisable to ask them to confirm whether, in the event of an application for pre-action discovery or proceedings being issued, the health authority should be named as well as the trust. This will be particularly important if the care complained of was prior to the creation of the trust.

If the care was given by a GP, the request should be made direct to him or her.

Requests for health visitor records should be made to the employing health authority. This is the case even where a health visitor's clinic is based at a local GP health centre.

The *Medical Directory* (published annually by Churchill Livingstone) provides a useful index of all hospitals and identifies by which health authority they are managed.

Where care was provided privately The request should be made to the individual doctor or, in the case of care in a private hospital, both to the manager of the hospital and to the doctor. It is important to bear in mind that the doctor will have separate notes which will not be stored in the hospital and that sometimes there will be important discrepancies between notes which ought to coincide exactly.

Application for pre-action discovery

Applications for discovery before the commencement of proceedings are made under RSC Order 24 r7A . This provides that an application for pre-action discovery shall be made by originating summons. The person against whom the order is sought should be named as the respondent on the summons.

The summons must be supported by an affidavit (RSC Order 24 r7A), which must:

a) state the grounds on which it is alleged that the applicant and the person against whom the order is sought are likely to be parties to subsequent proceedings in the High Court in which a claim for personal injuries is likely to be made;
b) specify or describe the documents in respect of which the order is sought;
c) show (if practicable by reference to any pleading served or intended to be served) that the documents are relevant to an issue arising or likely to arise out of a claim for personal injuries likely to be made in the proceedings; and
d) state that the person against whom the order is sought is likely to have or have had them in his possession, custody or power (see *Dunning v Board of Governors of United Liverpool Hospitals* [1973] 1 WLR 586).

Having regard to the purpose of the procedure, the phrase 'likely to be parties' should be liberally construed to include the case where the bringing of the action may depend on the result of the discovery, provided that the claim has a reasonable basis and is not irresponsible or speculative.

The affidavit must then be served with the summons on the person against whom discovery is being sought. A precedent of an affidavit is reproduced in appendix 3C.

On whom the summons should be served

The initial response to the request for records may have come from solicitors. As with any originating process, it should be checked whether they have authority to accept service of the summons or whether it should be served directly upon their client. In any event, it is wise to serve a copy set of documents on the respondent's solicitors, even where they require service to be effected directly upon the respondent.

The order

An order under Supreme Court Act s33(2) may be 'conditional on the applicant's giving security for the costs of the person against whom it is made, or on such terms, if any, as the Court thinks just, and shall require the person against whom the order is made to make an affidavit stating whether any documents specified or described in the order, or at any time have been, in his possession, custody or power and, if not then in his possession, custody or power, when he parted with them and what has become of them'. It should be noted that the obligations upon a health authority to make pre-action discovery do not include a requirement for it to provide an itemised list of every document disclosed (see *M v Plymouth Health Authority* (1992) *Times* 26 November).

The costs of and associated with an application

The normal rule is that the respondent's costs are paid by the plaintiff (RSC Order 62 r3(12)). In the case of *Hall v Wandsworth Health Authority* (1985) 129 SJ 188; *Times* 16 February, it was held that in a few cases the defendant's conduct in the pre-action disclosure proceedings would justify an order that he should pay his own costs and, in some cases, those of the plaintiff. The misconduct in the *Hall* case was delay in disclosing records to the plaintiff's solicitors.

What happens if the records are missing?

The reason given for the failure to disclose any documents or for giving incomplete discovery is not uncommonly that the records cannot be traced.

In order to be able to pre-empt or respond to such a situation, it is important at the outset to have ascertained from the client any names or addresses under which they may have been recorded, the hospital number, the approximate date of admission and periods of treatment, the name or number of any wards he or she was admitted to, and details of all treating departments.

If it is said that records cannot be traced it should be ascertained what searches have been made and whether all the wards and departments in which the client was treated have been searched. It should be also ascertained whether there is a system in the medical records department for signing out records to particular doctors and/or departments and, if so, the date on which the client's records were last signed out and to whom. If there is such a record, a request should be made for the search to be extended to that individual or department.

If there is a refusal to carry out such searches, it is unclear whether a master dealing with an application for pre-action discovery has jurisdiction to order that they should be, but the authors would argue that there is inherent jurisdiction to order this under RSC Order 24. Some masters have certainly been persuaded to make such orders. Unless defendants carry out thorough searches it is hard to see how they can properly comply with an order requiring them to serve affidavit evidence stating when they parted with documents no longer in their possession, custody or power and what has become of them.

County court procedure

The right to pre-action discovery in the county court emanates from County Courts Act 1984 s52 and the procedure for the application is that set out in CCR Order 13 r7(1)(g). What has to be shown to succeed on an application is identical to that which has to be shown in the High Court.

How to obtain records from non-defendants before proceedings commence

Since pre-action discovery can only be enforced against potential parties to the action, it can only be obtained on a voluntary basis from people or bodies who are unlikely to be parties to it. Often, once reassured that proceedings are not contemplated against them, health authorities and doctors will voluntarily disclose records.

Patient-held records

It is always worth checking with the client whether he or she holds any records personally. Where obstetric care is shared between GP and hospital, the expectant mother will carry what is called a co-op card on which notes about her condition and that of the foetus will be made at each ante-natal appointment. Some obstetric units are now providing women with a complete set of notes to carry with them.

If the client is on regular medication, such as drugs to control asthma or the risk of thrombosis, he or she may have been given a booklet to carry detailing the medication. If the client has retained these, it will be important to obtain them.

Summary

A meaningful investigation into whether or not care provided has fallen below an acceptable standard and what the consequences, if any, of that have been can commence only once the records have been obtained. How this investigation is carried out is examined in the following chapters.

CHAPTER 6
The records and how to respond to them

Not waving but drowning
Stevie Smith, *Poem title*

This chapter looks at what the practitioner should do with the records once they are received, whether by way of voluntary pre-action disclosure or as a result of an application for pre-action discovery having been made.

When the records arrive

Are they all there?

The first thing to be ascertained is whether the records that have been provided are complete. There are various ways in which this can be checked.

First of all, read through the records. Is the continuity or sequence interrupted in such a way that it suggests that a page or pages are missing? It may be that there has been a simple copying mistake and the reverse side of pages in the notes has not been copied.

On immediate examination, are the copies that have been provided complete and legible? It is not uncommon for the edges of pages to slip when being copied and as a consequence key details such as the dates and times of entries in the notes can be missing or incomplete. Similarly, sometimes the copying is of poor quality and the copy is too faint to read. In both cases further, complete and legible copies should be requested.

Next, read the notes in the context of the client's proof. For
example, where the client has been able to give details and dates

of appointments, check that there are records relating to these appointments. If there are no such records, does that suggest that the copy set may be incomplete or should the client be reproofed? Or, where a client has referred to a GP writing a referral letter to a hospital, is there a copy of that letter in the notes?

Having looked at the notes, consider again whether they are complete. Set out below are particular points which should be considered.

a) *Is there reference in the notes or the client's proof to tests for which there are no records?* For example, are there X-ray requests or reports, but no copy X-rays? If so, are copies needed of all or any of these? Does the client recall a histological test such as a cervical smear test being done, but there is no request form or report on the result in the notes? As well as requesting a copy of the missing record, should a request be made for confirmation that the original histological slides will be made available for inspection if the expert indicates that this will be necessary?

b) *Some types of records will be in booklet form.* For example, some hospitals use a booklet for obstetric records which will include the details relating to ante-natal care, labour, delivery and post-natal care up to and including discharge. If there are page numbers on any of the records, this may indicate that these notes are in booklet form. If there are numbers missing from the sequence, this may mean that the records are incomplete, or it may simply be that a blank sheet has not been copied. Whatever the possible explanation, the practitioner should check with the provider of the notes whether the numbers indicate that the notes are in a booklet and why there is an interruption of the sequence of numbers.

c) *Some types of records are not in their original form if on A4-sized paper.* For example, records from intensive care units are generally on large chart-type sheets. Other records which will almost always be on large-sized paper are prescription charts, obstetric partograms, and CTG traces. It will be necessary to have full sized copies rather than 'A4 chunks' since even if these are stuck together they may be incomplete and/or collated out of sequence. Consequently, information contained in them which may be central to the issues in the case may be missing or impossible to interpret.

d) *Compare the records with a checklist.* The authors have

included in appendix 1 a checklist of types of records which should be looked out for in particular cases.

Who should check the notes?

Some lawyers use someone such as a nurse to check and sort the records. This is a question of individual preference. The benefit of a nurse checking the records is that they will be checked by someone who is familiar with medical records and terminology. So far as the cost of employing someone to do this is concerned, it has recently been decided by the Legal Aid Board costs appeals committee that work carried out by an in-house medico-legal assistant will generally be recoverable as fee-earning work. They have said that, 'The hourly rate and mark-up applicable will be what is appropriate in all the circumstances having regard to the nature of the work carried out and the special skills and qualifications possessed by the person concerned.' (Decision No. CLA12, Status of medico-legal assistants as fee-earners, *Law Society's Gazette* 31 August 1994). Some firms use nurses to sort records who work on a freelance basis. In those cases, the fee charged by the nurse is treated like any other disbursement and will be recoverable if proved to be reasonable on taxation.

It is essential that lawyers become familiar with what medical records look like and with the detailed contents of records in individual cases. The fact that a nurse has read through the notes in order to sort them and check that they are complete should never persuade a lawyer that there is no need for him or her to read and familiarise him or herself with them.

The importance of this was emphasised somewhat brutally, but incorrectly, in the first instance decision in *Locke v Camberwell Health Authority* [1990] 1 Med LR 253. The solicitors acting for the plaintiff were ordered to pay the costs of the action because of a failure to note that the plaintiff's expert's contention that a particular drug had not been given (which should have been given) was contradicted by the records. The Court of Appeal reversed this order, having decided that the record concerned had probably not been disclosed before the trial. The Court of Appeal made some general observations about the circumstances in which a solicitor should be ordered to pay costs personally under RSC Order 62 and the extent to which a solicitor should rely on an expert and counsel.

Sorting and organising the records

The next step is to organise the records into a logical order. Individual practitioners will have their own preferred system.

The records should, at the very least, be sorted into chronological order within the separate types of record, for example, separate the clinical records, the test results, the charts and the correspondence.

In cases where the records cover a lengthy period and do not all relate to the condition and care at issue, consider separating the records relating to the condition or care relevant to the potential claim.

The copy records should then be paginated. This is essential because it means that the lawyers and experts involved in a case know that when discussing a particular entry in the notes they are referring to the same document. It is also a way of ensuring that all the lawyers and experts in a case have identical sets of documents upon which they have based their advice.

What to do if the records are incomplete

If the records seem to be incomplete, but it appears that it is only one or two identifiable pages which have either not been copied at all or which have been incompletely copied, a request should be made for new copies of these.

If it appears that there may be a number of records missing, consider asking for facilities to inspect the original records and check the copy set against them. This may also be a useful exercise where it is impossible to tell from the copy set what the sequence of undated pages of notes should be.

Generally such requests will be granted. If they are not, then an application for production and inspection should be made under the provisions of RSC Order 24.

If it is apparent there are records missing, it may be necessary to examine the original records. The job of checking copies against the originals may be harder after sorting them into a working order than whilst the papers remain unsorted.

It may be impossible to read handwritten notes or to get a legible photocopy of typed notes. If the former is the case, consider requesting a typed transcript. While practice varies amongst defence lawyers, many will provide a transcript without charge. If the problem is illegible copy typescript, and if the original is so faint that it will not copy legibly, inspection will mean that the lawyer can prepare a transcript of the note in question.

It is clearly in both sides' interests (in particular in terms of saving costs) that documents disclosed by way of pre-action discovery can be easily understood. Thus, if a document is illegible the defendant may well agree to a request for a typed transcript, but may require the administrative costs of producung this to be paid. If such a request is refused, arguably an application could be made under the provisions of RSC Order 24 r13, which provides that no order for production or inspection shall be made by the court unless it is of the opinion that the order is necessary for disposing fairly of the matter or for the saving of costs. That said, there is no obligation on a party giving discovery of a document in a foreign language to provide a translation (*Bayer AG v Harris Pharmaceuticals Ltd* [1991] FSR 170) and perhaps the same argument could be used by defendants objecting to the production of a typed transcript.

Reading and understanding the records

Having obtained a complete set of records and sorted them into logical and chronological sequence, the practitioner must now read and understand the records in detail.

This means grappling not just with bad handwriting, but with terms and abbreviations which, hitherto, have been quite unfamiliar. This may mean relying heavily on a medical dictionary, on the lists of commonly used abbreviations (see appendix 2) and possibly on more specialised texts on the particular area of medicine and/or a book on anatomy. The daily nursing notes and the correspondence in the records can often be a simple way of understanding the more abbreviated, and generally handwritten, clinical notes.

To understand the notes and to enable the plaintiff's case to be considered in the light of their contents, it is frequently helpful to prepare a chronology of events. Such a chronology can cross-refer the contents of notes from various sources and also the client's recollection of events. As well as being a useful aid for the practitioner in beginning to understand the case, the chronology prepared at this stage will usually take on a life of its own and form the draft for a document that will be relied on by lawyers and experts alike throughout the course of the case (see chapter 8 on instructing counsel).

Having read the records, what action needs to be taken?

Having read the notes in detail, the practitioner needs to consider the following questions:

a) *Is it immediately apparent that this is a hopeless or an indefensible case?* For example, is it apparent that there has been no injury? If so, and there is no financial loss, then there is no basis for a claim. Or on the other hand, is it apparent that a surgical swab was left in the patient following surgery and that this remained undetected, resulting in the need for further surgery? If so, it is almost certainly an indefensible case.

b) *Does the client need to be re-proofed about particular entries in the notes?* For example, does it appear that there is a discrepancy between his or her account and what is recorded?

c) *Do any other witnesses need to be proofed?* For example, is it apparent from the records that someone else was present at a key appointment or at a crucial point during a hospital admission who might be able to give an account of what they saw and heard?

d) *Do the contents of the records entail a revision of the initial assessment of the expiry of the limitation period?*

e) *Do the contents of the records indicate that an amendment to the legal aid certificate is necessary?* For example, does it appear that there may be another defendant?

f) *Do the contents of the records indicate that there are other records that will need to be obtained from other hospitals?* Will they be potential defendants?

g) *Do the records indicate that there may be other documents which need to be obtained and which the plaintiff is entitled to by way of pre-action discovery?* For example, does it appear that there was an internal investigation into what happened? If so, ask for the documents relating to the investigation. In an obstetric injury case, does it appear that midwifery and medical staff were absent for long periods? If so, consider whether it would be helpful to see the delivery register, in order to establish how busy the labour unit was that day or night. Does it appear that some types of records are missing and that they may be stored elsewhere? For example, X-rays and X-ray reports are sometimes stored in the X-ray department.

h) *Is a colour copy of any page required?* Occasionally a colour copy can be useful, especially where, on the face of it, it appears that there has been a material alteration or addition to the notes in respect of recorded facts which may be at issue. Obtaining a colour copy may help the lawyer and the experts to determine whether the alteration was an entirely innocent one or whether it was an attempt to change the records to fit the outcome. For example, what colour and type of ink are the respective entries made in? It may be that not even a good colour copy can resolve such problems and it may be necessary to arrange to see the originals.

i) *Do the records provide an indication of what speciality the expert or experts will need to be drawn from?* If it is clear that experts from several different specialities will be required to comment on both quality of care and causation of injury, consider whether any amendment to the limitation on the legal aid certificate is required.

j) *When reading the records, it will be useful to make a note of particular points arising out of them which will need to be addressed to the expert or experts.* For example, if there is reference in the records to a deterioration in the client's condition before the critical event, it will be important to seek the expert's opinion on the significance of the deterioration and any recorded response to it.

k) *On reading the records, is it apparent that because of the quality or type of a document it is likely that the original records will need to be made available for the plaintiff's expert to examine?* For example, sometimes however well a CTG (cardiotocograph) trace is copied, the copy does not adequately reproduce poor quality sections of the original. Generally, original documents will be made available to plaintiff's solicitors if the defendants can be assured that an original document will be carried and transported by an employee such as a clerk and kept in a fireproof safe overnight. Alternatively, defendants will usually allow an expert to examine an original document in their client's hospital. If this is what is proposed, careful thought needs to be given about this as it will disclose the identity of the expert then instructed for the plaintiff but who may subsequently prove unhelpful to the plaintiff's case.

l) *Is it apparent that pre-action inspection of the ward or machinery or equipment is necessary?* For example, is it apparent from the documents that have been disclosed that the layout of the ward may be crucial in determining whether a bedside monitor could have been seen by a nurse sitting at a central desk? If so, consider an application under Order 24.

Difficult issues arising from the notes

Generally, reading client's patient records is a routine and time-consuming, but essential, task. Sometimes, however, they can raise difficult ethical issues. Two examples are given below.

Concealing true nature of illness from patient

What if it is apparent from the notes that the doctors treating the client have decided on clinical grounds not to inform the client of the true nature or prognosis of his or her condition? Is it the lawyer's job to inform the client? The authors' view is that, initially, it should be ascertained from the plaintiff's family doctor whether the client has been told. Where the doctor in question is a potential defendant or employed by one, the question should be addressed to the defendant's solicitors. If the client has not been told, the lawyer would be well advised to discuss the matter with the Law Society's Ethics and Guidance Committee.

In *DHSS v Sloan* [1981] ICR 313, the employer's contention that it would be detrimental to the employee's mental stability to see the medical records was upheld on appeal by the Employment Appeal Tribunal.

Notes may be to client's discredit

It may be necessary to discuss the contents of some of the records with the client, but the notes in question may be unpleasant or derogatory about the client. Careful thought has to be given as to whether such discussion is really necessary for the purposes of properly investigating and pursuing the claim. If it is, great care and tact is going to have to be used. In some cases it may be helpful to seek advice from the experts instructed about the best approach to the issue.

Conclusion

Grappling with records is demanding and time-consuming. However, it is one of the key areas where experience really does bring rewards in terms of speed and accuracy. Even if it is economical for the task of sorting and collating the records to be delegated, the solicitor must read the records thoroughly him or herself and become familiar with them, both for the sake of the case in hand and for future efficiency in approaching other files. The practitioner should persevere.

CHAPTER 7
Choosing and instructing the expert

*We all know,' I said, 'your eminence as a witness, but would you
tell me what you have done as an engineer? What works have you
designed or constructed?'*

'Not very much,' he answered.

*'Can I help you? You designed a floating dock for Bermuda, did
you not?'*

He assented with a 'Yes' that sounded like a grunt.

'And it would not float?'

Again he grunted.

*'And you designed, if I am not mistaken, the Caterham Lunatic
Asylum?'*

J H Balfour-Browne KC, *Forty Years at the Bar*

This chapter will discuss how to select the expert or experts to be
instructed both during the investigation of the potential claim
and during the conduct of the litigation. It will outline what
information and guidance the lawyer should give to the expert
when first instructed to advise in the case.

Which expert?

The authors have indicated elsewhere in this book that at each
stage of the investigation and litigation, the progress of the case
must be reviewed with an eye to what has to be proved in order to
succeed. Medical cases can become so complex that time and
money may easily be spent in travelling down blind alleys. It is
important at every stage to keep the focus on what may bring
success in the action, and to choose and instruct experts
accordingly.

At the stage of the investigation reached in this chapter, the lawyer must decide what expert advice is necessary to determine whether or not the client has any claim to pursue and if there is a claim with a reasonable prospect of success. We suggest the following questions should be asked:

a) What medical speciality or specialities provided the care or treatment complained of by the client?
b) Will the expert who can advise decisively on whether the care was negligent come from that speciality? Normally, but not always, the answer will be yes.
c) Is there anything in the client's proof or the medical records which raises questions about the quality of care provided by doctors from a different speciality, even if the client has not focussed on that other care?
d) If so, are more experts from allied specialities required to advise on the quality of care provided?
e) What was the medical speciality of the consultant or consultants responsible for the client's care after the injury which it is suspected may have been caused by negligent care?
f) Is it from this speciality that the expert or experts on both causation and condition and prognosis will need to be drawn? Is an expert from the 'treating' specialty sufficient to deal with causation, condition and prognosis?
g) Is there any intervening treatment or condition which may have (i) caused or contributed to the current condition and prognosis and/or (ii) broken the chain of causation?
h) If so, is an expert from this field required?

Some or all of these questions may be impossible to answer until after one or more experts have advised. However, they are key questions for the practitioner to ask both because of the need to select the right type of expert and because of the costs involved.

Sadly (although, perhaps understandably, given the complexities of medical science) it is not uncommon to see experts being asked to advise on the quality of care given by a doctor in a field of practice quite different from their own. For example, even though obstetric care may be shared between a GP and a consultant obstetrician, only a GP can properly and reliably advise on the quality of care provided by the GP. Similarly, even though following surgery a patient may have some neurological damage, it is a surgeon, not a neurologist, who will be needed to advise on the quality of care. The neurological input may, however, then be required to prove causation.

In legal aid cases it will be essential to ensure that the limitation on the certificate covers obtaining the number of reports that are needed. As indicated in chapter 4, initially a certificate may be limited to obtaining one report per speciality. It may be necessary to seek an amendment to cover instructing further experts if the initial limitation is too restrictive.

A private client will have been advised at the outset of the probable need to instruct more than one expert and the potential costs. Clearly, the practitioner must inform the client if it is decided that further expert advice should be sought, why it is necessary and what the costs of doing so are likely to be.

What type of expert should not be approached to advise

It is *never* right to seek a report on liability, causation or condition and prognosis from the doctor responsible for the care which is the subject of the investigation, or from a doctor working in the same immediate area or for the same trust of health authority. Even if they do not feel a sense of personal loyalty to the colleague or colleagues concerned, they will have a conflict of interest in advising a plaintiff in a claim to be pursued against their employing authority.

Generally, the authors consider that it is not advisable to obtain reports on condition and prognosis from doctors treating the client. There are two reasons for this. The first is that a treating doctor may not always be able to be wholly objective about a patient for whom they have cared. The second is that in writing an objective report a doctor may be forced to be more blunt about the patient's personality than is necessary during medical consultation and thus a doctor-patient relationship which is important to the client may be jeopardised.

Occasionally, however, because of time constraints, it will be necessary to obtain a report on condition and prognosis from a treating doctor. If so, the lawyer should be aware of these potential problems and indicate this awareness in the letter of instruction.

How to find the expert

It is highly desirable that the expert should be someone who has had experience of advising in medical negligence cases, who has proved him or herself to be objective in giving such advice and has proved to be a good witness at trial. This may all seem self-evident, but medical negligence claims are won or lost by expert opinion and these are key factors which can determine whether a case succeeds or not.

Advising in medical negligence litigation is demanding and time-consuming work for the medical expert. Those who have not been involved in cases previously will not appreciate this and may find it increasingly difficult to afford the client's case the time and the attention to detail which is required.

Some doctors feel uncomfortable about advising plaintiffs and prefer to advise only defendants. The majority of these will simply refuse to advise plaintiffs. Others perhaps will fail to recognise this reluctance, but will find it difficult to be objective about the shortcomings of care provided by other doctors and health carers. For this reason, it may be wise for the inexperienced practitioner to use an expert who is known to have advised plaintiffs and to have advised positively.

Giving evidence and being cross-examined can be a stressful experience for the medical practitioner, however eminent and practised at speaking in public. The attention to detail which is so central to the forensic process means that the expert must be fully conversant with the client's medical history, the detail of the client's proof, medical records and the medical literature upon which both they and the experts advising the opponents seek to rely. The expert who is not is in danger of being led into contradicting him or herself under cross-examination.

Finding the right expert can be a daunting task for the practitioner. Probably the most useful starting-point is AVMA. By paying an annual fee to be a member of the lawyer's resource service, a practitioner can obtain details of experts who have advised in similar cases. Sometimes experienced counsel or an existing expert will be able to advise on who else should be instructed. The inexperienced solicitor will always do well to check any proposed expert with counsel or the experts already involved in the case.

Another starting-point is to read reports of cases where similar medical issues have been the subject of litigation and to see which experts were instructed for the plaintiff. The lawyer should always look to see how the expert has fared in the judgment – some experts have become well known and are often instructed without ever being successful in making their evidence effective in court.

However the expert is found, it will be essential to check his or her details in the *Medical Directory* to ensure that there is no close connection with the proposed defendants.

Other points which should be borne in mind when deciding on which expert to instruct are:

a) The expert advising on liability should be someone who was practising in the relevant speciality at the time of the alleged negligence and should have experience of the precise procedures or treatment in point.
b) As long as the expert has experience contemporaneous to the alleged negligence, she or he should either still be in clinical practice, or if retired, only very recently so. It is likely to be two to four years before the case comes to trial, by which time someone already retired will be at risk of being shown to be out of touch.
c) If, because of the complexities of the case, a decision is taken to instruct more than one expert in the same field, consider instructing consultants of differing generations, ie, someone who has been a consultant for five years and another who has held a consultant post for fifteen.
d) It is not necessary for the expert instructed on causation to have had clinical experience contemporaneous to the alleged negligence. What is essential is that causation experts are experienced in the field today and able to argue using current research in support of the plaintiff's claim.
e) The type of hospital where the alleged negligence occurred is relevant. Try to match experts. Thus an expert in a case involving a teaching hospital should, ideally, be someone who has or has had a consultancy in a teaching hospital rather than a district general hospital.
f) Some experts have acquired a reputation for always adopting a particular stance in relation to particular issues. Using such an expert may make the plaintiff's claim vulnerable to a particular line of cross-examination and it may be wise to consider a different expert.

What has to be done once an expert is found

It is inadvisable to instruct an expert without first checking with him or her that he or she is willing to act. Obvious as this may sound, it is surprising how many experts complain that large bundles of documents have arrived on their doorstep with no prior warning and in cases in which it is not appropriate for them to be instructed. For example, they may be from the wrong speciality, or may be employed by the potential defendant or may already be advising the defendant!

Where the practitioner is instructing an expert for the first time, that expert should be asked whether he or she has any objections to advising in a medical negligence claim and in particular that there are no objections to advising a plaintiff. The expert should also be told who the potential defendant is and the name of the consultant in charge of the care which is the subject of the investigation. By doing this it should be possible to avoid any potential conflicts of interest. Consider whether it is advisable at this stage to give an expert who may be advising the defendants the full name of the plaintiff or other experts involved in the case.

Those experts who undertake medico-legal work will often have lengthy waiting lists. Thus the expert should be asked how quickly the report will be ready. This is especially important in cases with a potential time problem. It is also advisable to find out what fee will be charged for reading the records, examining the client (if appropriate) and attending a conference with counsel. The private client will need to sanction incurring the expert's fee. Information about the fee will also be needed if prior authority has to be sought from the Legal Aid Board (see chapter 3 on legal aid).

Instructing the expert

Limitations on legal aid certificates used to provide that counsel could be instructed to draft the letter of instruction to the expert if the solicitor considered it appropriate. The standard limitation now does not provide for that, probably because experienced specialist solicitors in the field consider there is no need to involve counsel at this stage. The authors consider that if a solicitor has undertaken the research and preparation referred to in the preceding chapters and is instructing a recommended expert it should rarely be necessary for counsel to be instructed to draft the letter. That said, the prudent beginner will ensure that legal aid cover is available for counsel to check and approve the draft.

No expert should be asked to advise without sight of the medical records. Unless the expert indicates that it will not be necessary to see all of the records, a complete copy set of paginated records should accompany the letter of instruction. This must be a separate copy set for the exclusive use of that expert, which he or she may mark. It is *not* sufficient for one or two sets of records to be shuttled between lawyers and experts.

There are exceptions. One example of where it will not initially be essential for the expert to have a complete set of records is the obstetric mismanagement claim, where the obstetric expert will not need all the paediatric records, but rather just the obstetric and neo-natal paediatric records.

For reasons previously indicated in chapter 6, the expert should be provided with a paginated copy set of records identical to those retained by the solicitor and those which will be sent to the other experts and counsel. By doing this there is little or no scope for misunderstanding about which entry in the records is being referred to.

The records and proofs should be accompanied by a detailed letter of instruction and where appropriate a chronology prepared by the solicitor. A precedent of such a letter appears in appendix 3E. The letter should include the following:

a) a summary of the facts and why the client has sought legal advice;

b) an explanation of what has to be proved in order to succeed in a claim for compensation arising from medical care and the balance of proof. Thus, there should be a précis of the *Bolam* test of negligence and an explanation of the requirement that the causational link between the identified negligence and the injury is proved;

c) specific questions to be answered by the expert, arising either from the practitioner's perusal of the records or raised by the client;

d) some guidance about what should be incorporated into the medical report. In the case of the liability expert this should include:

   (i)   a summary of the material records and witness proof/s;

   (ii) where appropriate, a commentary on the quality of care indicated by the entries in these;

(iii) a commentary on what care would have been appropriate and what the outcome would and should have been had this been done; and

(iv) references to medical texts in support of any conclusions. The report on condition and prognosis should detail the current condition and prognosis. In addition to referring to the findings of any examination it should, where appropriate, refer to the contents of the records and the client's proof. It should also refer to any treatment which may be available and comment on the prospects of success and the costs of such treatment;

e) in cases where there is a conflict of evidence between what the client says and what is recorded in the notes, a request to give alternative opinions based on each of the two scenarios;

f) the date by which the report should be available and in those cases where there is a tight time-limit, an explanation of the potential prejudice to the client if this deadline is not met;

g) confirmation that prior authority has been granted for the expert's fee, if appropriate.

What to do on receipt of the expert's opinion

As has been said before, it is not sufficient for the solicitor undertaking medical negligence litigation simply to act as a postbox.

On receiving the expert's report, its contents and conclusions must be considered in the light of the contents of the records and the witness proofs. The following points need to be considered.

a) Has the expert addressed any or all of the issues identified by the solicitor in the letter of instruction? If not, these questions should be raised again with the expert in clarificatory correspondence.

b) Where there is a conflict of evidence between the records and the witness proofs, has the expert commented on the discrepancies and advised on the alternative scenarios? If not, the expert should now be asked to do so.

c) Does any part of the expert's report require clarification? If so, ask for this clarification straightaway by letter. For example, is the expert saying that intervention should have occurred and a baby been delivered earlier than it in fact was? If so, it will be necessary to know how much earlier in order to determine whether the negligent delay was causative of the child's brain damage.

d) Is there any indication that the expert may not be wholly objective? For example, does it appear from the tone or content of the report that there may be an over-identification with either the plaintiff or the defendant? Should another expert be instructed either in addition or as an alternative? If so, is legal aid authority required to do so?

e) Does the expert raise queries which require a further proof to be taken from the client or from other witnesses? If so, ensure that these are taken and then made available to the expert swiftly, before memory fades and the expert loses focus on the case.

f) Does the expert indicate that other specialist advice is required before a final opinion either on liability or on causation can be reached? If so, is there an indication of what type of expert and why their advice is necessary? Does the solicitor consider it necessary? Will legal aid authority be required for this additional expert?

g) Does the expert indicate that further records exist and should be obtained? If so, seek authority from the client to obtain these and then request them.

No claim should be initiated without a conference with counsel and the experts. Because of the highly technical nature of these cases, the authors consider that even where there has been a negative report, a conference should usually be arranged. The purpose of a conference in such a case is to ensure that the case has been thoroughly investigated and that a key issue has not been ignored. Where it is clear that the conference is a part of the investigation, the reasonable costs of and associated with the conference should be recoverable on taxation.

Depending upon how many of these points remain to be dealt with, it may be possible to press on and organise the conference especially as where more than one expert is involved, it is likely that there will be some delay before the conference can take place. Thus the outstanding points may have been dealt with by the time of the conference.

The importance of the conference and preparation for it are described in chapter 9.

Legal liability of expert witnesses

It may be helpful to close this chapter by touching on the legal position of expert witnesses who consent to act in litigation. This topic has been examined in *Palmer v Durnford Ford* [1992] 1 QB 483, where Simon Tuckey QC, sitting as a deputy High Court judge, concluded that there was:

> no good reason why an expert should not be liable for the advice which he gives to his client as to the merits of the claim, particularly if the proceedings have not been started. . . . The problem is where to draw the line, given that there is immunity for evidence given in court and it must extend to the preparation of such evidence to avoid the immunity being outflanked and rendered of little use. This problem was considered by the House of Lords in *Saif Ali v Sidney Mitchell & Co* [1980] AC 198 in the analogous but not identical situation of the advocate's immunity from suit. . . . I think a similar approach could be adopted in the case of an expert. Thus the immunity would only extend to what could fairly be said to be preliminary to his giving evidence in court, judged perhaps by the principal purpose for which the work was done. So the production of a report for disclosure to the other side would be immune but work done for the principal purpose of advising the client would not. Each case would turn upon its own facts . . .

CHAPTER 8

Choosing and instructing counsel and arranging the first conference with experts

> *The advocate must have a quick mind, an understanding heart, and charm of personality. For he has often to understand another man's life story at a moment's notice, and catch up overnight a client's or a witness's lifelong experience in another profession; moreover, he must have the power of expressing himself clearly and attractively to simple people, so that they will listen to him and understand him. He must, then, be histrionic, crafty, courageous, eloquent, quick-minded, charming, great hearted. These are the salient qualities which go to make a great advocate . . .*

Sir Edward Marshall Hall, *Marjoribanks*

There are various stages at which counsel will be instructed in a case. The question of whether and when counsel should be instructed is dealt with below (see p78). It is the question of whom to instruct and how to instruct them that is at the heart of this chapter.

To some extent, the stage at which counsel is first instructed will vary from case to case. For the purpose of this chapter it is assumed that counsel is being instructed for the first time to have a conference with experts after pre-action discovery has been given, and after expert reports on liability and causation have been obtained, but before proceedings have been issued. It is also assumed that the private client's authority to instruct counsel has been obtained or that, if the client is legally aided, the certificate covers instructing counsel.

Choosing counsel

Medical negligence litigation is a specialist field and, therefore, not one for dabblers. Recognition of this has led to the establishment   75 by the Law Society of a specialist medical negligence panel for solicitors.

At the moment there is no equivalent for barristers. However, for a number of reasons (including franchising requirements) there has been some recent discussion about whether or not there should be some accreditation scheme for barristers who hold themselves out as specialists in the field. That debate continues and may or may not have gathered force or led to changes by the time this book comes to print. There are particular difficulties in any scheme which might be devised, relating to the 'cab-rank' rule. In any event, the authors believe that the question of accreditation of lawyers who will be chosen by lay people raises very different considerations from the process by which solicitors, who should be knowledgeable about those they engage, choose barristers. Regardless of the outcome of that debate, one thing is clear: a client will be badly served if his or her solicitor instructs a barrister inexperienced in the field.

The various legal directories can give the solicitor a guide to the areas of law in which particular counsel or chambers specialise. However, the listings are a result of subjective judgments and gossip assembled by the compilers and give the practitioner no reliable guide as to whether or not an individual barrister can truly be described as a medical negligence litigation specialist. This applies more strongly to those directories where the barrister must be included, or where any number of specialisms are claimed.

That said, the authors would suggest that for those instructing counsel in a medical negligence action for the first time it is prudent to use chambers which purport to have several counsel specialising in medical negligence litigation. Help in selecting specialist counsel may also be derived from looking at reported cases, and speaking to AVMA or APIL or other experienced solicitors. As always, the most reliable guide to choosing counsel will be to follow the consensus of anecdotal response from experienced specialist solicitors.

The authors would also suggest that when instructing an individual barrister for the first time his or her clerk should be asked to provide details about the number of medical negligence cases in which counsel has acted, whether any of those cases have concluded with a settlement or trial (ie, to ensure that counsel's experience is of more than simply the initial stages of an action) and whether or not counsel will act for both plaintiffs and defendants.

Particular qualities are required from barristers in this field. The barrister must be prepared to work very hard at mastering complex facts: the approach needs to be much more 'Roundhead' than 'Cavalier'. The ability to challenge the propositions of eminent experts in their own field, to test the consistency and thoroughness of their views, does not come without application. Given that the client will believe that he or she has have been let down by medical professionals, the barrister chosen should be capable of good client relations and in particular of good client communications. Further, the conduct of such a case calls for a high degree of co-operation over a sustained period between the solicitor and the barrister instructed. Where there is a choice of suitable counsel to instruct, the solicitor should not feel ashamed to choose a barrister with whom he or she will feel comfortable working for such a long time.

All these considerations should enter into the initial choice of counsel. They should also be borne in mind when considering whether to instruct a given barrister a second or a third time. Indeed, if counsel chosen in a given case seems to be failing to deliver in any significant way, the authors do not hesitate to say that the solicitor should *consider* removing instructions in the case before the case is concluded. Responsible solicitors will clearly only do so where there is good reason. If there is good reason, then no sense of embarrassment should prevent the case from being moved.

Organising the conference

Preparation for the conference by the solicitor

Organising a full conference with medical experts and counsel is frequently a scheduling nightmare. The gaps in professional commitments rarely seem to coincide, particularly where the medical experts remain in clinical practice. It is thus very common for such conferences to be organised months in advance, sometimes only to fail on the day because of unexpected clinical or forensic demands on the expert's time. No magic can prevent this. One of the characteristics of medical litigation is that it is slow, and these scheduling problems play an important part in that. The prudent solicitor will simply seek to keep the timetable of the case well advanced, and will try to instruct experts and counsel who have a record of keeping to arrangements.

In recent years it has become professionally proper for counsel to confer other than in chambers or at court. Where there is an advantage, solicitors should now think of arranging conferences at their offices, in an expert's consulting rooms or hospital, or even at the client's home if the client is disabled or finds movement painful. Counsel's chambers often remain the most convenient place, since they are usually central, but the solicitor should not hesitate to choose another venue if that is sensible. The question of costs should always be borne in mind when planning the location of a conference: the travel and time costs incurred by lawyers and experts will often have to be justified on taxation.

Experts or counsel who are asked to travel to conferences will thank the instructing solicitors if the arrangements do not mean an excessively early start or late finish, and will also thank solicitors who arrange two or even three conferences to follow one another, rather than setting up one meeting giving rise to a very long round trip.

It sometimes happens that not all the experts in the case can be present at a conference within the necessary timescale. It is then the solicitor's responsibility, having consulted counsel on the telephone, to prioritise the experts and get the best range of expertise present in the flesh. It is also sensible to arrange for those who cannot be present to be available to be consulted during the conference. It is also now possible to hire video-conferencing facilities in the Temple through the Bar Council, and in most major cities commercially. We suspect that this facility will be used very much more in the future, as the technology improves and the cost comes down. It is probably already cheaper than to travel from Newcastle to London. Legal Aid Board approval can be sought to protect the position in a legally aided case.

When to instruct counsel

It is good practice to instruct counsel at an early date, well before the conference, given the amount of material and the complexity of technical information and advice which is often involved. It is obvious that one consideration in planning the conference must be whether two counsel are required at this point in the case. This decision should be made with a number of factors in mind, such as the complexity and size of the claim, how far advanced the case is, and whether decisions which are irrevocable and which will determine the conduct of the trial fall to be taken.

Instructions for counsel

To some extent it is true to say that counsel is only as good as the instructions that are delivered. If counsel is to be in a position to be able to advise and/or plead properly, the instructing solicitor must ensure that all the relevant material is made available and that counsel is made aware of any relevant facts which are not recorded in the documents.

The written instructions to counsel should neither be a bare back-sheet nor an exhaustive recital of all the facts. A summary of the history, if possible with a chronology of events, and a discussion of the important issues in the case is the best form. Such an approach has the dual function of ensuring that the solicitor has thought through the issues in the case thoroughly and that counsel focusses on the essentials when studying the brief.

Ideally, the format of instructions should enable counsel to find out the following from perusing the instructions alone:

a) the essence of what the case is about,
b) what the factual or medical issues are,
c) what the legal aid position is,
d) what the state of the evidence is on behalf of the client,
e) what stage proceedings have reached,
f) what counsel is being instructed to do,
g) what the timetable is and whether there is any urgency,
h) whether there are any factual, procedural or medical complexities or problems,
i) what documents are enclosed.

The documents for counsel

Invariably in medical negligence cases it will be necessary to send a sizeable file of papers with the first instructions to counsel. If both counsel and the solicitor are to be sure of what papers counsel has and that no papers have been omitted, it is essential that there should be a specific and itemised list of enclosures – ie, listing letters individually, rather than simply as 'correspondence between the parties'.

Many practitioners who are new to medical negligence work are perturbed by the amount of photocopying that such cases necessitate. If a claim is to be properly investigated, each expert and counsel must have their own copy set of records to which they can refer as and when necessary and on which they can note their own comments. It is *not* satisfactory to give to counsel a copy bundle which has previously been used by an expert.

Where the volume of photocopying is more than the average case the taxing master can be asked to exercise his or her discretion to allow something in respect of that copying where the documents copied are unusually numerous in relation to the nature of the case (RSC Order 62, Part C; *Practice Direction (Supreme Court Taxing Office) (No 1 of 1986)* (1986) 9 April; [1986] CLY 2166).

On first being instructed, counsel should be provided with the client's statement or statements and those of any witnesses. Counsel should also be provided with a complete set of medical records and the reports of, and correspondence with, the experts. If the solicitors have obtained relevant medical texts, these should also be sent to counsel. If those texts were referred to in the expert's reports, this should be made clear. Any relevant correspondence between the parties and with the client should also be included.

It is never satisfactory for counsel to be provided with an unchecked, unsorted and unpaginated set of medical records. If he or she is, the costs of counsel's time spent sorting the records will not be recoverable on taxation. If the records have been sorted and paginated in the manner described in chapter 6, this is a problem which should not arise and it should be possible to provide counsel with a copy set of records identical to those sent to the experts. If counsel is to understand the case properly and to discuss the issues with the experts, it will be as important to provide him or her with full-size copies of key records such as CTG traces as it is to provide them to the experts.

It is rarely helpful to enclose all the legal correspondence in the case with instructions. Unless some procedural point arises or the correpondence bears on the possibility of settlement or factual evidence, for example, correspondence need not be enclosed.

In legal aid cases, the wise clerk to counsel will always check that the work counsel is being asked to undertake is covered by the current limitation on the certificate. A copy of the legal aid certificate and any notices of amendment should, therefore, be included with the papers. A copy of the original certificate is in any case essential so that counsel may operate the interim claim system under the legal aid scheme – given the customary time scale of this class of case, that is essential to maintain a sensible cashflow for specialist counsel.

It is usually helpful for the solicitor to prepare some outline material on the quantum of damage. It is inappropriate to prepare this fully, before the decision to proceed is taken. On the other hand, when considering the cost/benefit of an action, it is needful to have a brief but considered idea of how much there may be by way of special damages. Too often this question arises almost as an afterthought in discussion with the lay client in conference, and answers given then may not be well thought through. The potential value of a claim is central to its viability from the beginning.

What is counsel instructed to do?

It is never satisfactory for counsel to be sent a set of instructions which are in the most general of terms and which effectively simply ask him or her to advise or do what he or she considers fit. The risks of doing so are that an opportunity to assess the case and/or progress will be lost and that the costs of instructing counsel and counsel's advice may not be recoverable on taxation. When instructing counsel it is essential to be clear about what this step in the case is designed to achieve and why counsel is being instructed.

In the case of the first pre-action conference with experts, the purpose is to clarify the medical issues, test the strength and state of the evidence, determine whether or not there is a reasonable prospect of the claim succeeding on the current evidence and decide whether proceedings should be issued. The instructions should, therefore, make clear to counsel why he or she is being instructed and exactly what he or she is being asked to do.

It may be useful for the solicitor to ask counsel to draft an agenda in advance of the conference. This can then be circulated to the experts to ensure that minds are concentrated on key issues and that time is not wasted. It will also serve to demonstrate counsel's grasp of the case and thus may be particularly important where counsel is being instructed for the first time. If counsel is not to be asked to prepare an agenda the solicitor should consider whether he or she should prepare one for circulation and inclusion in counsel's papers. The costs of preparing the agenda can properly be treated as part of the preparation of the papers for counsel by the solicitor and as preparation for the conference by counsel.

It may be helpful to ask counsel to draft pleadings or part pleadings in advance of the conference, although the solicitor should be careful to ensure that such work is within the the current legal aid cover, if applicable, and that it can be justified on taxation. It is clearly a waste of time to draft a whole pleading where the case may well not proceed. In what appears on paper to be a weak case, even drafting allegations of negligence in advance will not usually be appropriate or even possible. However, in an apparently strong case, draft allegations can form the focus of the discussion, as long as the participants are wary of asssuming too much because some criticisms have been formulated in writing. One central purpose of the conference with the experts is to test all propositions: the fact that counsel has been able to draft allegations in black and white must not be allowed to muffle or elide discussion of the fundamentals of the case.

Further preparation for the conference and the conduct of the conference is discussed in the next chapter.

CHAPTER 9
The conference

Mr Harding was shown into a comfortable inner sitting room, looking more like a gentleman's bookroom than a lawyer's chambers, and there waited for Sir Abraham. Nor was he kept waiting long: in ten or fifteen minutes he heard a clatter of voices speaking quickly in the passage, and then the attorney-general entered . . . .

'And so, Mr Warden,' said Sir Abraham, 'all our trouble about this lawsuit is at an end.'

Mr Harding said he hoped so, but he didn't at all understand what Sir Abraham meant. Sir Abraham, with all his sharpness, could not have looked into his heart and read his intentions.

Anthony Trollope, *The Warden*

Introduction

Since the medical case commonly lives or dies by the opinion of experts rather than hingeing on a difference of primary fact, the testing and refinement of that expert opinion in a conference usually decides whether the case will proceed or not. It is the best opportunity for the lawyers to assess the potential of the experts as witnesses. It is the best opportunity for solicitors to assess the strengths or weaknesses of counsel, with implications for the instant case and future cases. If the action is to proceed, the shape of the allegations of negligence are determined in conference, and usually decisions are taken about any further necessary evidence. It is also the time when the client's understanding of the technical, medical and legal issues that govern the case must be checked and renewed.

As with most things, the successful conference depends upon good preparation (see chapter 8).

Preparation by counsel

The first essential, if it is practicable, is to prepare for the conference far enough in advance to change things if need be. Counsel should read the papers with an eye to all the matters set out in the previous chapter. Whether or not the instructions ask for an agenda to circulate, it is wise to draft one. It is usually helpful to draft pleadings or allegations of negligence, although the authors entered a caveat in the previous chapter about this. The drafts are useful to focus discussion, but should not be a cramp upon thinking. Counsel will not be paid for drafting pleadings which are not issued, but the time spent can be properly claimed as part of the preparation for the conference, if the work is done to maximise the usefulness of the conference.

Since the first objective of the conference is clarification, counsel must be sure of what he or she does understand, and of what he or she does not. If there is any doubt about a point, it should be placed on the agenda. Propositions made by experts should not just be taken at face value, and if common sense gives rise to a question, it should be asked.

If scientific or medical literature is enclosed with reports, it should be read in advance, not taken as read. Only by doing so will counsel be in a position to test the views of the experts.

If more material or another expert report is necessary to get to the crux of the case, counsel should not hesitate to say so, even if that means an unravelling of existing arrangements. For obvious reasons this should be done early, if counsel is not to antagonise the instructing solicitor, who will have to explain this to busy experts and a disappointed client. However, a conference which is plainly going to be inconclusive should not go ahead through inertia.

The conference itself

It is essential to begin by explaining to the lay client the objectives of the discussion. Far too many counsel launch into the detail of the case, leaving the client at sea. It is suggested that it is useful to plan the conference in two parts, the first dealing with the medical issues and the second, after the experts have gone, dealing with the legal and administrative decisions that follow.

These points and the objects of the conference should be explained to the client at the beginning of the meeting. This structure reassures the client that he or she will have the chance to comment on what the experts have said to their representatives. The client (or the lawyers) may have formed a view on the basis of the reports that a given expert is over-cautious, unfocussed or biassed. If it is clear from the outset there will be an opportunity to raise such things in the absence of the expert, conflict in the conference can usually be minimised.

The client should normally be encouraged to correct what he or she believes to be factual mistakes or to add details which are relevant. Apart from being a valuable check on accuracy, this will serve to involve the client in a worthwhile way. In cases turning on esoteric expert points, this may otherwise be difficult. The client should also be reassured that he or she will have an opportunity at some point to ask questions in an open-ended fashion.

It is absolutely essential that the solicitor takes a full note of the conference. It is very rare that counsel can lead the discussion and take a full note at the same time. Indeed, it is often a good idea to try and get exact formulations of words agreed and placed in the note. This will help to ensure that complicated medical issues have been understood by all, and that there is true agreement between the participants.

It may be helpful to give an example, however compressed, of the level of complexity that commonly arises. In treating hyperthyroidism (over-active thyroid gland), doctors use the drug Carbimazole in an attempt to produce long-lasting thyroid balance without resort to surgery. In the course of such treatment, the patient is likely to suffer a period or periods of hypo-thyroidism (under-active thyroid gland) before a balance is established. This artificially induced hypothyroidism is often treated by a further drug, Thyroxine, and thus the patient is simultaneously treated with drugs having the 'opposite' effect. However, the drugs operate in different ways.

Various permanent effects can arise if this balance is never achieved, or if it is achieved too slowly. The discussion in conference will need to establish what are the *Bolam* limits of treatment at the time of the events complained of. What were the acceptable limits of dose for this patient at that period? How often and in what ways should the patient's progress have been monitored? How often was he monitored and was he monitored adequately? Were the permanent neurological or cosmetic consequences (for example, prominent eyes) avoidable? Were the consequences complained of the result of *negligent* treatment or could they simply be the result of the condition itself, even if adequately treated?

The endocrinology of all this is extremely complex. Yet in such a case, the medical issues will have to be resolved into a combination of precise scientific data and accurate but plain English so that the legal team can understand the case. Only then will counsel be able to plead the case in a way which is comprehensible.

It is best to get this account agreed almost word for word in such a case. The expert will then have focussed on the wording and there is less likelihood of change thereafter. It will be seen whether the expert can express things in a clear but accurate way. The agreed wording can be incorporated into the pleading and the client ought to have a version of events which will be comprehensible to him or her.

Testing the evidence

This is one of the most demanding skills for counsel. It is necessary to test the propositions of experts who have been chosen for their seniority and distinction and who ought if possible to be forensically experienced. It is necessary to do so economically, without appearing callow and without giving offence.

To illustrate the breadth of issues which can arise, we take an example of a very serious case involving brain-damaged babies, where negligent perinatal care leading to oxygen starvation is suspected. Such a case is the basis for the pleadings in chapter 11. The case papers from this hypothetical case are to be found in appendix 3.

In such a case, the following areas frequently arise for medico-legal analysis:

a) assessment of the risk of the labour, whether by midwife or doctor;

b) assessment of the size of the maternal pelvis for delivery: was there a disproportion between dimensions of the baby and the pelvic outlet?

c) whether gestation was allowed to proceed too long before labour was induced;

d) the method and timing of the induction of labour;

e) the adequacy of foetal monitoring before and during labour;
f) reading the cardiotocograph (CTG) or foetal monitor; what in fact was the condition of the foetus during labour?
g) assessment of the progress of labour;
h) the need for and timing of intervention in labour: did the second stage of labour go on too long?
i) whether the mechanical assistance to delivery was appropriate; were the forceps or the Ventouse suction extractor used reasonably skilfully?
j) whethers the decision to perform Caesarean section was appropriate;
k) whether the time-lapse from the decision to deliver by Caesarean section to delivery itself was within reasonable limits;
l) assessment of the state of the baby at birth;
m) the resuscitation of the baby;
n) the immediate aftercare for the mother, with consideration of the gynaecological and other consequences.

Naturally, not all subjects will arise in every case, but the list is by no means exhaustive. In many instances, an issue will need to be considered in the separate contexts of negligence and causation. There will be the obstetricians who will consider negligence: how did the matter appear to the staff who had the care then? What was the minimum acceptable response to that? There will be the paediatric neurologist and/or neonatologist, who will attempt to reconstruct what was actually happening to the foetus, however it may have appeared contemporaneously to the obstetric and midwifery staff.

To illustrate how such an issue may develop in conference, we take one from that list: the reading of the CTG. The CTG will need to be considered both on the adequacy of the reading at the time and as evidence which must be considered with the benefit of hindsight so as to establish the true condition of the foetus along the relevant timescale. Only when the latter has been clarified, can the decision be made whether better care would have prevented or reduced harm.

In the hypothetical example chosen as the basis of the case papers in appendix 3, this discussion would centre on paragraphs 7.1 to 9.1 of the report of Mr Hawk-Monitor (pp 278–280).

In the course of the discussion of that issue, the lawyers should be watching such things as:

— how well are the experts explaining their point of view?
— is any one expert appearing to take a markedly different line from that taken by the others?
— how familiar do they appear to be with the notes and records?
— have they compared the timings in the automatic tracing and the manual records and found any discrepancies?
— are they reasonably familiar with the relevant legal principles?

Obviously, only experience will enable lawyers to get real depth of field on medical experts, but anyone beginning in the field must attempt from the start to go beyond a deferential acceptance of the views of experts.

Formulating allegations of negligence

In many cases the first conference will be held at a stage before it is clear the case can proceed. Even there, however, if the experts on liability on balance feel that there was negligence, then the authors suggest that counsel should aim to formulate allegations of negligence at least during the conference, and that something quite well developed should be put before the experts in conference. In addition, in the hypothetical example the analysis of the CTG should have been clarified and the descriptive or narrative basis (paras 12 to 19 of the Statement of Claim at p287 of appendix 3) should be agreed as far as possible.

In one sense, the time and effort spent in getting precise formulations will be wasted if the case cannot proceed. However, it is not truly a waste. The discipline of close formulation of propositions has a good effect on the quality of thinking in conference. Moreover, if this is not done, and the case does eventually proceed, much more effort is required to get the lawyers and liability experts back to a high concentration on the case.

The opportunity presented by the conference should also be taken to explore potential weaknesses in the case as fully as possible, and to assess the quality of the experts in the process.

The close of the conference

After the experts have given their views and all present have asked their questions, the experts may be released and the discussion turns to the more familiar interchange between lawyers and client.

The first task is to ensure that the client has in fact followed the expert evidence, if that is not already plain. It is often the case, particularly where the expert advice has been negative, that the client will wish to make points which run counter to the experts' views.

The lawyers will next wish to consider whether further advice needs to be obtained. The law must be explained, if it has not already been debated in the meeting. No counsel should assume that the client understands the law because his solicitor has already explained it on a previous occasion. The explanation should now be related directly to the evidence in the case.

The final point to consider is whether an amendment to the legal aid certificate limitation needs to be sought (or indeed, an amendment to the description). It is probable that the limitation will need to be extended to cover issue and service of proceedings. If the national standard limitations have been used, then it is likely that the next limitation will be, 'Limited to all steps up to and including setting down, to include mutual exchange of factual witness statements under RSC Order 38 r2A and mutual exchange of expert evidence under RSC Order 38 r37 and to the preparation of papers for counsel and obtaining counsel's opinion on merits, quantum and evidence'.

When any consequential advice has been given, the conference can be drawn to a close. In a field where, by definition, the client believes or suspects he or she has been let down by one set of professionals, it is unwise to close a conference without giving him or her every opportunity for comment and response and to ask any questions he or she wishes, even if they are not relevant to the narrow legal issues.

After the conference

Whatever the outcome of the conference, favourable or unfavourable to action, or inconclusive, it is highly desirable that the note taken by the solicitor is circulated for approval by all experts and counsel. It is often many months before counsel (in particular) will return to that case. If the note is misleading or incomplete, memory will have faded and distortions may enter without detection. It is good practice to ensure that any action which is required following the conference is highlighted in the note and diarised by the solicitor.

Preparing such a note can be time-consuming. Solicitors should note the decision in *Brush v Bower Cotton & Bower* [1993] 4 All ER 741 and the legal aid costs appeals committee decision No. CLA13 (*Law Society's Gazette* 31 August 1994). Both cases indicate that in principle the time taken in preparing attendance notes in order to record and preserve information necessary for the proper conduct of a client's affairs is recoverable.

If a pleading is drafted following the conference, then that too should be circulated, preferably soon after the conference and before memories fade.

A tiny proportion of medical negligence cases proceed to trial: the great bulk of such cases settle. It follows that the settlement is reached on the basis of discussion in conference. The need for thorough and intelligent analysis cannot be overstated: whether as the basis for declining to proceed with a weak case; accepting a settlement; formulating a case with maximum effect so that the defendants accept the inevitable and make an offer; or deciding on the bold and expensive step of actually proceeding to court.

Conclusion

In a real sense, the conference room and not the courtroom is the proving ground for most medical cases. There is a good reason for this. As previously stated, relatively few medical cases turn upon conflict of primary evidence. In a sense, a medical negligence trial represents a failure, since it usually means that one or other team of lawyers and experts has misread the case. The conference deserves as careful preparation as the trial itself.

CHAPTER 10

Limitation

Time present and time past
Are both perhaps present in time future,
And time future contained in time past.
If all time is eternally present,
All time is unredeemable.

T S Eliot, *Burnt Norton*

Introduction

Medical negligence cases often throw up particularly difficult limitation problems. The solicitor may be confronted with a claim arising out of surgery carried out 20 years ago, where the client has recently seen a television programme featuring a 'similar' case where the plaintiff was awarded £1m. Medical treatment can fail by omission, with no obvious time when negligence has led to damage. In such circumstances, what is the client's 'date of knowledge', from which the limitation clock starts to run? Has the psychiatric client had relevant periods of disability which affect the date of his or her knowledge? Is there a history of psychiatric illness which is relevant to the exercise of the court's discretion to let the claim go forward under Limitation Act 1980 s33 where the primary limitation period has expired? Does knowledge arise before an expert identifies the act or omission which caused the damage, and hence should a 'protective' writ be issued before a thorough investigation of the claim? Or is it better to instruct experts to comment on liability and await their reports before commencing proceedings?

The intention of this chapter is to provide a straightforward guide to the provisions of the Limitation Act 1980 as it affects medical negligence cases, and to help the reader establish a system of working which will ensure that limitation issues are handled correctly and given the priority they require in the overall management of the plaintiff's claim. References to 'the Act' in this chapter are references to the Limitation Act 1980.

The primary limitation period

The reader will be aware that where an action is for damages for negligence or breach of duty (including breach of contractual or statutory duties), and the damages claimed consist of or include damages in respect of personal injury, the primary limitation period is three years from:

a) the date on which the cause of action accrued; or
b) the date of knowledge (if later) of the person injured (see s11(4) of the Act).

The reader will also be aware that if the action is begun after the expiry of the primary limitation period, the plaintiff must rely upon the exercise of the discretion of the court under s33 of the Act.

Where the claim is for assault, the limitation period is six years from the date of the assault and there is no question of establishing 'date of knowledge', nor is there any provision which allows the court to exercise a discretion under s33 of the Act to allow the claim to go forward after six years (see *Stubbings v Webb* [1993] 2 WLR 120).

The six-year limitation period may also apply where the claim is an entirely economic one arising from a 'wrongful birth'. This turns upon whether a failed sterilisation or a failed vasectomy can be held to constitute personal injury. There are conflicting authorities on this point. In *Allen v Bloomsbury HA* [1993] 1 All ER 651, Brooke J suggested that if only economic loss was claimed in a case of failed sterilisation, then it 'is hard to see how s11 of the Limitation Act 1980 would apply'. In the failed vasectomy case of *Pattison v Hobbs* (1985) *Times* 11 November, CA Transcript 85/676, a similar approach was adopted. However, in *Walkin v South Manchester Health Authority* (1994) 19 May, Supreme Court Practice News Issue 6/94 the opposite view was taken by Potter J. So far as the authors are aware, this difference remains unresolved. With diffidence it is suggested that it is hard to say that a claim by a mother who has to undergo the pain of labour does not comprise personal injury. On the other hand, a claim by a father whose vasectomy has not been effective, and whose only loss is financial, can be more easily seen as not comprising personal injury.

By s28(1) of the Act, a person under a disability 'on the date when any right of action accrued' may bring an action within the period which is the normal primary limitation period in question, beginning on the day when the disability ceases. Thus, in personal injury cases, the clock starts to tick when a child becomes 18 and the relevant primary period would normally be three years from that date. Thereafter, the same limitation period applies – three years from the date when the cause of action accrued or, if later, the date of the plaintiff's knowledge. A disability which *begins* after the clock starts to tick does not affect the primary period at all – the clock goes on ticking. It is important to emphasise that a disability which arises even a day after the action crystallises, will not stop the clock. The moment when the action accrues can be a complex issue, particularly where there are multiple causes of an action. This needs very careful thought. A disability arising after the action accrues will be highly relevant to the exercise of s33 discretion (see below).

At the outset the solicitor will need to establish from the plaintiff the facts which will determine both when the cause of action accrued and the plaintiff's date of knowledge. These dates may not be immediately obvious. Even if they seem clear, they may need to be revised when medical records are received or an expert's report is available. It is prudent always to take the earliest date as the date from which time starts to run and make the appropriate diary entries to ensure that proceedings are commenced within the limitation period. In extreme cases, where the limitation period is about to expire, it may be necessary to issue proceedings, even though legal aid has not been granted.

The cause of action accrues at the time when the plaintiff suffers damage. The damage need only be minimal and it is irrelevant that the plaintiff was unaware of it. The plaintiff's lack of knowledge of the nature and degree of his injuries is however relevant to his 'date of knowledge' and this important concept is considered below.

If the injured person dies before the expiry of three years from the injury without starting a claim, it can be brought within three years of the deceased's death or of the personal representatives' or dependents' date of knowledge of the accrual of the action, whichever is the earlier. The court can exercise its equitable discretion under s33 of the Act on behalf of dependents but not on behalf of personal representatives (see ss11(5), 12(2) and (3) and 13 of the Act).

Date of knowledge of the act

Limitation Act 1980 s14 lists all the factors which must be present before the clock begins to run. The plaintiff's lawyers need to establish the *first* date on which the plaintiff knew *all* of the facts set out below:

— that the injury in question was significant;
— that the injury was attributable to the acts or omissions which are alleged to be negligent; and
— the identity of the defendant.

Significant injury

The injury is significant if the plaintiff would reasonably have considered it sufficiently serious to justify making a claim against a defendant who admits liability and has the money to pay any damages which may be awarded (see s14(1)(a) and (2) of the Act). At first sight this seems an odd definition, since it may be thought that if a defendant is prepared to admit liability and is good for the money, any plaintiff would regard the injury as significant. The courts have held that this is partly a subjective and partly an objective test. The question which must be asked is – would the client have been reasonable in considering the injury *not* sufficiently serious to justify bringing the claim? If the answer to this question is 'yes', the client does not have the requisite knowledge. In the case of *Broadley v Guy Clapham* (1993) 4 Med LR 328 one of the issues which was considered by the Court of Appeal was whether Mrs Broadley had actual or constructive knowledge that her injury was 'significant'. She had an operation in 1980 for the removal of a loose body from her left knee. After the operation she was unable to dorsiflex her left foot. Over the next seven months she got on with her life, the trial judge finding that her attitude was, 'This is something that has happened to me. I must just get on with it.' Later he commented, 'Even a person as uncomplaining as Mrs Broadley would . . . have thought there was something significantly wrong with an ankle that was still ineffective [seven months] after the operation . . .'. The trial judge found that Mrs Broadley had actual knowledge that her injury was significant.

The approach in *Broadley* was followed by a different Court of Appeal in *Dobbie v Medway Health Authority* (1994) 5 Med LR 160 at 164, where Sir Thomas Bingham MR commented,

> Time does not run against a plaintiff, even if he is aware of an injury, if he would reasonably have considered it insufficiently serious to justify proceedings against an acquiescent and credit-worthy Defendant, if (in other words) he would reasonably have accepted it as a fact of life not worth bothering about. It is otherwise if the injury is reasonably to be considered as sufficiently serious . . . time then runs . . .

In cases where damages are claimed for the effects of a prescribed drug, the injury is not significant until the plaintiff recognises that he is not suffering from an accepted or expected side-effect of the drug but from an injurious or unacceptable consequence of drug ingestion (see *Nash v Ely Lilly* [1993] 1 WLR 782).

Injury attributable to the defendant's fault

It should be noted immediately that knowledge that the act or omissions involved negligence, nuisance or breach of duty as a matter of law is irrelevant – it is knowledge of the *facts* which matters. The plaintiff acquires knowledge when she or he knows of the essence of the act or omission to which his injury is attributable (see *Nash v Ely Lilly* above). In *Broadley v Guy Clapham* (above) the defendant's counsel set out four possible criteria of knowledge of the acts or omissions which could amount to knowledge within the meaning of ss11 and 14 of the 1980 Act:

a) *Broad knowledge*: carrying out the operation to her knee in such a way that something went wrong, namely that it caused foot drop (an injury to her foot).
b) *Specific knowledge*: carrying out the operation in such a way as to damage a nerve, thereby causing foot drop (an injury to her foot).

c) *Qualitative knowledge*: carrying out the operation in such a way as unreasonably to cause injury to a nerve (unreasonably to expose a nerve to a risk of injury).

d) *Detailed knowledge*: knowledge sufficiently detailed to enable the plaintiff's advisers to draft a statement of claim.

Balcombe LJ considered that qualitative or detailed knowledge went beyond the standard necessary for the purposes of s14(1)(b). Only broad and specific knowledge were required. The Court of Appeal specifically disapproved the test applied in *Bentley v Bristol and Weston Health Authority* (1991) 2 Med LR 359 that a plaintiff only acquires knowledge when he learns from his expert that the cause of an injury might be the incompetent use of a specific procedure (in that case excessive traction of the nerve).

Plaintiffs' lawyers will need to establish at what date the client had knowledge of the essence of the act or omission which might amount to negligence. In the authors' view, where a case involves surgical procedures the plaintiff does not have 'knowledge' simply because something went wrong ('broad knowledge'). He or she must know *what* was damaged during the operation ('specific knowledge'). He or she must also know that the injury is significant and attributable; see *Driscoll-Varley v Parkside Health Authority* (1991) 2 Med LR 346.

These recent cases put the plaintiff's lawyers and experts in a difficult position. It may be that from a very early stage the plaintiff him or herself had 'specific knowledge'. However, this is wholly insufficient to enable the plaintiff's lawyers to commence proceedings. At the very least, the plaintiff's solicitor is likely to require a report from an expert giving some detail as to what went wrong and identifying whether the act or omission fell below the standard which could reasonably be expected in such a case. Nevertheless, the current state of the law does suggest that a plaintiff's legal team may be forced into commencing proceedings in order to prevent the claim becoming time-barred with only the bare essentials of allegations of negligence.

The identity of the defendant

The identity of the defendant is usually straightforward enough. In most cases of National Health Service hospital treatment it will be the relevant trust or health authority. If the client knows only the name of the hospital or of the consultant, a telephone call to the hospital or a check through the *Medical Directory* to establish where the consultant was working will enable the proper name of the defendant, corporate or individual, to be found.

Individual GPs, dentists or opticians should be sued personally. The plaintiff may not be able to recall which GP in a practice he or she saw on a particular date and the handwritten note may not identify him or her. The solution is to write to the GP who has been identified, enclose a copy of the relevant entries in the notes and ask for the identity of the author of each entry. This may be a good opportunity to ask for a typed copy of any illegible entries.

In private hospitals the position is more complicated. The managers are responsible for the nursing and administrative staff. The individual surgeon or physician is almost always sued individually because he or she is not an employee of the hospital or clinic. The position of the junior doctors and the anaesthetists will need to be established. Wherever there is any doubt as to the contractual relationship between the managers or owners of the hospital and the staff, write to the managers, ask them who was involved in the operation and the aftercare, and ask them to clarify their contractual relationship with the staff.

Constructive knowledge

Once the date of knowledge has been established, it is necessary to go on to establish whether or not the plaintiff might have had constructive knowledge at an earlier date, because he or she ought to have made enquiries earlier.

Constructive knowledge may be attributed to the plaintiff under s14(3) of the Act in respect of each of the elements or circumstances set out in the previous part of this chapter. The plaintiff's knowledge includes knowledge of facts which he or she could have been expected to acquire directly or with the help of medical, legal or other expert advice which it was reasonable to seek. The plaintiff is not assumed to have knowledge of facts which he or she could only have obtained with expert advice if he or she has taken reasonable steps to obtain and, if appropriate, act on such advice.

The difference between knowledge and belief

A belief by the plaintiff that, for example, his or her injury is significant (in the sense that it is worth suing for) may not be the same as 'knowledge' and so may not start the clock. Most, if not all, plaintiffs require reassurance and confirmation by medical or legal experts of their beliefs. When such confirmation is given, then the plaintiff will have the requisite knowledge. 'Knowledge' may, of course, be constructive knowledge if the plaintiff delays in seeking confirmation of the belief, in circumstances where it would be reasonable to seek confirmation. If negative advice is given, the plaintiff does not acquire knowledge. Similarly, if the plaintiff believes that 'something went wrong during the operation', this does not amount to actual knowledge of the act or omission which is alleged to be negligent. Once again, if a plaintiff believes that something has gone wrong, he or she may be penalised if prompt action is not taken to have that belief confirmed or denied by experts.

Attributability

The plaintiff must have knowledge that his or her injuries are attributable to the act or omission alleged to constitute negligence. How specific does the plaintiff's knowledge have to be? The answer is that at the very least the plaintiff must know the essence of the act or omission alleged to be negligent. This does not mean that he or she (or the lawyers and experts advising him or her) must be aware of each and every particular act of negligence likely to be pleaded. In many cases both plaintiff and solicitor will merely suspect the general nature of what has gone wrong.

For example, in *Broadley v Guy Clapham* (see above) Mrs Broadley was held to have had constructive knowledge (specific knowledge) that her nerve had been damaged within 12 months of the operation. She could and should have asked her GP and consultant 'What went wrong?'

If the solicitors and counsel involved know the essence of the acts or omissions but need further information before the claim can be fully pleaded, they should realise that the limitation clock has begun to tick. The appropriate diary entries must be made.

A final word of warning on the question of the plaintiff's knowledge. If the claim is against a hospital and his or her instructions as to the significance of the injury or the attribution of it suggests that he or she does *not* have the relevant knowledge, it is always sensible to check this. A very useful source of information is the plaintiff's GP's notes. The *absence* of complaints by the plaintiff to his or her GP about the treatment or the significance of the injuries may be helpful if the limitation period is a problem. The *presence* of such material, on the other hand, may well indicate that he or she has already acquired the necessary knowledge for time to start running.

Conclusions on date of knowledge

The lawyers ought to address the issue of date of knowledge at the outset and should constantly revise their views as to when the plaintiff has actual or constructive knowledge of all of the three elements:

— that the injury was significant;
— that it is capable of being attributed to the essence of the act or omission which will form the basis of the claim; and
— the identify of the defendant(s).

The solicitor is justified in asking counsel to advise on date of knowledge at any stage. Counsel is entitled to be given all the relevant information in order to give such advice. Provided full instructions are taken, the plaintiff, the medical experts and the lawyers should be able to make a fairly confident conclusion as to the timetable they will need to work to.

Section 33 discretion

As mentioned above, the courts have an equitable discretion to direct that the three-year time-limit shall not apply. A court has to balance the prejudice to the plaintiff of having his or her action dismissed as out of time against the prejudice to the defendant of allowing the action to proceed. This discretion is unfettered, but the court is required by ss33(3) of the Act to have regard to all the circumstances and in particular to seven specific factors. These are:

a) the length of the delay on the part of the plaintiff (s33(3)(a));
b) the reason for the delay on the part of the plaintiff (s33(3)(a));
c) the extent to which the plaintiff's or defendant's evidence will

be less cogent than if the action had been commenced within three years(s33(3)(b));

d) the defendant's conduct after the cause of action arose, including the extent to which he responded to the plaintiff's reasonable requests for information to establish relevant facts (s33(3)(c));

e) the length of any disability of the plaintiff arising after the cause of action accrued (s33(3)(d));

f) the extent to which the plaintiff acted promptly and reasonably once he knew whether or not the act or omission of the defendant to which his injury was attributable might be capable at that time of giving rise to an action for damages (s33(3)(e)); and

g) the steps the plaintiff has taken to get medical, legal or other expert advice and the nature of any such advice (s33(3)(f)).

Whether preparing a proof of evidence or drafting an affidavit, it is sensible to divide up the plaintiff's evidence so as to deal with each of the factors which are relevant to the exercise of the s33 discretion.

It is not possible in this chapter to cover every possibility and contingency which arises. However, set out below is some advice on material which will usually need to be covered in a proof or affidavit under the specific factors set out above. We have also provided an example of an affidavit on behalf of a plaintiff in appendix 4.

(a) and (b): Length of and reason for delay

All relevant personal details about the plaintiff and his or her family should be included. Where these appear in the medical records (as they usually will), it is important to correct any errors set out in those records. It is important to try to convey the character of the plaintiff and give details about his or her education and ability to understand information received from lawyers or experts from time to time. A full chronological account must be given. Once again, cross-reference this to the medical records. Although the court is primarily concerned with delay after the expiry of the three year primary period of limitation, the paragraphs on delay should also cover the history up to the expiry of that period because the court is also bound to consider the overall delay in commencing proceedings (see *Donovan v Gwentoys* [1990] 1 WLR 472).

(c) Cogency of evidence

The medical records assume paramount importance under this heading. Since the defendants are required to make and keep full and accurate records, the plaintiff is entitled to point out that both parties will have the benefit of such records when evidence is given. Problems arise when the plaintiff alleges that facts or conversations were not recorded by the defendant, that they have been erroneously recorded or that the records have been tampered with afterwards. The reasons why the plaintiff has a cogent recollection of events should be set out in full. Sometimes the defendant's witnesses may have died or gone abroad. In such cases, point out the date when the plaintiff asked the defendant for the medical records or indicated that proceedings were contemplated. At that stage the defendant had the opportunity to take a statement from any witnesses who may no longer be available.

(d) The defendant's conduct

Was the defendant unhelpful or obstructive when asked for disclosure of records or other information? Has the defendant refused further and better particulars or answers to interrogatories? Were the records illegible or disordered when they were disclosed? If the plaintiff sought an explanation for bungled treatment from the hospital, did the defendant put forward an edited, distorted or false explanation? Has the defendant evaded service?

The provisions of Limitation Act 1980 s32(1)(b) should be noted. If any fact relevant to the plaintiff's right of action has been deliberately concealed from him or her by the defendant, time does not run until the plaintiff has actual or constructive knowledge of the concealment.

(e) Disability

This refers to technical disability in the sense of the plaintiff's inability to manage or administer his or her property and affairs by reason of mental disorder. We have dealt with the effect of disability on the primary period above. If disability in the sense of mental disorder starts after the clock has started to run, it does not have the effect of stopping the clock but will be an important and perhaps crucial factor in the exercise of the discretion of the court (as well as in determining the plaintiff's date of knowledge). Was the Court of Protection involved? When was a next friend appointed? What was the reason for any delay in appointing the next friend? Were instructions available from another source, eg, parent or spouse?

(f) Prompt and reasonable action by the plaintiff after he or she had 'knowledge' within the meaning of s14

Once again, full details of the action taken by the plaintiff and his or her advisers must be set out. A plaintiff who does not act promptly may still be acting reasonably. What were the factors which prevented him or her from acting earlier? Personal details such as family, work or disablement may all be relevant.

(g) Action taken by the plaintiff to obtain expert advice and the nature of any advice received

The chronology of seeking advice should be set out. The plaintiff need not disclose the whole of the expert advice received (which is privileged) but should disclose the general nature of that advice so far as is necessary.

In the absence of an act of unequivocal waiver of privilege, a party need not disclose reports or statements referred to in another document (see *Booth v Warrington Health Authority* [1992] 1 PIQR 137), and attempts by defendants to use such a reference in an affidavit to obtain reports should be strongly resisted.

Other areas to consider

Other matters which may need to be covered are the relative strengths of the plaintiff's case on liability and quantum and the extent to which the plaintiff may have a claim against his former solicitors for failing to take action on his behalf. If he or she has a good claim against the solicitors, the court may decide that he or she should pursue the lawyers rather than the doctors. The fact that the defendant is insured or is otherwise good for the money may be relevant.

Procedural matters

This chapter has looked at some of the practical aspects of establishing the plaintiff's date of knowledge followed by practical guidance for the preparation of a hearing in which the court's discretion under s33 is sought. In many cases the court may be called upon both to determine date of knowledge and exercise s33 discretion at the same time. This may arise in the following circumstances:

— a striking out application by the defendants;
— a preliminary issue; or
— at the full trial.

Striking out

The striking out procedure is dealt with in RSC Order 18 r19 and CCR Order 13 r5.

The defendant may seek to strike out the plaintiff's claim on the grounds that it is out of time, frivolous, vexatious or otherwise an abuse of process.

In the face of an application to strike out the pleading, the burden of proof is on the plaintiff to show a date of knowledge within three years of the date when proceedings were commenced. If the action was issued more than three years from the date when the cause of action accrued, the plaintiff must plead in the statement of claim that he or she did not have knowledge until a date within three years of the date the writ was issued. The defendant may deny this and put the plaintiff to proof. Alternatively, the defendant can allege an earlier date of knowledge, in which case the burden of proof is on the defendant to establish that date. The significance of the burden of proof will become apparent on any striking out application. There is usually no evidence other than affidavit material, and discovery may not have taken place. The plaintiff's action will only be dismissed if it is unarguable that his date of knowledge was within three years of the commencement of proceedings.

It should be noted that the plaintiff's pleadings can and in appropriate circumstances should rely on an application for discretion under s33 in the alternative to a pleaded date of knowledge which will preserve the action. If the exercise of discretion is sought in the pleading, then full particulars should be pleaded.

Preliminary issue

The provisions for splitting the trial and dealing with a preliminary issue are found in RSC Order 33 r3 and in CCR Order 13 r2(2)(c).

The plaintiff may have pleaded a late date of knowledge and, alternatively, invoked the s33 discretion. The defendant may have pleaded an earlier date of actual or constructive knowledge on the part of the plaintiff, or may have simply raised the question of limitation, putting the plaintiff to proof that the claim is within time. It may suit the parties to have limitation tried as a preliminary issue. The advantages from the defendant's point of view are obvious. From the plaintiff's point of view there may be advantages also. Success on the preliminary issue is likely to provoke a settlement on the substantive issue of liability and quantum. The disadvantages usually arise where the plaintiff's case is weak on limitation but strong on liability. If both issues are tried at the same time, the court may be more inclined to exercise its s33 discretion in favour of the plaintiff. If one party objects to limitation being tried as a preliminary issue, the other party should take out a summons setting out the grounds in favour.

If a preliminary hearing is ordered, directions are given whereby the parties exchange affidavit evidence. It is then open to each party to indicate which of their opponent's witnesses are required to attend to give evidence. Otherwise the witness affidavits are read out in court. The mini-trial which then takes place will finally dispose of all aspects of the issues of limitation which the case raises.

In *Fletcher v Sheffield Health Authority* (1994) 5 Med LR 156, the Court of Appeal upheld the decision of the county court judge that a preliminary trial of the limitation issue would be wrong since expert evidence would have been required at both the preliminary hearing on limitation and the later substantive hearing. The limitation issues in that case could not readily be separated from issues of causation and negligence.

Conclusion

Limitation is a minefield in any area of litigation, and medical negligence is no exception. The solicitor's highest priorities must be:

a) to analyse the time-scale of a case, in terms of limitation, as early as possible;

b) to diarise appropriately from the very beginning;

c) to try and manage the case with limitation pitfalls in mind.

Plaintiffs in medical cases can *usually* avoid defeat on limitation if the level of presentation and preparedness by the lawyers is high, and if full use is made of the s33 discretion.

CHAPTER 11

Issuing proceedings and pleading

> *To succeed in the profession of the law, you must seek to cultivate command of language. Words are the lawyer's tools of trade . . . When you are advising your client – in writing or by word of mouth – you must use words. There is no other means available. To do it convincingly, do it simply and clearly. If others find it difficult to understand you, it will often be because you have not cleared your own mind upon it. Obscurity in thought inexorably leads to obscurity in language.*

Lord Denning, *The Discipline of Law*

The approach

The essentials of pleading a negligence case were simply stated in the last century by Willes J in *Gautret v Egerton* (1867) LR 2 CP 371. He said that the statement of claim 'ought to state the facts upon which the supposed duty is founded and the duty to the plaintiff with the breach of which the defendant is charged.' Pleadings have changed a great deal since the high Victorian period, but the essential ingredients are the same. Those who plead on behalf of medical victims would do well to have one other governing principle in mind: pleading is at least in part an exercise in advocacy. In addition to meeting the technical requirements, the successful pleader will take care to make the pleadings present the case in a persuasive way.

Pleading cases of extreme technical complexity is naturally difficult. The pleading will hardly be persuasive, unless it achieves to a sufficient degree Lord Denning's objective of being as simple and clear as possible. He is right in saying that such clarity depends on the person drafting the pleadings having a thorough understanding of the subject in hand.

The practice in this field is for pleadings to be markedly longer than in the conventional personal injury action. Some specialists in the field have carried this principle too far, and create pleadings of enormous length and very discursive tone. We believe this is rarely persuasive. A balance must be struck.

Longer pleadings will naturally emerge from a complex and technical story, particularly where the medical terms and acronyms, scientific and medical concepts, and perhaps even the anatomy and pathology in question will be wholly unfamiliar to the judge. However, the pleading which extends to more than 30 pages and 60 paragraphs is usually unapproachable and over-burdened with narrative detail and will tend to lose the attention of the reader. The authors recognise there can be no hard and fast rule. There are exceptional cases which justify gargantuan pleadings, but they are indeed exceptions.

In the course of this chapter, references will be made to the sample pleadings from the case papers in appendix 3. These are illustrative only. It is not claimed that the pleadings in the annex are perfect, and indeed some critical comments are made below. They are intended as useful and perhaps typical examples of specialist pleadings in a case in the field, rather than as examples of perfection; it is doubtful if perfection is achievable. Naturally they reflect the style of the pleaders, and many will have different stylistic preference.

It would be quite impractical to give a full range of pleadings dealing with even the commonest medical 'accidents'. There are too many circumstances which arise. It would also be misleading, since no prescriptive approach can truly be helpful. The pleader in this field must ensure that each pleading is carefully and freshly thought through in the light of the particular facts. Save for a few formulations, the medical negligence statement of claim cannot properly be constructed by reaching for the standard clause from the memory of the computer.

The initiation of proceedings

High Court

In the High Court, a writ allows a case to be begun without any full pleading of the case. This can be extremely useful in a field where usually much time must be spent in research on a case before an informed judgment can be reached on whether the case is viable and justifies the issue of proceedings. An example of a suitably endorsed writ is included in the case papers in appendix 3(I) p286.

County court

In the county court, with initiation by writ impossible, the solicitor may be in the position of needing to issue proceedings while the case has not yet been sufficiently refined to permit full and accurate pleading. This presents a real problem.

In some county courts, district judges will permit the issue of initial particulars of claim which contain little more than a writ would. Depending on local practice, there may be a need for an ex parte order permitting one or more of the following:

a) extension of time for filing full particulars;
b) extension of time for filing of a medical report on condition and prognosis; and
c) extension of time for filing a schedule of loss.

If this is the practice locally, the problem is easily solved. Indeed one solution for those practising away from such courts, is to ascertain the practice in another county court or courts where proceedings could be issued within the terms of CCR Order 4 r2. If another such court will permit the short-style initial particulars of claim, then the claim can be issued there and if necessary transferred later to a nearby court, convenient for interlocutory hearings.

Many courts will not permit 'bare' or general particulars of claim. If the solicitor does not wish to become a migrant for these purposes, then there is no alternative to pleading the case as fully as possible in the knowledge that the pleadings will require subsequent amendment. This is never satisfactory, and the best approach, if driven to this, is to plead as briefly as possible whilst satisfying the court's practice, so that there is the least chance of subsequent amendment becoming embarrassing.

Persons under a disability

Where a plaintiff under a disability wishes to take proceedings in respect of an act or omission which purports to have been done under powers in the Mental Health Act 1983, he or she may need leave (Mental Health Act 1983 s139). If however the proposed defendant is a health authority within the meaning of the National Health Service Act 1977, or (it appears) an NHS trust, or the Secretary of State, then leave of the court is not required (s139(4)). On the other hand, if the proposed defendant is a GP or a social services department, the plaintiff has two steps to take. First, he must apply to the High Court for leave (s139(2) and RSC Order 39 r9(1)(b)). The application is made to a judge and is usually in chambers. Second, he must be able to show that he has an arguable case that his cause of action discloses bad faith or lack of reasonable care on the part of the proposed defendant (see s139(1)).

The practitioner will be aware of the need to file the next friend's consent to act and a solicitor's certificate confirming that there is no conflict of interest between the next friend and the plaintiff.

The full pleading

The approach to the full pleading of the case is the same whether the claim is in the High Court or the county court. For brevity, we refer to the statement of claim in the rest of the chapter, meaning the first full pleading at either level.

The structure of the statement of claim

It is convenient to analyse various segments within the statement of claim, which make up its essential structure:

A. the legal duty
B. the recital of essential fact, which may incorporate or be completed by a recital of minimum acceptable practice
C. the allegations of breach of duty
D. causation
E. damage and loss
F. the claim for interest and the prayer.

If this general structure is adhered to, all the essential elements will be covered. The structure may vary slightly: for example, it may be convenient to deal with causation before the allegations of breach, if the causation is inherent in what happened. However, all these elements must be present or the pleading will be defective.

A. The legal duty

Tortious duty can be pleaded in a more or less formulaic way. The statement of claim in appendix 3J provides a typical example. Some writers suggest that a NHS hospital has a primary duty to provide proper care, and any reference to the employment or engagement of the medical or other staff is otiose, but the authors feel it is wise to include it. The question of whether to sue the individual doctor as well as the hospital, in the context of NHS hospital care, has been discussed elsewhere. We feel it adds little to do so.

The term 'the hospital' above means the relevant health authority, usually the district health authority, or the relevant trust or other governing body. Naturally, the identity of the party needs to be established for the purpose of the issue of the writ and for pre-action discovery and should already be clear when the matter comes to pleading.

The duty of care of the NHS general practitioner (medical or dental) can be equally simply pleaded. The central phrase is that the doctor owes to the plaintiff the duty to provide 'reasonable professional skill and care'. The pleader must consider whether the partners should be sued as having joint and several liability with the errant GP. The authors believe that it is not normally necessary to do so, but if the fault lies with a receptionist, a practice nurse or some other employee, then it will be prudent to do so, pleading the vicarious liability of the whole partnership and/or each partner jointly and severally. A locum should normally be sued in his or her own name, although there may also be partnership responsibility for the actions of a locum.

If the medical care has been offered privately, then different principles apply. First, the duty of care will arise contractually as well as in tort. The nature of the duty will rarely be any different, but the pleader should consider some circumstances touched on below and in chapter 2, where a different duty may arise. Secondly, it is unsafe to rely upon the hospital where the patient was treated as having any liability for the actions of senior medical staff with a contract for services with the plaintiff.

It is necessary in all such cases to sue individually all doctors or surgeons whose care is in question. If the failure of care is alleged to be that of nursing staff, paramedical staff, or very junior employed doctors working for a hospital and treating the patient privately, then the hospital can be sued, on the ordinary principle of vicarious liability by employers. Even here, it is the authors' practice to sue all doctors individually, since it is much more likely that a private hospital will attempt to defend on the basis that a doctor was exercising an independent professional judgement not within their control, and thus that there was no vicarious liability. Since the law is not crystal clear, we recommend caution and suggest that both private hospital and junior doctor be joined.

Sometimes it may be possible to claim that the contract was to provide services above the *Bolam* level, for example if there have been express representations as to the level of expertise of the surgeon concerned which caused the plaintiff to enter into the contract. There appears to be no reported case in this field where this has been litigated, but there is no reason on first principles why such a special duty of care should not be imported by representation or warranty. As noted in chapter 2 on substantive law, this proposition appears to be supported by dicta of Lord Donaldson MR in *Hotson v East Berkshire Health Authority* [1987] 1 All ER 210 at 216. The case of *McLeish v Amoo-Gottfried* (1993) *Times* 13 October should be borne in mind, if pleading any case with an alleged special duty, and perhaps in any private case. This case is analysed at p149 in chapter 14 on damages.

In the great majority of cases, the duty will be uncontroversial, and will be admitted by the defence.

B. Recital of essential fact

It is in the process of pleading this section that the greatest skill in advocacy can be displayed. The objective should be to set out a series of clear, germane propositions of fact; the aim is to make the propositions impossible for the defence to deny, or at least as difficult as possible. Allegations which it is predicted will be denied may often best be placed in a separate paragraph from those it is hoped will be admitted.

The factual propositions must be logical and clear. Any medical or scientific exotica must be explained as the pleading proceeds. A statement of claim which throws in an airy reference to Type II dips on a CTG will be intelligible to the defence and their advisers, but not to most judges. It is here that the pleader must remember that the statement of claim is likely to affect the judge's mind as he or she reads the case papers, possibly three years after pleading, on the eve of trial.

The pleading should be divided into short rather than long paragraphs. This increases clarity, but also has a more important effect. In addressing such a pleading, the defence is less able to blur the issues. A paragraph which has one, two, or at the most three factual propositions is more likely to provoke a defence which meets the case, rather than a defence which departs entirely from the structure of the statement of claim.

The pleadings in the appendix are interesting in this context. The recital of fact in the statement of claim (appendix 3J) is, on the whole, clear and sensibly divided. It provides a judge with a coherent and intelligible narrative on behalf of the plaintiff. However, the skilful defence (appendix 3O) departs from the structure of the statement of claim. The pleader for the defence has set up his own competing narrative, rather than being trapped into a piecemeal response following the plaintiff's pattern. This may succeed in displacing the plaintiff's case from the attention of the judge. On the other hand, it may equally irritate the judge, since he or she will be unable easily to sort out what is accepted and what is rejected by the defence.

The examples in the appendix demonstrate that no pleading approach is certain to gain all its objectives. The pleader for the defence felt able, on advice, to reject almost all the plaintiff's expert's interpretation of the CTG and the allegations of the degree of foetal acidosis which would have been revealed by foetal blood sampling (defence para 6). In most cases, such a wholesale rejection of the plaintiff's expert's case will not be possible. A short, clear recital of fact is much more likely to confine the defence to a responsive pattern of denial, admission or non-admission, which will favour the plaintiff.

The statement of claim will be brought as close as possible to sounding inexorable, by maximum reliance upon observations made and recorded by the defendant's own staff. 'At 8pm Nurse Gamp noted that the plaintiff was cyanosed [blue from lack of oxygen]' will be understood to contain the factual allegation that the plaintiff *was* cyanosed at 8pm and also that such was the nurse's observation at the time. This maximises the difficulty for the defence, since a denial of the allegation will tend to undermine the judgement of its own nurse.

It is essential that clear propositions as to what was the appropriate practice should be made during or at the end of this part of the pleading. In the statement of claim in the appendix, these propositions are spliced into the narrative, since there are multiple propositions as to what was the appropriate response at different times. An example is the last sentence in para 11. Re-reading the pleading after its creation, the authors feel it was correct to make these points along the way. However, it could be argued that the pleading would be improved if the allegations of the minimum standard of care were always in separate paragraphs. This pattern would have separated the last sentence of para 11, the last clause in the first sentence of para 13 and the two sentences in para 14 into small separate paragraphs.

The reader will understand that there is always a high degree of stylistic choice in such decisions. This discussion has, it is hoped, drawn attention to the problems, which the reader faced with pleading such a case will have to solve for him or herself.

C. Recital of breach of duty

In form, this will follow the conventional 'particulars of negligence' familiar from all tort pleadings. The recital of the criticisms should be brief, clear and without duplication. Judges are often reluctant to find that fellow professionals have been negligent. They are extremely unlikely to find that a doctor or restricted group of doctors have been negligent in 28 particulars. A confined set of clear allegations is more likely to prevail. If there is truly only one particular, then that one is the only one which should be pleaded.

A helpful test is to stand back from the pleading after completing the first draft, and consider whether all the particulars are necessary. Is there duplication? Are there allegations of negligence which could not be thought causative of damage? It may even be wise to ask, if allegations A, B and C fail, is it conceivable that allegations D, E and F could succeed? If allegations A, B and C succeed, can the defendants escape liability? If the answer to the last two questions is no, then are D, E and F necessary? They may be worth discarding. There is an obvious risk in pruning too far, but few pleaders do that. Many are too prolix in settling particulars of negligence.

Where it is possible to do so, it is suggested it is good practice to specify the individual responsible for a failure, even if he or she is not being sued individually. The particulars in the appendix exemplify this. There are allegations specifically directed to Sister

White and Mr Rasputin, and also allegations where no individual can confidently be nominated. Where it is possible to name individuals without risk that the particular will be too narrow, then to do so lends an air of confidence and precision to the pleading.

A final principle in pleading particulars is that they should represent the culmination of what has been pleaded already. They must be based on:

a) fact already pleaded – what was in fact done and not done; and
b) necessary practice already pleaded.

It is poor practice to set out particulars which introduce new material. This makes the document confusing and will almost always lead to requests for further and better particulars. It is poor advocacy. It permits the pleader of the defence merely to enter a traverse of the particulars, leaving the plaintiff's team wondering whether the denial is directed solely to the assertion of negligence, or extends to the factual material introduced in this way.

D. Causation

This can be dealt with briefly. The alleged chain of causation should be clearly set out. The issue may arise in a negative sense during the narrative; an example is in the last sentence of para 13 in the statement of claim in appendix 3J. Here the pleader is making it clear that damage was *not* caused by a certain act or by a given time. The period when the damage was caused and the connection with the treatment complained of should be clear.

E. Injury, loss and damage

In most medical cases it will not be sufficient to recite that the plaintiff has suffered injury, loss and damage as a result of the pleaded negligence. These matters require to be pleaded with sufficient particularity. It is not sufficient to recite that the medical report which accompanies the statement of claim deals with the issue. In RSC note 18/12/1, the editors of the White Book state expressly that the duty to serve a medical report 'does not dispense with the need to plead brief particulars of the injuries sustained and the prognosis'. This sits ill with the suggestion at note 18/12/4A that the medical report 'served under this rule will operate as the particulars of the allegation of the personal injuries sustained or suffered in the statement of claim'. The prudent course is to place brief particulars in the body of the pleading which are expanded in the medical reports served.

In *Sion v Hampstead Health Authority* (1994) 5 Med LR 170 at 172, Staughton LJ considered the effect of the medical reports served with pleadings, suggesting that the report(s) should be regarded as 'a general outline of the plaintiff's case' and that the plaintiff would not be 'wholly and rigidly confined to what is said in the report'.

The same principle applies to the question of financial loss. A sentence or two in the body of the pleading indicating the nature of the loss will usually suffice. The construction of a schedule of loss is considered in chapter 15. Often the only schedule which can be served with the pleading in a medical case is very much a preliminary guide or skeleton. Such a schedule has been incorporated into the hypothetical case of Brown (appendix 3K, p291), which can be compared with the full schedule in Smith (appendix 7, p326).

In some cases, particularly where it is proposed to have a split trial, it may be sensible to seek an order relieving the plaintiff of the obligation to serve a schedule at all.

F. Claim for interest and prayer

These should be pleaded in the same way as in an ordinary personal injury action.

Reading the defence – further pleadings

As noted above, the defence will either follow the structure of the statement of claim or will set up a competing narrative. Whichever approach is taken, the defence must make it plain what the defendant's case is, and the first step when contemplating further pleadings after receipt of the defence is to decide if the defence case is sufficiently clear. There is undoubtedly a trend, being advanced by the judiciary, for more open handling of medical cases. Useful dicta, noting and supporting the 'open-handed' approach, are to be found in *Khan v Armaguard* (1993) 18 BMLR 86.

The authors' anecdotal experience is that High Court judges favour the open-handed approach to pleading and other aspects of procedure, much more than district judges and masters of the Queen's Bench. The latter, who usually take the decisions on whether to order interrogatories, further particulars or amendments to defences, are generally more conservative in their approach to pleading.

The general principles governing further and better particulars and interrogatories should be familiar to the reader. It is however worth noting some specific points.

Requesting further and better particulars

Further and better particulars will usually be ordered not merely to establish what the defence say was actually happening, but also to establish what the medical professionals believed was happening. By definition, it was the latter which governed their actions. The basis of their belief is also a relevant consideration.

Very often it is thought the doctors have acted on a reasonable but mistaken belief of fact, and acted so as to damage the patient by omission or commission. Where this is or may be the case, three interlocking questions of fact must be clarified:

a) what was actually happening?
b) what did the professionals believe was happening at the time?
c) as a matter of fact, what was the professional thinking at the time, based on his or her contemporaneous beliefs as to what was happening to the patient?

It is the last question of fact which will have determined the medical decisions taken. All of these are matters of fact, which must be elucidated before the experts advising the plaintiff can make final judgments about the case.

It is necessary for the pleadings to throw sufficient light on these matters, so that the issues between the parties can be adequately defined. The multi-layered factual ingredients of the medical negligence case should be borne in mind when framing requests and in arguing for particulars to be ordered. Often there will be resistance to pleading a sufficient or any summary of layers (b) and (c) above. A request for such particulars of the defence will be met with rejection and an assertion that the request is directed to matters of evidence. This is misconceived, but can often be successful before a master unless the request makes clear the relevance of the point sought, and unless the intellectual basis of the request is made plain in argument. Naturally, particulars of mere evidence are inappropriate. It is very often problematic to identify the line between mere evidence and relevant issues.

One particular point to note in the context of requesting further and better particulars is how to address the 'pregnant negative'. This is not a medical term, but a reference to a denial of an allegation that something significant was not done by the defendants. Let us suppose that an allegation is made that the defendants had no proper system to guard against swabs being left inside a patient undergoing surgery. A denial of that allegation will in fact be an assertion that there *was* a proper system in place. The normal rule, that no particulars can be requested of a denial, does not apply here, precisely because the defence is actually making a positive assertion.

This principle was established long ago (see *McLulich v McLulich* [1920] P 349 and *Pinson v Lloyds Bank* [1941] 2 KB 72). However, it appears that many practitioners have not attended to this. The matter received a good deal of comment in 1994; see *Hockaday v S W Durham H A* (1994) PMILL Vol 10 No 6.

If the traverse is pregnant, then it is not safe to assume that no positive evidence of system (or of any other implied positive allegation, to which the pregnant negative gives natural birth) can be given by the defendants at trial, without further pleading by the defendants. It is incumbent on the plaintiff to analyse the defence and observe the pregnant negative. If a proper request for further particulars is made, then further particulars will be ordered. If no request is made, then the evidence will be permitted, and may well completely undermine the case of the unwary plaintiff.

Giving further and better particulars

The ordinary principles apply to giving such particulars. In the nature of things, the plaintiff tends to have possession of less primary information than the defendants. Nevertheless, some defence pleaders in the field have established the practice of settling enormous requests for particulars. The authors'

tentative suggestion is to err on the side of generosity in responding to requests,

a) since there is little to lose, if the plaintiff and witnesses have
been well proofed and in the context of the modern system for
exchange of witness statements;
b) since the judicial trend is to favour 'open-handedness'; and
c) provided any trespass towards communicating the expert
judgments being made on the plaintiff's side is prefaced by
qualification.

It will often be appropriate to reply, 'The request directs itself
towards matters of expert evidence and the defendants are not
entitled to particulars of evidence. Notwithstanding, for the
avoidance of doubt, and subject to the expert evidence which
will be furnished in due course, the plaintiff is prepared to
make the following reply.' Such a disclaimer may read rather
ponderously, but it is a necessary precaution.

Under no circumstances should a specific medical report be
identified in any pleading, unless it is absolutely vital to do so.
There can be circumstances where the plaintiff's knowledge is in
question for the purposes of limitation, when mention of expert
advice is unavoidable. Even there, the reference should be kept as
general as possible. If a specific expert's report is mentioned, then
the defendants are likely to seek production of that report under
RSC Order 24 r10 or CCR Order 14 r4.

The tactics of what response to make to a request for
particulars vary so much from case to case, that it is difficult
to offer any more useful suggestions here.

Interrogatories

The modern procedure for interrogatories, whereby a notice is
served and an obligation to reply arises unless a counter-notice is
served (see RSC Order 26 passim), has changed only the
procedure surrounding interrogatories. Their use and purpose
have remained the same, as has the very wide test for their
propriety, namely that they are necessary for disposing fairly of
the cause or matter, or for saving costs. Order 26 consists of a
compendious code and set of notes dealing with this whole topic,
and is required reading before a pleader settles his or her first set
of interrogatories and many times thereafter.

The principal use of interrogatories in this field is to flush out weaknesses or clear up lacunae in the other side's case. If the pleader for the plaintiff senses that there is a gulf between different professional witnesses of fact on a relevant issue, the interrogatory is an impressive weapon for exploiting such a weakness. The question should recite quite simply the discrepancy: 'The note compiled by Sister White indicates that the first vaginal examination by Mr Rasputin was at 4.10 am. The note made by you [Mr Rasputin] indicates that the first vaginal examination by you was at 5.00 am. When was the first vaginal examination you made of the plaintiff's mother on 17 October 1990?'

Provided the question gives rise to a simple answer by the person interrogated, the question may often be quite long and involved. In appendix 3Q (p309), other examples of interrogatories and answers to interrogatories are framed in the case of *Brown v Barchester Health Authority*, which give a flavour of what may and may not be achieved.

Interrogatories may properly be served after witness statements have been exchanged. The authors have had experience that interrogatories served at this point, exploiting a pregnant silence in two doctors' witness statements as to a crucial conversation between them, produced an admission of liability in a previously heavily defended case worth over £1m.

The pleader must constantly have a weather eye to the contents of RSC Order 26, to the area of overlap between particulars and interrogatories, and to the difficult question of where the interrogatory goes too far or too wide, and is likely to be refused by the defendants and the court. No pleader will achieve a 100% 'strike rate', only serving interrogatories which are answered or ordered to be answered. It is essential that instructing solicitors consult with counsel who settled an interrogatory which has been refused before seeking an order. Counsel may not wish to risk the costs of a contest on the point, and should be given the opportunity to say so.

Conclusion

Pleading the medical case is taxing, and should not be done loosely or on automatic pilot. The essential point is that the pleading must be clear to be persuasive, and must be persuasive to do its job for the plaintiff.

CHAPTER 12

The summons for directions and other interlocutory applications

Another interesting case was dealt with recently at the Cruiskeen Court of Voluntary Jurisdiction. A man called Smoke sued a well-known Dublin surgeon for grievous bodily injuries. The defendant claimed professional privilege and counter-claimed for fees amounting to £457.12.3. His Honour Judge Twinfeet, mounting the Bench, said 'Now, no jargon. Whoever uses jargon is for it.'

Opening the case for the plaintiff, Mr Juteclaw said that his client was a decent working man, a trade unionist and a member of the Trinity College Fabian Society . . .

Proceeding, Mr Juteclaw said that his client's object in visiting the defendant was to seek treatment for his complaint. He received no treatment whatever and was at no time given even what is commonly known as 'the lamp'. But after an interval of inaction, the defendant cut the plaintiff's hand off, when the latter was suffering from the effects of some vapour or potent drug, no doubt administered by the defendant. Mr Smoke now found himself crippled for life. He came to court seeking substantial damages.

His Honour: 'I am perished up here.'

Myles na gCopaleen,
The Cruiskeen Court of Voluntary Jurisdiction

The summons for directions

It is important for the plaintiff, through his or her lawyers, to be in the driving seat of the litigation. The summons for directions (the pre-trial review hearing in the county court) sets the procedural timetable. It is, therefore, a key stage for the plaintiff if he or she is to maintain control of the action.

High Court actions

In the High Court the automatic directions which apply to personal injury actions do not apply to medical negligence actions. RSC Order 25 r8(5) states: 'This rule applies to any action for personal injuries except . . . (b) any action where the pleadings contain an allegation of a negligent act or omission in the course of medical treatment'. For this reason a summons for directions has to be issued.

When to issue the summons in the High Court

Under RSC Order 25 r1, 'the plaintiff must within one month after pleadings in the action are deemed to be closed, take out a summons (in these rules referred to as a summons for directions) returnable in not less than 14 days'. It is not uncommon for the defence to ask for a lengthy extension of time for service of the defence in order to enable them to investigate the claim. In most cases, extensions of three months are not unreasonable.

If a lengthy extension is being granted, it is in the plaintiff's interest to rely on RSC Order 25 r1(7), which entitles any party to an action to take out a summons for directions at any time after the defendant has given notice of intention to defend, or if there are two or more defendants, at least one of them has given such notice. Allowing for listing delays, the effect is that the summons for directions is likely to be heard either shortly before the defence is due (in which case it can incorporate provision for service of the defence) or immediately after.

County court actions

Unlike in the High Court, CCR Order 17 r11 does not specify that the automatic directions do not apply to medical negligence actions. Hence, if those directions are not to apply, the plaintiff must make application for a pre-trial review date to be set, so that directions other than the automatic ones are made. Since the automatic directions take effect as soon as pleadings are deemed to be closed, the application for the pre-trial review should be made no later than that date.

The authors consider that it is never advisable to have the automatic directions in a medical negligence action. It will rarely be possible in a medical negligence action to meet the tight timetable imposed by the automatic directions. Further, the automatic directions provide that witness and expert witness evidence be exchanged at the same time (CCR Order 17 r11(3)(b)(i) and (iii)). The importance of lay witness evidence being exchanged before expert evidence is discussed below.

What directions should be sought?

When considering what directions should be sought, thought needs to be given to what evidence it will be necessary for each party to serve in support of their respective cases and what the sequence and timetable for this should be.

A precedent High Court summons for directions is set out in appendix 3P. The authors have not included a precedent for a county court order for directions because each county court tends to have its own style of order and if the application for directions other than the automatic ones is to go smoothly, the prudent lawyer will familiarise him or herself with the local format and adapt the wording of the directions sought accordingly.

In the following sections we set out the directions that should be sought. Where special considerations apply, county court directions are discussed separately.

The precedent summons has been drafted on the assumption that the defence has been served. Clearly if it has not or if there are further and better particulars of pleadings which have not been replied to, provision needs to be made for these and the rest of the timetable adjusted accordingly.

The steps which the precedent summons provides for are:

— discovery
— exchange of witness of fact statements
— exchange of expert evidence on liability and causation issues
— exchange of expert evidence on condition and prognosis
— service of the schedule of loss with supporting documentation
— service of the counter-schedule with supporting documentation
— numbers of witnesses
— setting down for trial.

Discovery

Discovery by the defendant

Even though pre-action discovery will have taken place, the defendants must still serve an itemised list of documents.

If full pre-action discovery has been given, the only additional documents that the defendants will have to disclose are those records relating to the plaintiff which have come into being since pre-action discovery was given.

When considering the defendant's list of documents the plaintiff's lawyers should consider it in the light of the plaintiff's evidence and the defence. For example, does it list all the documents already disclosed by way of pre-action discovery? Is the defence pleaded in such a way that it indicates that other documents exist which have not been disclosed? If so, specific discovery of these documents should be sought.

Plaintiff's discovery

During investigation of the plaintiff's claim, medical records from a number of sources will have been obtained and these will probably have been updated. These records should be listed in the plaintiff's list of documents, even if the defendants have been given pre-action discovery of them.

Consideration then needs to be given to what other documents the plaintiff has in his or her possession or control which are discoverable. There may be documents relating to the special damages claim such as wage slips or receipts. If the plaintiff is a child who has suffered brain damage as a result of the negligence, any education statements or reviews that have been prepared and with which the family have been provided should be disclosed.

Exchange of statements from witnesses of fact

The importance of factual and expert witness evidence is discussed elsewhere, as are the steps in response to the defendant's witness evidence (ie, specific discovery, interrogatories). It is imperative that the summons for directions provides for exchange of witness evidence in advance of the exchange of expert evidence.

Exchange of expert evidence on liability

When determining the timing for this exchange, sufficient time must be allowed after the date for service of the witness statements to ensure that the experts will have time to consider the witness evidence and to incorporate their opinion on the contents of the statements into their final reports.

Thought should also be given to whether there is any intervening event which might affect the timetable – for example, if the Christmas and New Year holiday will fall during the period between exchange of witness and expert evidence, it might be wise to allow two extra weeks.

Service of plaintiff's schedule and documents in support

The importance and preparation of this is discussed in chapter 15. Frequently the preparation of the final schedule is a lengthy and complex task and sufficient time should be allowed for this to be completed.

Service of counter-schedule and documents in support

It is important to ensure that there is a realistic period for the defendant to investigate the financial claim, between service of the plaintiff's schedule and the last effective date for a payment into court before the trial begins. How long a 'reasonable period' may be will vary from case to case, depending on the complexity of the financial claim.

Numbers of expert witnesses

As the automatic directions in the county court provide for expert witnesses to be limited to two per party, it can be difficult to persuade the court to grant more. Clear reasons must be given.

In both the High Court and the county court, the practice is to specify in the directions the maximum numbers of expert witnesses to be called by both parties. Careful thought will have to be given by the plaintiff's solicitor about the likely specialities from which liability, causation and quantum experts will be called and, therefore, what the maximum number is likely to be. If in doubt between two figures, the larger should be inserted in the summons. Whilst, obviously, an application to vary the numbers of witnesses can always be made if it is necessary to do so, the costs of the application will almost certainly have to be borne by the plaintiff.

Defendants may seek to try to limit the number of specified witnesses. Unless they can satisfy a master or district judge that the plaintiff cannot explain why so many are required or unless the number sought is clearly excessive, they are unlikely to succeed. The plaintiff's advisers will still have to prove on taxation of costs that the number of experts called was reasonable and necessary for the preparation of the plaintiff's claim.

Setting down for trial

The High Court summons for directions should make provision for setting down the action for trial. The authors consider that plaintiffs are always well advised to seek a direction enabling them to set the matter down for trial within a short period, for example 56 days.

The plaintiff will be able to set the case down and get an appointment to fix the date for trial within three to four months of the hearing for directions. The fixture can be tailored to allow time for the procedural timetable to be completed and to ensure the availability of experts, witnesses and counsel (see below). The benefit of this is that by setting down and fixing the date of trial so early, the plaintiff maintains tight control over the procedural timetable. In addition, it will mean an earlier date for trial. A direction that the case should not be set down until after a specified time following close of pleadings or until after exchange of expert evidence means that there is likely to be a delay of about a further twelve months in getting a fixture. It also means that if the defendants delay in serving their defence or their expert evidence, then they have effective control over when the trial is listed.

Practice about fixing dates for trial in the county court varies from court to court and the prudent lawyer will check local procedure. Some county courts feel uncomfortable about listing cases as far ahead as it is necessary to list medical negligence cases. The authors' view is that an application to fix a date for the trial should be made and listed for hearing at the same time as the application for a pre-trial review for directions. Prior to the hearing, it is advisable to check that the listing diary for the appropriate period will be available so that the trial date can be fixed. The benefit of doing this is that it prevents the delays caused by defendants failing to provide the court with dates to avoid and also cuts out any administrative delay in fixing a date for trial. If this practice is to be followed, it will be essential to know in advance on what dates the plaintiff's experts will not be available to attend a trial.

No lawyer should underestimate how important it is for a plaintiff or a plaintiff's family to know that there is a date when the claim will be over, however far ahead that date may be.

Place and mode of trial

Medical negligence cases will generally be category B cases in the High Court and will always warrant a circuit judge in the county court.

There may be circumstances (for example convenience of witnesses) which will lead one or other side to decide to try to have the case listed for trial in a court other than the one in which it has been issued. If the application is made by the defendant, careful thought will have to be given by the plaintiff's advisers as to whether or not such a move will benefit the plaintiff and his or her expert witnesses.

Other directions to be considered

Transfers between High Court and county court

Under RSC Order 25 r3, the High Court must consider on the hearing of the summons for directions whether the matter should be transferred to a county court. RSC Order 25 r6(2A) requires the plaintiff to lodge a statement of the value of the action and to serve a copy on the other party(ies) not later than the day before the hearing of the summons. Order 25 provides that failure to comply with this provision will result in the proceedings being automatically transferred to the county court.

The High Court and County Court Jurisdiction Order 1991 article 7(5) sets out the criteria to be considered by both the High Court and the county courts in deciding whether to exercise their power to transfer actions to the other court. The *Practice Direction* of 26 June 1991 [1991] 1 WLR 643 indicates that cases involving professional negligence and fatal accidents will be considered important and therefore suitable for High Court trial.

Trial of preliminary issue

Reference has already been made in chapter 10 on limitation to the possibility of limitation being tried as a preliminary issue. Clearly, if it is decided that this should happen, the directions will have to be tailored to meet this.

Split trials

There are probably as many opinions as to whether or not a split trial benefits a plaintiff as there are lawyers who specialise in medical negligence litigation.

The authors believe that a decision has to be taken on a case-by-case basis. If the prognosis is clear and, therefore, unlikely to be affected by a delay, and if work has already started on preparing the plaintiff's claim for a trial on liability and quantum, arguably a split trial will only delay the final resolution of the claim. On the other hand, if the plaintiff's evidence on liability is strong and a shorter liability-only trial can be listed considerably sooner than a full trial, it might be in the plaintiff's interests to have a split trial; in that case, if the plaintiff succeeds on liability, the defendant will have difficulty resisting a request for a substantial interim payment.

Even in those circumstances, it is difficult to generalise with any confidence. In some cases, one would make the judgment that the plaintiff is more vulnerable without the tactical scope afforded by a full trial listing; it may be more advantageous to negotiate with all the uncertainties weighing upon the defendants.

Clearly, if it is decided that there should be a split trial, then the directions being sought will have to be tailored accordingly. The directions relating to quantum will not, obviously, need to be included.

It should be borne in mind that while the conventional split trial merely directs that liability and quantum should be tried separately, some cases may need more refinement or imagination than that. It may make sense to try a short crucial issue of liability first. It is perfectly possible to get a direction that causation be tried on its own. If that is the most crucial issue, and can be dealt with relatively quickly, it may be right to have it tried anticipating that a settlement is likely to flow if the plaintiff is successful.

Another point to consider is whether the location of the liability/quantum split is clear, since the boundary can be blurred. Care needs to be taken that experts do not have to attend both trials. For example, the authors know of a case where a patient's heart condition went undiagnosed, leading to a 'coronary'. A direction was given to try liability and causation separately. The medical evidence in the first trial established liability *and* 'causation', namely that the plaintiff's heart attack would not have occurred or would not have been so significant if it had occurred, but for the negligence. However, because of the court's order, the evidence stopped short of depicting the detailed medical consequences for the plaintiff, since to do so was clearly to decide issues of quantum. In the event, after the plaintiff succeeded on the first trial, a most difficult negotiation ensued. It would have been much more sensible to have had more fully developed directions specifying that all medical issues should be decided at the first trial, which would have equipped the two sides with full judicial findings for the negotiation and would also have meant that no further attendance would be required of the medical witnesses.

After the directions have been made

If the summons for directions or plaintiff led pre-trial review is to fulfil its potential of placing the plaintiff in the driving seat of the litigation, it is essential that all of the deadlines for service and exchange are diarised and that so far as possible those deadlines are met.

Fixing the date for trial in the High Court

In a medical negligence claim it is essential that all the experts upon whose evidence the plaintiff will rely will be available to attend trial. For this reason it is important to get a fixed date for the trial rather than running the risk of an expert or experts being unavailable when a case gets into the warned list.

As soon as the case has been set down for trial in the High Court, an application to fix the date for trial should be made. Before the appointment to fix, the plaintiff's experts should be asked to provide a list of dates on which they will not be available to attend a trial in order to ensure that the date that is fixed is convenient for all.

Other interlocutory orders – Order 14 and interim payments

Occasionally, it is appropriate to consider an RSC Order 14 summons in a medical case. This should only usually arise in a case of the very grossest kind, such as the amputation of the wrong limb, or the administration of a large dose of the wrong drug. In truth, such an application should only be made if it can be confidently anticipated that the other side will not sustain opposition to the summons. If this procedure is followed, then a good approach is as follows.

a) Review the medical evidence for the plaintiff, which will have to be disclosed much earlier than otherwise. Is it watertight? Are the experts experienced, confident and good enough not to be rocked?
b) Consider whether the district judge or High Court judge can be presented with a fairly clear line through the case. Can it be presented so clearly that the application is likely to succeed, if the other side do resist?
c) If the application is made, it should be accompanied by a simultaneous summons for an interim payment, since that (i) will increase the likelihood of settlement, (ii) arguably has a slightly lower threshold for the plaintiff to jump, and (iii) will avoid any frustrating delay after victory under Order 14 before the plaintiff begins to see the rewards of victory.
d) The dates for service of affidavits should be fairly generous. If the affidavit for the plaintiff is delivered not less than eight weeks before the hearing date, then it is difficult for the defendants to resist a date for their affidavit(s) in reply not less than four weeks in advance of the hearing. With such a timetable, it will be possible to withdraw the summons with minimum cost, if there really is something revealed in the defendants' affidavits or reports which discloses a triable issue.

It is stressed that Order 14 applications are very much the exception in professional negligence cases. This caution is reflected in dicta in *European Partners in Capital (EPIC) Holidays BV v Goddard and Smith* [1992] 41 EG 118. The question at issue in that case was surveyors' negligence, but the dicta are capable of general application.

Applications for interim payments in medical litigation are otherwise to be dealt with exactly as in other personal injury cases. It is important for the plaintiff's advisers to consider whether an interim payment should be sought and, indeed, whether it is essential to do so – for example, because a severely disabled plaintiff cannot be properly cared for in the current home and an interim payment is required to purchase and adapt a new property. Many other interlocutory orders are mentioned throughout the book as they naturally arise, and it is not intended to deal with them all separately here.

CHAPTER 13

Exchange of evidence with the defendants

Here is the classic example of circumstantial evidence. A witness in a railway case at Fort Worth was asked to tell in his own words just how Hole, a mate of his, came by his death. He said: 'Well, 'Ole and me was walking down the track, and I heard a whistle, and I got off the track, and the train went by and I got back on the track. I didn't see 'Ole, but I walked along, and pretty soon I saw 'Ole's hat, then I walked on and saw one of 'Ole's legs. After that I seen one of 'Ole's arms, and then another leg; and then, over on one side, I seen 'Ole's head, and I says to meself: "My Gawd, something muster 'appened to 'Ole."'

Reginald Hine, *Confessions of an Uncommon Attorney*

After the documentary discovery, pre-action or on issue of the writ, there are usually four (and sometimes five) stages of exchange of evidence with the defendants. These are: exchange of witness evidence; exchange of expert evidence on liability and causation; exchange of expert evidence on condition and prognosis; exchange of expert, witness and documentary evidence in support of the schedule of damages; and in some cases exchange of supplementary or consequential expert reports on liability and causation or condition and prognosis.

This chapter will look at how the factual witness and medical expert witness evidence is prepared for exchange and the process of exchange. The directions which it is advisable to seek in relation to the exchange of witness and expert evidence are discussed in chapter 12. The preparation of expert evidence in support of the schedule of damages is discussed in chapter 15.

Preparation of witness evidence for exchange

The exchange of evidence of witnesses of fact is a key stage in the preparation of a medical negligence claim. Because it is a stage at   131 which both sides have to review the strength of their factual evidence, it can be the spur to an early admission of liability.

The directions will provide for exchange of witness evidence between the parties. As discussed in chapter 12, it is essential that the exchange of the witness evidence on liability and causation issues takes place before the exchange of medical evidence on liability and by way of mutual and simultaneous discovery between the parties. Such a method of exchange is tactically important for the plaintiff because it will ensure that the defendant's evidence is not simply a tailored response to the plaintiff's witness statements or expert evidence.

The directions may provide that the initial exchange of witness evidence will only relate to liability and causation issues or they may provide for statements to deal both with liability and causation issues and issues relating to quantum. The authors would argue that, except save in cases where the plaintiff has recovered from all the physical, emotional and financial effects of the negligent care, the initial exchange of witness evidence should be confined to liability and causation issues. It is considered that quantum issues are more appropriately addressed in witness statements to be served with the schedule of damages because they will relate to issues relevant to the schedule. The preparation of witness evidence relating to quantum is accordingly discussed separately.

Orders for exchange of statements

RSC Order 38 r2A and CCR Order 20 r12A empower the court to order that witness evidence should be exchanged. There should in fact be no need to seek a separate order, since it is critical that the order for directions in a medical negligence claim provides for the exchange of witness statements. The note in the White Book to Order 38 indicates that:

> The overriding features of the written statements which may be served under the Order are:
> (1) that they are intended for use at the trial itself; and
> (2) that they relate to issues of fact to be adduced at the trial.
> Accordingly, the written statement of such a witness must contain only such material facts as the witness is able to prove from his own knowledge.

Order 38 also indicates what form the statements should follow. They should be expressed in the first person and state:

a) the full name of the witness;
b) his place of residence or, if he is making the statement in his professional business or other occupational capacity, the address at which he works, the position he holds and the name of the firm or employer;
c) his occupation, or if he has none, his description; and
d) the fact that he is a party to the proceedings or is the employee of such a party (if such is the case).

Witness evidence relating to liability and causation issues

The preparation of witness evidence begins with the taking of the initial proof from the plaintiff (or in the case of a child or person acting under a disability, the person giving instructions on the plaintiff's behalf). What the proof should cover has been discussed in chapter 4. That document and other initial witness statements that were taken during the investigation stage of the claim will form the basis of the witness statements for exchange.

Once it is apparent that a claim is not only going to be pursued, but that it is going to be defended – and the plaintiff's advisers know from the pleadings what the nub of the defence will be – the preparation of witness evidence in a form fit for exchange should be commenced. It may well be that if any further documents are received or served prior to exchange (ie, further and better particulars of the defence or replies to interrogatories), the witness statements will have to be reviewed and amended prior to service.

The first stage in the preparation of witness evidence for exchange is to check who may be able to give evidence relevant to the issues. If it is apparent that there may have been other witnesses who can give evidence relevant to liability and causation issues, but only the plaintiff has been proofed, the other witnesses must be contacted and proofed.

Before the witness or plaintiff's proof is prepared for exchange its contents must be reviewed in the light of the contents of the medical records, the plaintiff's expert's reports, the statements of other witnesses and the pleadings. If there are factual discrepancies the witness should be reproofed on these points in order to ascertain whether the initial proof really records what he or she can remember and does so accurately and fully, or whether it only partially records what the witness recalls or perhaps records what he or she assumed happened or when it happened.

If the discrepancy is, for example, between the contents of the plaintiff's statement and the defence and relates to an event which is either ambiguously recorded in the notes or not recorded at all, clarifying and checking the plaintiff's evidence on the point may be crucial to the outcome of the case. For example, the plaintiff's statement may indicate that during a specified period there was no examination by a doctor. The defence may plead that a doctor reviewed the plaintiff's condition during that period and may specify a time for the review even though the records provide no specific indication of the time of the examination. In such a conflict it is essential to check the point with the plaintiff. It may be that the plaintiff's evidence remains the same. It may, however, be that the plaintiff means that no detailed physical examination took place, but does he or she recall a doctor coming into the room?

There is no doubt in the minds of the authors that there are some medical events about which people retain an extraordinarily clear, accurate and detailed memory – for example, the events surrounding the birth of a child. Equally, where a witness is giving evidence about a series of appointments which took place over a number of months or years, separating the memory of one from the other may be difficult if not impossible.

If a witness remains certain that his or her recollection of events is accurate and that recollection conflicts with the contents of, say, the records or the defence, it will be necessary to explore the reason for the witness's confidence. It may, for example, prove to be the case that the witness is certain because a letter or diary note was written immediately after the event and that the witness has retained or seen that record. If so, the document should be obtained.

Should counsel approve the witness evidence before exchange?

There should be no need for the experienced medical negligence solicitor to ask counsel to approve witness evidence before exchange except in the most factually complex of cases. The authors would, however, urge practitioners who are not experienced to ask counsel to advise on and approve the contents of such statements. The costs of counsel doing so should be recoverable on taxation as a step that was necessary and reasonable, although, of course, additional resort to counsel is likely to affect the level of mark-up or standard fee enhancement on profit costs the solicitor is entitled to recover.

If counsel is to be instructed to advise on the witness statements, the question of any legal aid limitation needs to be addressed. In privately funded cases, the client's authority to instruct counsel must be sought and obtained.

Exchange of witness evidence

There is no magic to effecting exchange with the defendant when the order for directions provides that it is to be by way of mutual and simultaneous exchange. All that the plaintiff's solicitor does is to contact the defendant's solicitor on the day before exchange is due to take place in order to see if they are also ready to exchange. Assuming that they are, both sides can then agree to put the witness statements in the post or document exchange that day and thereby comply with the order. If the defendants breach the timetable, a summons should be issued. No disbarring order is likely on a first application, but breach of a revised timetable will often make a debarring order achievable.

What to do once witness evidence is exchanged

It is essential that exchange of witness statements of fact takes place before exchange of expert evidence. It is nonsensical as well as wasteful of costs for it to occur either at the same time or after exchange of expert evidence.

As soon as the defendant's witness statements are received, the solicitor must consider the contents carefully and compare them against each other, against the plaintiff's statements and the records. He or she must consider whether there is an irreconcilable conflict between assertions in different witness statements as to time or place. For example, is one defence witness saying that a patient was being kept under minute-by-minute observation, but another witness states that all the staff concerned were involved in serving lunch to the other patients on the ward at the material time?

The plaintiff and his or her witnesses should always be sent copies of the defence witness statements for comment. If a version of events is entirely at odds with the plaintiff's evidence, or if new and/or different issues are raised in the statements, it will be essential to take a further detailed proof from the plaintiff and/ or other witnesses, including witnesses employed by the defendant. For example, if the medical staff indicate that any failure in care was the result of acts or omissions by nursing staff from whom there are no statements, the plaintiff's solicitors should consider themselves tracing and interviewing the nursing staff.

The experts advising on liability and causation should also be sent copies of the defence statements. This is discussed below.

Preparation for exchange of expert witness evidence on liability and causation

The first step in the preparation of expert evidence for exchange will have been taken when the expert or experts were initially instructed.

The second step will have been taken by seeing the expert or experts in conference before the issue of proceedings.

The third step is that the experts should be sent copies of the final form statements served on behalf of the plaintiff, the defence witness statements and the comments of the plaintiff and the plaintiff's witnesses on those statements. The expert should be asked whether the contents of the statements affect his or her opinion in any way and/or whether he or she wishes to amend his or her report to deal with issues raised in any of the statements. This is discussed in more detail below.

The fourth step in the preparation is the pre-exchange conference with the experts.

Organising the pre-exchange conference with the experts

The authors take the view that it is unwise in any action where liaibility is in dispute to proceed to exchange of expert evidence without a pre-exchange conference with the client and experts.

A conference should be arranged with the experts on liability and causation at which the contents of the records, all the documents that have been served (ie, pleadings, further and better particulars, interrogatories and replies to the same, and witness evidence) and the reports and comments to date of the plaintiff experts should be reviewed. The importance of this conference cannot be overestimated. It is the first post-issue stage at which a really thorough assessment of the relative strengths and weaknesses of the opposing cases can be made. It is the stage at which the plaintiff's experts have to 'pin their colours to the mast'.

It may also be that at this conference it is necessary to refocus the medical discussion because of the contents of the statements on pleadings served by the defendants. This is the first time that the plaintiff's experts will be told explicitly what was the reasoning (or what are the excuses) of the treating doctors or surgeons. Previously, the experts will have been speculating as to why the witnesses acted as they did. The question should be addressed directly – are the reasons or excuses good enough? The plaintiff's experts must be prepared to go right back to basics, and consider afresh what happened. They must decide again whether or not an act or omission was negligent. The consequence of this may be that the way in which negligence has been pleaded requires amendment, or even on occasion requires to be abandoned.

If the conference is used as a fundamental review of the case, it should not be a problem justifying it on taxation. If there are any fears about justifying the conference, it will be prudent for counsel or solicitor, or both, to prepare a note explaining its importance which can be lodged with the papers for taxation and which can be referred to at a full taxation hearing.

If the timetable for exchange of witness and expert evidence has followed the precedent directions (see appendix 3P), there will only be three months between service of witness evidence and exchange of expert evidence. Given the very great difficulties in finding a conference date which is convenient for all the experts, and the fact that there will need to be sufficient time after the conference for the follow-up work to be completed, the wise solicitor will arrange a provisional date for the conference in advance of exchange of witness evidence.

Before the conference takes place the legal aid cover needs to be checked. Is there provision for counsel to see the experts and advise before exchange? If not, it should be sought. For the reasons set out above, it should not be difficult to persuade the Board of the need to make the appropriate amendment. Similarly, the privately paying litigant should be advised of the importance of the pre-exchange conference and his or her authority to arrange it should be obtained.

Solicitor's preparation for the conference

The solicitor's preparation for the conference begins with sending the experts the disclosed witness evidence. It is likely that the statements that are served by the defendant will follow closely what is recorded in the notes. However, if an account is given of events which are either not recorded or poorly recorded, the expert should be asked specifically (a) to consider whether such a version of events is possible and or probable in the light of the contents of the records and the statements of other witnesses (including the plaintiff), and (b) whether the statements support, undermine or alter the allegations of negligence.

The experts should be asked whether from a medical or medical practice point of view further information should be sought and if so, whether this information is likely to be in documentary form and, therefore, in records which have not already been disclosed. For example, it may be essential to be able to show at what time a consultant was called and/or the delay between the call and the consultant's arrival at the hospital. Some hospitals keep records of all external telephone calls. In a case where the timing of a call is crucial it will be important to ask for these records. Ambulance records may not have been obtained: these may resolve a crux of timing between statements and notes.

Once the experts' comments or revised opinions have been received, the solicitor should consider those comments with reference to each expert's previous opinion, the contents of the records, the contents of the witness evidence and the comments of the other experts. If there are any discrepancies or contradictions or if it appears that the contents of a witness statement or an entry in the records has been overlooked, the solicitor will need to consider whether the points can usefully be pursued in correspondence or whether further discussion should be left to the conference itself. If the latter, then the need for such a discussion will have to be made explicit in the instructions sent to counsel.

In the majority of cases, with more than one expert, the experts should be sent each others' comments or revised opinions in advance of the conference. Any queries the solicitor has should be made known to those experts and in the instructions sent to counsel.

Often a key additional, clarifying or qualifying opinion is given by the expert in conference or in correspondence. In every case, the expert and the lawyers will have to give thought to amending the expert's initial report before exchange. For example, in an obstetric injury case the obstetric expert may have expanded comments on the acceptable response time between the initial evidence of foetal distress, as evidenced by a drop in the foetal heart rate, and any intervention. Even if the solicitor has not discussed with the expert whether this should be included in the final report, the point should be raised in any instructions sent to counsel.

The solicitor should ensure that the instructions delivered to counsel in advance of the conference are accompanied by:

— the complete revised witness statements;
— the plaintiff's comments on the defendant's statements;
— the experts' comments on the statements and any revised opinions;
— any correspondence between the solicitor and the experts about the comments or opinion; and
— any comments the solicitor has on the key liability issues raised by the documents.

Where appropriate, any previous chronology prepared by the solicitor should be updated to incorporate any fresh information. This should also be included in counsel's papers.

Counsel's preparation for the conference

It is important that counsel, who has already advised and pleaded the case, and who should already have met the experts in conference, does not make the assumption that little fresh preparation is required prior to this meeting. The focus of the case may have changed radically. The memory of the case which seems clear is often muddled or skewed by the passage of time. Proper preparation time should be allowed for this second conference, so as to avoid waste of time and potential embarrassment during the conference itself.

The conference itself

A central task at this point is to check that the opinions being expressed by the experts are consistent with the medical literature on which they seek to rely. Any inconsistency or ambiguity can open an evidential gap which the alert defendant's experts and counsel will seek to exploit. For example, in an obstetric injury claim success may depend upon proving that intervention within a specified period would have avoided a damaging lack of oxygen. If the timing is tight, any imprecision on the part of the expert may be damaging to the outcome of the case.

If there are any such inconsistencies or contradictions, these must be discussed in conference. The object should be to ascertain whether these difficulties are the result of a failure on the expert's part to take account of all of the evidence; simply the result of ambiguous or imprecise wording; or the result of firm, but differing views on what actually happened and what should have happened. The first two problems may easily be resolved by discussion and, if appropriate, by permitting the expert to re-work the appropriate section of the report. The third problem may lead to tough decisions having to be taken on whether to serve and rely on an expert's opinion.

In many cases, the experts will be glad of guidance on the final shape of their reports. Clearly, the expert content of the reports is a matter for them but often they can be helped on the architecture and presentation. There is discussion elsewhere (see chapter 16) on the recent clarification of the duties of an expert witness given by Cresswell J in the case of *National Justice Compania Naviera SA v Prudential Assurance Co Ltd (Ikarian Reefer)* [1993] 2 Lloyd's Rep 68 at 81. Those guidelines are not repeated here. However, it is wise to direct an expert to the guidelines if there is any doubt as to his or her forensic experience, and it may be sensible to provide copies of the guidelines to the experts, and make sure they understand them during the conference.

Counsel should also consider, in the light of the witness statements and the experts' comments on them, whether interrogatories or a request for further and better particulars of the defence should be served. If so, where the information being sought relates to medical practice or to medical issues, the questions to be asked should be clarified with the experts before being placed into pleadings.

Follow up to the conference

Counsel should be instructed to draft any interrogatories or request for particulars. Any indications from the witness evidence and the experts' comments that there are further documents which should be disclosed by the defendants should be followed up with a request and, if refused, an application for specific discovery.

It is emphasised again that the solicitor should take a detailed note of the conference for circulation to the experts and to counsel. The experts should be asked to give thought to their opinion and whether they consider it appropriate to clarify or expand it ready for service.

Where it has been clear in conference that there are significant gaps or ambiguities in an expert's report and/or where the expert make significant amendments to his or her report, the amended reports together with the conference note should be sent to counsel, who can then advise on whether the reports should be served on the defendants. That additional advice should be covered by any legal aid limitation which covered counsel seeing the experts in conference and advising on expert evidence. Given the importance of the exchange stage, that additional consideration of the evidence by counsel should be justifiable on taxation. The question of whether it will affect the level of mark-up/ standard fee enhancement recoverable by the solicitor will depend largely upon the extent of the solicitor's involvement in the process and the complexity of the case.

Exchange of expert evidence

The direction which should be sought in relation to expert evidence is discussed in chapter 12.

After exchange of expert evidence

Once the defendant's expert evidence has been received, copies of the reports shoud be sent to the client and to the experts for comment. The experts should specifically be asked to comment on:

— whether the opinions expressed by the defendant's expert(s) are ones which are likely to succeed;
— whether he or she agrees with them in whole or in part;
— whether any further expert opinion should be sought, given the speciality of the defence expert and/or the opinions expressed.

Once the client's and experts' comments have been received, the papers should be returned to counsel for advice on merits and, if appropriate, on quantum.

Knowing what opinion the legal and medical advisers have of the prospects of success will be very important for any client. Legal aid cover will almost certainly have been extended to this stage. Further amendments to the limitation will probably be dependent upon counsel's views on merits and quantum following exchange of evidence with the defence. For the privately funded litigant who must pay his own costs and who runs the risk of a costs order, it will be crucial in determining whether or not to go on.

From this stage on, the preparation will be leading up to trial with all the attendant risks and costs. The costs of the trial itself are likely to be equal to, if not in excess of the costs to date.

CHAPTER 14

Damages

And if any mischief follow, then thou shalt give life for life, eye for eye, tooth for tooth, hand for hand, foot for foot, burning for burning, wound for wound, stripe for stripe.

Exodus chapter 21 verses 23 to 25

The principle of due compensation is deeply rooted in history, and underpins almost all systems of law. The measure by which the due level of compensation is to be assessed was re-stated in more modern times by Lord Blackburn in *Livingstone v Rawyards Coal Co* (1880) 5 App Cas 25, HL at 39:

> Where any injury is to be compensated by damages, in settling the sum of money to be given . . . you should as nearly as possible get at that sum of money which will put the person injured . . . in the same position as he would have been in if he had not sustained the wrong.

The practical problem for the lawyer is how to achieve it.

In Lord Blackburn's time, a jury would have set damages in any personal injury case, including a case of medical negligence. Even in the case which is the foundation of our modern law in the field (*Bolam v Friern Hospital Management Committee* [1957] 1 WLR 582), it is to be noted that McNair J was directing a jury when he stated the principle by which they had to decide. If they had decided against the defendants, the jury would have gone on to fix the level of damages. Since *Ward v James* [1966] 1 QB 273, save in very rare circumstances perhaps now of academic interest only, this no longer applies. Juries are no longer involved.

It will be the everyday experience of the lawyer in this field that the client says, sometimes repeatedly, 'The money doesn't matter: I just don't want this to happen to anyone else'. It is important to meet this by explaining that the money *does* matter, indeed that the damages justify the action. The adviser should try   143 to avoid seeming heartless in putting across this message. However, it is a vital step in the education of the client into realistic expectations of the legal system.

In some other fields of litigation, non-compensatory damages can be achieved. However, in *Kralj v McGrath and St Theresa's Hospital* [1986] 1 All ER 54 Woolf J stated that it would be entirely inappropriate to introduce the concept of aggravated or exemplary damages into the field of medical negligence. In the general field of personal injury damages, the decision of the Court of Appeal in *AB v South West Water Services Ltd* [1993] QB 507 that the award of exemplary damages should be limited to causes of action which could give rise to such damages in 1964, when *Rookes v Barnard* (below) was decided, points the same way.

The decision in *Kralj* is understandable on its facts, but the authors believe it might be capable of challenge in the right case. It is not impossible to see how a case could arise in the field which would bring the defendants into one of the categories laid down by Lord Devlin in *Rookes v Barnard* [1964] AC 1129, where exemplary or punitive damages are appropriate. An example would be where a doctor could be shown to recommend and carry out useless or even harmful treatment for profit, and where the profit to the doctor exceeds the damages calculated by the principle of compensation. It would be prudent in such a case to depart from the normal parameters of pleading and include a claim for battery, if possible, in order to lay the ground for the court to distinguish *Kralj*.

At the time of writing, the Law Commission has stimulated a debate on whether the availability of non-compensatory damages should be extended by parliament, and it appears possible that the result of that debate will be a change in the law.

Compensatory damages

For the vast number of cases, compensation is the only measure of damage which will be in question. In most respects, the calculation of damages will be exactly similar in medical cases and in non-medical cases. The authors do not intend to duplicate or summarise any of the leading textbooks in this field, nor to give an account of the general principles applying to damages, or, for example, to fatal accidents. The exception is to deal below with the current and fast-developing debate on the assumptions as to real return on money which underpin awards of damages, and with the allied question of multipliers, so important in establishing the adequacy of compensation.

The practitioner is presumed to have access to one or more of the regularly updated looseleaf works which provide precedents for quantum of general damage and much detail on the calculation of special losses. The position is now simplified in some ways by the publication by the Judicial Studies Board of the *Guidelines for the Assessment of General Damages in Personal Injury Cases*, (Blackstone Press, 2nd edn 1994) (the Guidelines), which aim to codify the existing reliable precedents for damages, and indicate what is the broad range of damages which may properly be awarded in a given category of case. No practitioner in the medical field is safe in conducting such litigation without ready access to such books.

Medical cases do throw up some problems which rarely arise in other personal injury cases, or at least arise more often in the medical field. Where specific authorities are quoted, these are intended as examples or indicators only. This chapter is not intended to be used as a substitute for a proper search for quantum precedent. The purpose of it is to give an account of the problem of valuation and how it may best be addressed in practical terms. The cases quoted are signposts.

Failure of treatment generally

A failure of treatment will often mean that a disease which should have been 'cured' or a trauma which should have been avoided or the consequences of which should have resolved has in fact caused injury. This arises in so many ways that it would be impossible to list them here. A crucial element in valuing such damage is to ensure that the correct expert evidence is in place. It is important for the practitioner to remember that the proper expert to advise on liability may not be able to give conclusive advice on damage. An example would be where there has been a failure to move to Caesarean section, leading to a traumatic emergency delivery using forceps. If any kind of nerve palsy is suspected, then advice will be needed from a neurologist as well as from the obstetrician who will have been brought in to consider the standard of care.

Competent treatment would very often have produced a better, but still imperfect, result for the patient or client. Thus a complicated 'before and after' picture will need to be investigated. Experience shows that a hidden injustice may arise in this calculation if the *Bolam* test is wrongly applied. For the purposes of establishing the benchmark test for negligence in the case, the legal and expert team will seek to decide what would have been the minimum acceptable treatment. However, when it comes to considering what 'would have been', a *Bolam* minimum standard will often not be the appropriate inference. A missed diagnosis in a generally excellent teaching hospital would probably have prevented the patient from receiving outstanding care. The assessment of the treatment which has been lost and its benefits must be based on the care which would actually have been received if the negligent doctor(s) had acted to at least a *Bolam* standard.

The complexity of this exercise means that there are few instances when the ordinary run of reported quantum cases will provide direct precedents for general damages in the medical case. In the absence of a reported medical quantum case which is a close parallel, the practitioner will be forced to make broader comparisons with awards in ordinary accident cases, and with the categories of damage in the Guidelines. Sometimes inventive and ingenious logic will need to be applied.

A good source for direct medical precedents on quantum of damage for pain, suffering and loss of amenity is the *Personal and Medical Injuries Law Letter* (PMILL). The journal is annually indexed and easy to use. Another good source is the *AVMA Journal*.

Pure pain or pure loss of amenity

Pure pain

It is very rare that there will be a case of pure pain other than in a medical context. Almost always in accident cases, pain is accompanied by some kind of damage to the body (or mind). However, pure pain is not uncommon as the damage in the medical field. In *Ackers v Wigan Area Health Authority* (1991) 2 Med LR 232, a mother who was delivered of her baby by Caesarean section whilst paralysed but not anaesthetised was given £12,000 for pain and suffering on the operating table, and consequent psychological upset. This award was made in 1985. In

Phelan v East Cumbria Health Authority (1991) 2 Med LR 419, a case decided in 1991, the plaintiff was given £15,000 for pain and suffering. He had also been paralysed but not anaesthetised on the operating table, while his leg was opened, four holes in the bone drilled and screws inserted. He was conscious and immobile throughout, able to hear and smell perfectly. He was traumatised and relived his experience thereafter. His award consisted of £5,000 for his time on the operating table and £10,000 for the psychological sequelae. Other cases can be found, but not always containing a clear delineation of the components of the award.

There have however been many settlements of 'pain' cases, which have gone unreported or unpublicised, and which differ very widely in the amounts agreed for broadly comparable experiences.

Pure loss of amenity

The allied case is of pure loss of amenity, without pain. This essentially occurs only in the unconscious patient. An example of an award is *Anwar v Wandsworth Health Authority* (1990) 31 January (unreported), Butterworth's PILS IX [1406 -1407], where a woman was rendered brain-damaged and unconscious by anaesthetic mistake for the period of three weeks between her accident and her death. She was awarded £900 for loss of amenity.

Repeat or extra surgery

This too usually only arises in the medical context. In *P v K* PMILL Vol 8 p63, £2,000 was awarded (it appears in 1992) by agreement to a baby for the pain, suffering and loss of amenity occasioned by a repeat circumcision operation under anaesthetic and with full, speedy recovery. In *Bovenzi v Kettering Health Authority* (1991) 2 Med LR 293, the plaintiff sued for damages for pain, suffering and loss of amenity. During a dilettage and curettage, the gynaecologist pulled down what he thought were retained products of conception after a spontaneous missed abortion, only to find he had pulled down a piece of bowel, having unwittingly penetrated the wall of the uterus. Other surgeons were immediately called in and the damage was surgically repaired before the plaintiff ever regained consciousness. She had a laparotomy, a scar and a recovery which took some time. She was unable to resume intercourse for about six months. She recovered £6,000 under this head in 1990. In

Lofthouse v North Tees Health Authority (1992) (unreported), Butterworth's PILS IX [1450], where judgment was given in April 1992, the plaintiff received £10,500 for four operations and continuing problems.

Settlements for single further procedures, such as a repeat sterilisation, or an abortion, have generally run at between £2,000 and £5,000, depending on the date of the settlement and on how demanding the procedure was for the patient.

Trauma and distress, nervous shock

This kind of award is by no means confined to medical cases, but does arise frequently in the field, and sometimes precedents from medical cases can provide closer parallels when negotiating. A useful award to consider is that in *Kerby v Redbridge Health Authority* (1993) 4 Med LR 178, where a mother claimed damages for the depression which resulted from the negligently caused brain damage and death after three days of one of her twin sons. The judge awarded her £10,000 for 'all her sufferings from the first uncertainties of delivery in the hospital until the present'. On a close reading of this case, it seems likely that the award went beyond compensating only that element of the mother's feelings which was pathological, but compensated her for all her sufferings because some of her reaction was pathological.

Another award of this kind is the case of *Salih v Enfield Health Authority* (1991) 3 All ER 400, CA; 2 Med LR 235; 7 BMLR 1. In this case a baby was born with congenital rubella syndrome as a result of diagnostic negligence. The Court of Appeal refused to disturb an award to the mother of £5,000 for her pain and suffering, although it commented that there was 'no evidence of any consequential psychological effects nor of any very serious physical defects'. In fact, no evidence is reported of any physical defects on the part of the mother which could be thought to be attributable to the negligence. The *Kerby* and *Salih* cases demonstrate how difficult and uncertain this area of the law can be. A further useful case on the topic is *Withington v Central Manchester Health Authority* (1993) *Times* 2 February.

Many Scots cases are reported in the specialist journals, and it is important for lawyers in England and Wales to recall that the Scots law on compensating for feelings is, or has been thought to be, very different from English law. The Scots authorities can only be used with great caution.

In *Grieve v Salford Health Authority* (1991) 2 Med LR 295, a mother who had a 'vulnerable personality' underwent a Caesarean section in order to deliver a stillborn child, following a failed attempt at forceps delivery. She was compensated for the 'loss of the child and of the satisfaction of bringing the pregnancy to a successful conclusion. . . . In addition, the psychological damage she suffered . . . and the prognosis . . .' She was awarded £12,500 general damages.

The *Grieve* case was decided before the re-statement of the law on 'nervous shock' by the House of Lords in *Alcock and others v Chief Constable of South Yorkshire* [1992] 1 AC 310. *Alcock* has been explicitly applied in two recent medical cases: *Sion v Hampstead Health Authority* (1994) 5 Med LR 170, and *Tredget v Bexley Health Authority* (1994) 5 Med LR 178. In each case the necessary high degree of proximity of damage and the restrictive nature of the category of 'nervous shock' is emphasised, and there is a formal consistency between the decisions. Indeed the judge in *Tredget* expressly applied *Sion*. However, the authors believe that different tribunals might well have applied the principle differently, on the facts of either case. In *Page v Smith* [1994] 20 BMLR 18, the Court of Appeal emphasised that the experience giving rise to the nervous shock must be such that it would be foreseeable in a person of ordinary fortitude.

These cases show how the compensation of a number of different elements of 'suffering' or 'trauma', on very individual facts, in the face of a definitely limited body of reported quantum law, throws the valuation of a case back onto the judgment of the practitioner and the marketplace of negotiation. Those acting for plaintiffs must remember that these uncertainties hit just as hard at the lawyers acting for defendants.

Peace of mind

The principle of compensating for 'feelings' or 'distress' has been restated or possibly expanded in the comparable field of legal negligence, in the case of *McLeish v Amoo-Gottfried & Co* (1993) *Times* 13 October. In that case, the plaintiff was suing his former solicitors, who had acted in his defence in a criminal case where he was convicted. He subsequently changed solicitors and successfully appealed against his convictions. He sued for negligence. Liability was admitted by the defendants, but quantum was contested. The claim was placed under two heads, distress and mental anxiety, and injury to reputation. The claim under the first head succeeded, and the plaintiff was awarded damages of £6,000 for his distress and anxiety between the point in time when he realised that he was not being properly represented, until the day the conviction was set aside. The basis of the claim, although not set out in the report, appears to have been that the contract between the plaintiff and his solicitors imported by necessary implication a term that the solicitors would provide for the plaintiff the maximum possible peace of mind by reason of their competent care of his defence.

The authors believe that if such a term can be implied into the contract between a legally aided criminal defendant and solicitor, then it is logically difficult to see how it should not be implied in contracts between patients and their doctors. This proposition appears to be untried in the courts. It may be that if the argument succeeded, it would open up a real difference between the rights of private patients and those of National Health Service patients when they are badly served by their doctors. On the other hand, the courts might be reluctant, as a matter of policy, to lay down a test which would have the effect of allowing private patients to recover more than NHS patients in respect of identical negligent treatment.

'Wrongful birth': failed abortion, sterilisation or vasectomy

These categories of case arise exclusively out of medical failure and need to be considered not merely in terms of general damages, but also as to special damages. Fortunately, there is a comprehensive statement of the relevant law and caselaw in *Allen v Bloomsbury Health Authority* (1992) 3 Med LR 257; [1992] PIQR Q50; [1993] 1 All ER 651, QB. The principles enunciated by Brooke J are that, in the face of an unplanned birth resulting from negligence:

a) *the mother* can recover general damages for the discomfort and pain associated with the continuation of her pregnancy and the delivery of her child (although the benefit of not having to undergo an abortion will have to be set against that in an appropriate case);

b) *the parent[s]* can recover damages for the financial loss incurred in the upkeep of the child through to adulthood and for the financial loss suffered because of the loss of earnings or the incurring of expense as a result of the obligation to the child which she or they would otherwise have sought to avoid.

Further, in an appropriate case, the parents have recovered general damages for the foreseeable additional anxiety, stress and burden involved in bringing up a handicapped child. A claim for damages for the tiredness and wear and tear involved in bringing up a normal child would not be allowed as it must be offset against the benefit of bringing a healthy child into the world and seeing it grow to maturity.

It is important to keep clear the distinction between the basis of 'wrongful birth' damages and the damages which will be awarded to a *child* damaged perinatally. As mentioned elsewhere, the child with a perinatal damage claim can recover for all his or her predicted needs, subject to the normal principles. The child in a wrongful birth case can recover nothing at all, since the basis of such a claim would have to be that the plaintiff should never have existed. Such a claim is disallowed on policy grounds. Only the parents can claim in such a case.

The claim by the parents of a child which has been 'wrongfully born' is for such support and expense as the parent will be called on to give, which would have been avoided if the birth had been avoided. There is a circularity about this. The award of damages is gauged to reflect the plaintiff parents' means and station in life. In *Allen*, the judge specifically considered that a well-to-do family, which would be expected to educate their children privately, may be able to recover for the cost of school fees. In making this kind of computation, the courts appear to look at the parents' capacity for expenditure on the child *before* the award, and quantify the award accordingly. This ignores the fact that once the parents have the award they will be obliged to spend more on the child and usually will. Thus they end up out of pocket even after receipt of the award. There is no easy solution to this short of calculating the child's needs as the basis of the award. No doubt in many instances this would make the 'wrongfully born' child much better off than his or her siblings.

These principles were followed, with an award varied to meet the different social and economic conditions of the family involved, by Moreland J in *Robinson v Salford Health Authority* (1992) 3 Med LR 270.

Major brain injury cases

At least in the case of infants, these cases are probably more often the result of medical negligence than otherwise, and they give rise to evidential and tactical considerations which are dealt with elsewhere in this book. However, the principles and practice involved in quantifying the loss are identical with major brain or spinal cord cases of any aetiology. Much material relevant to this kind of claim is included in chapters 15 and 17 on constructing a schedule and on structured settlements. A major case damages checklist is included in appendix 5 at p315. A full example of a schedule is included in appendix 6 at p317.

In addition to that material and to the major looseleaf texts, there are some authorities which are particularly useful when looking at how to construct such a claim, particularly when it is of medical origin. The case of *Almond v Leeds Western Health Authority* (1990) 1 Med LR 370 is extremely helpful, as is *Janardan v East Berkshire Health Authority* (1991) 2 Med LR 1. The case of *Charlie B*, of which an account is given in *PMILL* Vol 9 p12, is a useful report of a brain-damage case which was settled and structured. A further account of such a structure is given in *PMILL* Vol 9 p18/19 in the report of *Granger v Hagan*.

Further medical treatment

It may often arise that a client needs or may be recommended to have further medical treatment following a medical tort. Clients sometimes feel under a good deal of pressure about this, since almost by definition, their faith in doctors and medicine has been understandably diminished. They should be reassured that the choice whether or not to undergo treatment remains theirs. It is not at all clear whether a client who declines medical treatment can be thought to have failed to mitigate loss, save in a case where the prospects of a successful result of treatment is very high indeed (see *McAuley v London Transport Executive* [1957] 2 Lloyd's Rep 500 at 505). The authors believe that there will even be a greater doubt whether that will be the case where the injury to the client was iatrogenic. Most judges called on to consider a plea that the plaintiff has failed to mitigate his or her loss in this way will give great leeway to someone who has good reason for diminished trust in the medical profession.

Where the client does need further treatment, and does want to have it, practitioners must always bear in mind the provisions of the Law Reform (Personal Injuries) Act 1948 s2(4) – the client can choose to have the necessary treatment privately and to include the cost in the claim. If standards in the NHS decline, or are thought to be declining, this may be a more common claim than it has been over recent decades.

Multipliers and the return on money

Consideration has to be given to the different multipliers that are going to be applied in the claim. This has been a very vexed question for some time, and at the date of writing it is the subject of comment and proposals from the Law Commission.

From the two cases of *Mallett v McMonagle* [1970] AC 166 and *Cookson v Knowles* [1979] AC 556 emerged the practice of calculating multipliers with reference to a presumed 4.5% real return on money. This was because the House of Lords in those cases observed that the historic rate of return on money had been between 4% and 5%. Whether this was accurate or not then, the assumption of a 4.5% return on money became set and has underpinned almost all cases since.

Clearly the multiplier in a given case is closely bound up with the real return on money. The conventional 'judicial' multipliers are based on the assumption as to the real return on money set out above. The object of compensation is to place the plaintiff in the position he or she would have been if uninjured. In financial terms, this means that ideally the interest *and the capital* awarded to the plaintiff should be exhausted at the same moment as the need for expenditure arising from the tortious damage comes to an end. Notionally and actually, the plaintiff will begin by using mostly interest and only a small amount of capital, but as the capital is progressively diminished, the amount of interest diminishes, and the need for use of capital increases.

If the amount of interest which the plaintiff can actually obtain after inflation (the real return on money) is less than that assumed when calculating the multiplier, he or she will be short of money. Either the plaintiff will spend less along the way, and will thus be undercompensated, or, if the spending levels are as intended when the award is made, the capital will be exhausted too soon.

The real return on money which the plaintiff can obtain is clearly dependent on how the money is invested. Usually a plaintiff will wish to have a conservative investment strategy, and no court will suggest otherwise. When the Public Trustee invests money on behalf of a plaintiff under a disability, a conventional division of the money is adopted, with 70% going into a range of equities (stocks and shares) and 30% going into gilt-edged securities (government bonds). The forensic debate on what in fact the real return on money is, conventionally turns on an analysis of what the return is likely to be given that pattern of investment. Although the debate is very technical, it seems to be the consensus that a 70/30 split of this kind would not have produced a 4.5% return on money in recent years, or anything like it. If that is correct, then generations of plaintiffs have gone undercompensated.

There is an allied problem about the assumptions which underlie the decision in *Roberts v Johnstone* [1989] QB 878. The principle governing that case is the same as the principle underpinning multipliers – that the damages should be exhausted at the end of the time of need attributable to the tort. This presents a particular problem when the plaintiff requires a different house from the one in which he or she would have lived if uninjured. The plaintiff will need that house, usually, until death. If the award was of the purchase price of the house – or even the additional amount needed to buy the house over and above the amount which would have been used to buy the house he or she would have lived in uninjured – then that capital would still be there after the plaintiff's death and would become a windfall for the legatees. The courts regard this as overcompensation.

In order to deal with the point, the case of *Roberts v Johnstone* set out to compensate the plaintiff on the following basis: suppose the plaintiff will need to spend £20,000 extra in buying the house he or she now needs, because of the kind of house it is, and will need to spend a further £20,000 on special adaptations. Let us suppose also that when the house comes to be sold, it will only be worth £10,000 more by reason of the adaptations. The plaintiff has lost in two ways. Firstly, he or she has been forced to invest £20,000 more in house-buying than would otherwise have been the case. That money will be locked up until the house is sold, and will not produce interest during that time. Notionally, the plaintiff could have invested the money over the period. The plaintiff has lost that interest.

Secondly, the plaintiff has been forced to spend £20,000 more on altering and extending the house, only £10,000 of which will come back at all in the shape of a 'return' on the investment in property. On this basis, the plaintiff is entitled to £10,000 in damages for alterations, since the money is lost forever. The plaintiff is also entitled to *Roberts v Johnstone* compensation on the additional £10,000 which has been forcibly 'invested' in the house.

On this approach, the measure of the loss of opportunity to invest is the 'real return on money', which the prudent plaintiff could have obtained, less any profit to the plaintiff on the investment in the house. Instead of investing £30,000 on a 70/30 split in equities and gilts, the plaintiff has had to tie it up in a house. In *Roberts v Johnstone* the court of appeal decided this rate should be 2%. While this may have made sense in a rising market in 1986 when that case was decided at first instance, or in January 1988 when the Court of Appeal heard the case, it has not made sense at any time since the property market collapsed. Although the potential return on investment in the markets has fallen, and is perhaps 2% or 3%, the value of property has also fallen, rather than grown or remained stable.

Thus a plaintiff who had a damages claim decided in 1989 on the figures we have given by way of illustration above, will have:

a) had too short a multiplier for future costs and losses because of the assumption of 4.5% real return on money; and
b) will have lost out on the purchase and adaptation of a house.

In making the *Roberts v Johnstone* award, the courts must be taken to contemplate that the plaintiff would be losing a 4.5% return on investments, but with a 2.5% return on the investment in the house, which could be compensated by a 2% per annum award. Instead, such a plaintiff will probably have lost a 2% to 3% real return on investments, and instead will have suffered a significant loss on the investment in the house. From 1989 to 1994, such a loss might well have exceeded 25%. The proper *Roberts v Johnstone* figure over those dates would arguably be 25.5%.

The principle is that the whole sum of damages should be exhausted at the end of the period for which it is predicted the plaintiff will need compensation. Frequently, this is the predicted date of the plaintiff's death; less often the date when he or she would have retired; sometimes another date – such as the time when the need for a given kind of labour will probably come to an end. The multiplier is merely the figure which will put this principle into effect.

The 'Ogden' tables

In the case of a loss for life by a male aged 45, the latest government tables suggest that his life expectancy would be 30.35 years, as opposed to 35.04 years if the plaintiff were female. If for convenience we assume an annual need in today's values of £1,000, it is possible to turn to the 'Ogden' tables, produced by the Government Actuaries Department, to see what the 'actuarial' multiplier would be.

The 'Ogden' tables were produced at the instigation of Michael Ogden QC, to reflect the real return on money adjusted for population mortality. A revised second edition was published in 1994. Our notional plaintiff, Mr X, should receive compensation as follows, given varying assumptions as to the real return on money:

Assumed return on money	Damages for X
4.5%	£15,500
4.0%	£16,400
3.5%	£17,400
3.0%	£18,600
2.5%	£19,800
2.0%	£21,200

It should be noted with all these figures quoted that they assume the plaintiff pays no tax and will receive the full return on his investment to apply to his or her need. With most plaintiffs, this will not be the case.

Even if the assumption as to the real return on money adopted by the courts were correct, the judicial multipliers of the annual need (in this case, £1,000) would be low. This arises, it is submitted, from the refusal of the courts to look sufficiently carefully at actuarial evidence and the over-compensation for the 'exigencies of life' so as to reduce the multiplier. The 'Ogden' tables reflect mortality but do not reflect 'the other exigencies of life'. That judicial phrase is usually taken to mean that the tables do not reflect the chance that Mr X would have suffered some other disaster or misfortune anyway, which would have meant he needed such financial support as is now being compensated. The particular 'exigencies' are never defined. This is used to reduce the judicial multiplier below the 'Ogden' multiplier. The 'judicial' multiplier for Mr X could well be as low as 14 or even 12, giving damages of £14,000 or £12,000.

What this judicial adjustment forgets, in the authors' view, is that the 'exigencies of life' are just as likely to pull the award up as they are to pull it down. The plaintiff is just as likely to live longer than expected as he is to live a shorter time. He is just as likely to have had the prospect of a more fortunate, higher-earning or cheaper life than average, if he had continued uninjured, than to have suffered some other disaster.

In summary, the authors believe the system of judicial multipliers is unsatisfactory because it:

a) overestimates the real return on money before tax, to the detriment of the plaintiff;
b) ignores tax, to the detriment of the plaintiff; and
c) ignores or diminishes the importance of actuarial evidence, to reflect the 'uncertainties or exigencies of life', again to the detriment of the plaintiff.

Recent developments

In the case of *Hunt v Severs* [1994] 2 WLR 602, HL; [1993] QB 815, CA, an attempt was made to circumvent one aspect of the traditional approach to the multiplier. The plaintiff in question had an expectation of life of 25 years, according to the agreed evidence of the medical experts on each side. The Court of Appeal, on the plaintiff's cross-appeal, agreed to treat this as a fixed period for the period of computation of damages. The assumed return on money was taken as 4.5%, but the money tables were applied to the period of 25 years, rather than the 'Ogden' tables or any judicial multiplier, because the Court of Appeal found that the expectation of life of 25 years was 'a fact, or rather an agreed assumption, upon which the damages payable for future care must be based' (see Sir Thomas Bingham MR at p841G).

Whatever the merits of this approach, it was disapproved by the House of Lords, who gave a clear traditionalist re-statement of the law (see the speech of Lord Griffiths, passim).

The Law Commission report

In September 1994, the Law Commission published its *Report on Structured Settlements and Interim and Provisional Damages* (Law Com No 224, Cm 2646). The recommendations of the report are very wide-ranging, and in fact would affect all awards of damages where multipliers are in question. In summary, the Commission recommends:

a) that the 4.5% assumption be abandoned in favour of evidence as to the return of money available on the relevant index-linked government securities, with the option to vary that in a given case if circumstances make it appropriate
b) that the 'Ogden' tables should be admissible in evidence by production in court of a copy, and that there should be an end to 'judicial suspicion and ignorance' of the tables.

If these proposals are implemented, they would go a long way to remedy the undercompensation of plaintiffs. No doubt the insurance industry, and perhaps the health authorities, will fight tooth and nail against them. The authors await the outcome with interest.

A suggested approach to pleading multipliers

In the face of *Hunt v Severs*, and until the Law Commission proposals result in a change of the law, what approach should the practitioner take to pleading multipliers? The suggestion is that the pleader should use the 'Ogden' tables and should assess the life expectancy. If there is no expert supporting the claim who can address the real return on money, then the best that can be done is to use the 4% tables. The approach should be to suggest that judicial knowledge be taken of the currently low real return on money, sufficient at least to justify a claim based on the bottom end of the traditional 4% to 5% bracket approved in *Cookson v Knowles* (above) and *Mallet v McMonagle* (above). Thus a multiplier should be pleaded derived from a 4% return on money.

The practitioner must at the same time look to the reported cases to establish what would be the likely 'traditional' judicial multiplier. While that may not be pleaded, it must be known, at least for the purpose of negotiation. Pleading the 'Ogden' 4%

figure will tend to lift the level at which the defendants are likely to agree.

In a case of sufficient size, it may be justifiable to instruct an expert who will support a lower figure for the real return on money. If this can be done, then naturally a lower assumption as to the real return on money can be pleaded based on explicit reference to the evidence. A consequentially higher multiplier will emerge. Even here, in the current climate of judicial opinion and in the absence of a change in the law, the plaintiff's team will need to know what the traditional judicial multiplier will be, and bear that in mind for the purposes of settlement.

Conclusion

Assessing damages is always problematic, particularly in respect of general damages. The difficulty is particularly marked where the injury being valued is rare. Medical injuries are much rarer than others and most cases settle, and consequently the volume of reported cases is very small and the body of judicial precedent very underdeveloped. As litigation in the field continues to grow, and as the series of specialist reports and journals continues, the body of precedent will also grow. The authors' plea to the editors of the journals and reports is to report more quantum cases, and their plea to practitioners is to submit more cases to the editors for consideration. In the meantime, only energetic use of what specific precedents there are, and experience and good judgment to fill the gaps, will carry the practitioner to a consistently good valuation of claims. Since such a high proportion of medical cases settle, getting the valuation right is of the highest importance in this kind of practice.

A final word of caution is that the solicitor who is relatively inexperienced should always consider having the case valued by experienced counsel, even if the value may be relatively low. The level of damages is difficult to establish in so many medical cases, that the judgment of an experienced practitioner should always be sought.

CHAPTER 15

The schedule of damages

We shall point out for a start that unless the person who tries to use poison happens to be a diviner or soothsayer, he acts in ignorance of how his spells will turn out, and unless he happens to be an expert in medicine, he acts in ignorance of the effect he will have on the body. So the wording of our law about the use of poisons should be as follows:

If a doctor poisons a man without doing either him or any member of his household fatal injury, or injures his cattle or bees (fatally or otherwise), and is found guilty on a charge of poisoning, he must be punished by death.

If the culprit is a layman, the court is to decide the proper penalty or fine to be inflicted in his case.

Plato, *The Laws, Book Eleven*

Introduction

This chapter will discuss both the evidence needed to support the financial claim and the principles to be adopted in drafting the schedule of special damages and future losses and expenses. Precedent schedules appear in Appendices 6 and 8.

The way in which the financial loss claim should be approached in a medical negligence claim does not differ from that adopted in any other personal injury case. Much has been written on the subject elsewhere, and it is a topic which could sustain a book on its own. This chapter should be regarded as a practical summary of the approach to building a claim and drafting a schedule. The authors have tried to avoid duplication with the chapter on damages, but inevitably the reader will find some topics arising in both chapters.

Case models

This chapter focusses on two types of medical negligence claims because between them they help to highlight aspects of the financial claim which often arise in medical negligence litigation.

Case 1: a claim on behalf of a married woman with two young children of school age who works part-time and who has had to undergo radical surgery because of negligently performed minor gynaecological surgery.

Case 2: a claim on behalf of a child who is severely disabled with cerebral palsy but who is intellectually unimpaired.

Precedent schedules relating to these two types of claims are set out in Appendices 8 and 6 respectively.

Collecting the evidence

Special damages

Specific items of past expenditure

As with any personal injury case, the client or the client's family needs to be advised at the outset to keep a record of those expenses incurred as a consequence of the injury and which would not otherwise have been incurred. Keeping a diary will often be the simplest way. Clients should be advised to keep receipts, bank statements and credit card statements and slips as proof of the expenditure.

Additional everyday expenditure

The client is likely to recall major or specific items of expenditure incurred as a consequence of the injury. However, it may not be appreciated what types of additional everyday expenses can be recovered. Thus, some guidance will be needed.

Every case will be different, but almost invariably in a claim for a child with cerebral palsy (case model 2) additional expenditure will be regularly incurred on transport, heating, laundry, clothing, food, holidays and entertainment.

Some, if not all, of those expenses may also be incurred in case model 1. For example, for a period of weeks after major gynae-cological surgery the plaintiff may not be able to walk any distance and certainly will not be able to carry heavy shopping. There may, therefore, be considerable expenditure on taxi fares. Similarly, if she has to spend a lengthy period convalescing and/or her wound weeps there may be a significant increase in laundry or dry-cleaning expenditure. She may feel uncomfortable in anything other than very loose clothes and may have to buy clothes which would not otherwise have been bought. She may not be able to cook meals for the family or the husband, who would otherwise do the cooking, may be too busy taking over other household and child-care tasks to have time any longer to cook. Thus there may be additional expenditure on convenience or take-away food. During her convalescence she may need something to keep her occupied and entertained and thus there may, for example, be additional expenditure on books and videos.

If these additional costs can be proved to be the consequence of the negligently caused injury, they should be calculated (preferably supported with documentary evidence) and claimed.

Another example of almost hidden additional everyday expenditure may be child-care. In case model 2 the mother of the child plaintiff may have returned to work, but more expensive child-care than otherwise envisaged may have had to be purchased because of the nature of the plaintiff's injuries. The additional child-care costs should be quantified and claimed. In case model 1 it may have been necessary to employ a child-minder to take and collect the children from school during the mother's convalescence.

It is, obviously, advisable at the outset to tell the client that in addition to a record of future expenditure, any documentation relating to similar everyday expenses which were incurred before the injury occurred should also be retained so that, where appropriate, a comparison can be made. For example, because of the injury the client may get cold very easily and thus post-injury heating bills may be significantly higher.

Cost of care provided by family and friends
Where the client has required care from family or friends which would not otherwise have been required a claim in respect of this care should be made (*Donnelly v Joyce* [1974] QB 454, *Housecroft v Burnett* [1986] 1 All ER 332 and *Cresswell and others v Eaton and others* [1991] 1 WLR 1113). The amount of additional care that has been provided has, therefore, to be calculated.

Initially, the carer or carers should be proofed about what has been involved in caring for the plaintiff. For example, has the client required help with dressing, toileting and mobility throughout the period since the injury? If so, the number of additional hours of care will be considerably higher than in the case of someone who is less severely disabled and has really only required help with housekeeping, shopping and cooking.

Once this information has been obtained, the additional care will have to be calculated in hours and then costed. In case model 1 the care provided by (say) the plaintiff's mother or husband will have been for a very limited period and can probably therefore be calculated and costed quite easily. However, in case model 2, the care provided by the family will be ongoing and extensive. In such a case the care that is the consequence of the cerebral palsy will have to be differentiated from the care that the child plaintiff would have been provided with in any event. Clearly, in this sort of case it is advisable for the amount and cost of care to be calculated by an expert on care needs. In the case of the severely disabled this part of the claim may well amount to £50,000 or more if care has been provided over a period of years. It is, therefore, important that the claim can be supported by strong supporting witness and documentary evidence (see below under future care costs).

Plaintiff's past loss of earnings

If the plaintiff was working at the time of the injury or would have been old enough or able to start work or to work increased hours by the date of trial, thought needs to be given to whether a past loss of earnings claim can be made.

This will be relatively straightforward in the case of a plaintiff who was in employment at the time of the injury (as in model 1), as evidence of pre-injury income and career pattern should be easily available through the last employer or, failing that, a trade organisation. However, even in cases such as these consideration needs to be given to whether overtime or promotion were lost, or perhaps a planned increase in working hours.

In the case of a plaintiff who had not worked or who worked only briefly or for limited hours before the injury, it may be necessary to commission a report from an employment expert to assess and quantify this aspect of the claim.

Carer's loss of earnings

It is also necessary to consider whether a carer has suffered a loss of earnings as a consequence of caring for the plaintiff. In case model 2 it will be important to know whether the carer has given up work or given up a planned return to work in order to look after the disabled plaintiff.

In case model 1 the carer (whether partner, mother or friend) may have taken unpaid leave or given up the opportunity of overtime or, indeed, turned down offers of work. Thought needs to be given about how this loss can be calculated and proved by documentary and/or independent witness evidence.

Any loss of earnings suffered by the carer cannot be recovered in addition to the costs of care provided by that person, since this would be double compensation; see *Cresswell and Others v Eaton and Others* [above] and *Mehmet v Perry* [1977] 2 All ER 529. However, it is possible to value the care provided by a family member at the rate of the loss of earnings. This claim can succeed when the carer has lost earnings at a higher rate than the commercial cost of care. The basis of the claim must be that no-one else but the individual concerned could provide the care. This situation has usually arisen where there are bereaved children who need to be cared for by their surviving parent. A claim was upheld on this basis in *Mehmet v Perry* and in *Topp v London Country Bus (South-West) Ltd* (1992) 1 PIQR 206.

Future losses and expenses

As with other personal injury claims, the guiding questions for the lawyer preparing the future losses and expenses claim are: what does this client require in order to live his or her life as independently and as fully as possible? What is needed so that the plaintiff's life is brought as near as possible to what it would have been if the plaintiff had been uninjured? What expenses and losses will be suffered in the future as a consequence of the negligent injury?

The following sections address the various aspects of the plaintiff's life which will need to be considered in order to answer this question in relation to the two case models.

Case model 1

Clearly, whether there is any future loss or expense which can be claimed will depend in part upon how long after the injury trial or settlement takes place. However, the following should be considered.

Loss of earnings Is there any continuing loss? How can this be proved?

Loss of non-recoupable benefits Has the nature of the benefits received by the plaintiff changed so that they are now recoupable? If so, they must be claimed; see *Hassall v Secretary of State for Social Security* (1994) *Independent* 16 December.

Costs of care Is there any continuing need for care or help? For example, is further surgery going to be required and thus help needed in another convalescence period? If so, this will need to be costed. Consider whether a care expert's advice is required because professional help will be needed. If the help will be provided by the family and will not be extensive, consider costing it at home-help rates using the national earnings surveys produced by the Department of Employment each year and published by HMSO.

Future medical care Will the plaintiff need further medical, and in particular surgical, care? For example, does she need plastic surgery on her scar or a major repair to a damaged bladder? It does not have to be assumed that this will be provided on the NHS and thought should be given to assessing and claiming the cost of this being provided privately. This topic is dealt with in chapter 14 on damages.

Counselling Has the plaintiff suffered psychological damage as a result of the negligent injury? If so, does the psychiatric expert advise that she will benefit from counselling? If so, the amount and cost of counselling should be assessed. In a road accident case, *Rodrigues v Woods* (reported in *APIL Newsletter* Vol 4 Issue 3), such were the demands on the carer that it was possible to recover the costs of her having counselling.

Additional expenses Consider what other expenses there are going to be. For example, if the effect of the gynaecological injury is to leave the plaintiff with a problem of incontinence, does this mean that she will have long-term additional washing or clothing costs?

Case model 2
Care Unless the cerebral palsy is very mild indeed, children and adults with cerebral palsy require care and assistance throughout

their lives if they are to be able to fulfil their potential and live as independent lives as possible. The amount and the level of care must be assessed and quantified. Will the plaintiff need nursing around the clock?

There are a number of 'care experts' who can advise both on care and equipment needs. Many of them are occupational therapists. In quantifying the care needs, account will have to be taken of what care a parent would be giving an uninjured child over the coming years. This will need to be deducted from the total number of hours for which care is needed.

Additionally, a careful assessment is required of the likely degree of continuing involvement by the family as carers. As the family members and the plaintiff become older, their involvement will usually diminish – possibly to the extent that they are not involved at all or they fulfil only the role of care supervisor. Whatever their future care involvement is likely to be, it must be costed and claimed.

Accommodation   Is the plaintiff in need of specially adapted accommodation as a consequence of the disabilities that have been negligently caused? If the plaintiff is now wheelchair-bound, it is likely that the present home will require some adaptation to provide doorways sufficiently wide for easy wheelchair access and a bathroom and kitchen which are functional for a wheelchair user. The plaintiff's disabilities may be such that special lifting and bathing equipment will need to be installed. The cost of adapting the current home and equipping it with the appropriate and necessary equipment is recoverable, subject to any necessary credit for the increased capital value of the home following adaptation (see previous chapter and *Roberts v Johnstone* [1989] QB 878).

The current home may not be amenable to adaptation. There may be insufficient space for extension to provide wider doorways and passageways for a wheelchair or to provide the space for a specially equipped kitchen or bathroom or facilities for a residential carer if one is required. In such a case, new, larger accommodation will have to be purchased. If this is necessary it is not the entire cost of the new property which is recoverable, but rather, 2% of the net difference in value between the old and new property to which the multiplier is then applied (see *Roberts v Johnstone* (above)).

When considering the property claim, those drafting the

schedule should bear in mind the discussion on multipliers and the return on money in chapter 14 and at the end of this chapter.

Equipment The plaintiff in a catastrophic injury case will almost always require some special equipment. For example, the child with cerebral palsy may require special furniture and eating implements to help him feed independently, and special toilet and bath equipment. If the child plaintiff uses a wheelchair this will require replacement throughout the rest of his life not just because of wear and tear, but because the size, design and manoeuvrability that is required will vary at different stages of the plaintiff's development.

In order to assess and quantify this part of the claim, an occupational therapist or person with specialist expertise in assessing the equipment needs of the disabled will have to be instructed to advise on what equipment is and will be required, how much this will cost and how frequently it will have to be replaced.

Transport

The plaintiff may require a car that has been specially adapted to enable him or her her to drive. In cases involving more severe physical disability a car may have to be purchased which is large enough to transport the plaintiff and any necessary equipment such as a wheelchair. This may mean that a family has to purchase a larger and more expensive car than would otherwise have been the case. Alternatively, it may be necessary to purchase a second car: one to transport the plaintiff and his or her care attendant and one for ordinary family use. The additional cost of the car and the associated and replacement costs are recoverable (see *Cassel v Hammersmith and Fulham Health Authority* (1992) 4 PIQR Q1).

It is probable that the person instructed to advise on equipment needs will be able to advise on transport needs also.

Therapy

Advice will have to be sought on whether the plaintiff will require any form of therapy in the short or long term. If this is needed, it may be apparent from the fact that the plaintiff is already receiving some speech therapy, occupational therapy and/or physiotherapy. If so, or if the need is indicated by the client or other experts, a speech therapist, an occupational therapist and/ or a physiotherapist should be instructed to advise on the short and long-term needs and cost.

Speech therapist   Cerebral palsy can cause not only difficulties with speech, but also problems with feeding and drooling. The advice of a specialist speech therapist will need to be sought about what speech therapy will be required throughout the plaintiff's life and what improvements can be expected. The cost of providing this will then have to be calculated.

Physiotherapy   If other experts advise (as they almost certainly will in the case of a child with cerebral palsy) that physiotherapy is required, then the level of provision and the cost of that will have to be assessed and quantified by a specialist physiotherapist.

Occupational therapy   If an occupational therapist has been instructed to advise on the plaintiff's care needs, he or she should also be asked to advise on what, if any, occupational therapy the plaintiff will require for the rest of his or her life and this should then be costed.

Technological aids

The computer age has brought with it an increase in the potential for communication and thus for fulfilment and independence for the severely disabled. This is especially so for those whose physical disabilities prevent them from communicating by way of the spoken word.

For example, a child with cerebral palsy may be unable to speak. Many are taught useful systems of sign communication, but this limits their communication to interactions with those who have learned the system. Some children can be taught to use computers not only to write and create images, and thus to communicate on paper, but also to use computers with a voice, enabling them to communicate with their peers and the rest of the world. Technology is also now developing to such an extent that 'talking computer' systems can be made compatible with a telephone system, increasing the potential for independence and socialisation.

For the child or adult with cerebral palsy, severely physically disabled to the extent that he or she is unable to speak but intellectually unimpaired, such equipment may be of supreme importance, for emotional as well as practical reasons. An expert on technological and computer aids for the disabled is essential to advise on the plaintiff's special technological needs and to provide details of cost and the likely need for replacement.

Before instructing the expert on technological aids, advice should be sought from both the educational psychologist and the speech therapist on whether they consider the plaintiff is likely to benefit from such aids.

Education

What education is the child with severe disabilities going to require? Can this only be provided by placing her or him in a residential school? Does this mean that school fees are going to be incurred which would not otherwise have been incurred? If private education was envisaged before the plaintiff's birth, the cost of this will have to be deducted from the fees of a specialist residential school.

Is the child in case model 2 a child who is intellectually unimpaired and thus capable of being educated in a mainstream school? If so, can he or she fulfil his or her maximum potential without the assistance of a personal classroom assistant? If not, the cost of the classroom assistant will have to be costed and included in the claim.

In order to answer the questions about education needs, the advice of an educational psychologist should be sought. If the child already has a formal statement of special educational needs, this may provide a useful guide both about needs and potential.

Loss of earnings

In the case of a child plaintiff, an assessment must be made about what type of employment the child would have gone on to but for the disability. Generally, the approach adopted is that of looking at the education and employment profile of the family, in particular any adult siblings. This means that a detailed proof should be taken about the family's career and educational achievements. An employment expert can pick up that evidence and use it to assess the likely future employment profile of the child plaintiff, injured and uninjured, to quantify the level of lost earnings.

Other future losses and expenses

Finally, consideration should be given to what other expenses and losses the client will incur as a consequence of the negligent injury. For example, will there be additional heating, laundry, mileage, electricity and holiday costs? If so, these will have to be quantified and claimed. Probably the most effective way of quantifying and proving these will be to ask the care and equipment expert to incorporate them into his or her report.

Forensic accountants

There has been much discussion between lawyers specialising in the field of medical negligence litigation as to when it is necessary and appropriate to use an accountant to help to support and prepare the financial claim. It is fair to say that opinions differ widely. The authors take the view that a decision needs to be taken on a case-by-case basis.

In making the decision whether to use an accountant it may be necessary to consider the following points:

a) Is the breakdown of the costings in the experts' reports so detailed that quantifying the past expenses and the future annual costs will be straightforward? If so, how will the use of an accountant to carry out this task be justified on taxation?

b) If the costings (past and future) require financial expertise in order to organise them into a form suitable for a schedule, it may be necessary and more efficient to use an accountant. If so, it should be possible on taxation to justify his use, particularly if the fee charged is reasonable for the work undertaken.

The decision to instruct an accountant is one which should be discussed between solicitor and counsel (and with leading counsel, if instructed).

Without specific and detailed instructions, accountants are unlikely to produce a report which will provide what the lawyers require, or if they do, the cost of their doing so may not be justifiable on taxation. It is necessary to prepare a detailed letter of instruction indicating exactly what the accountant is instructed to advise on and what documents he or she is to prepare.

Legal aid and experts' fees

Experts' fees can be very high indeed. The types of experts referred to above may be charging fees of anything between £350 and £1,000, while accountants' fees may vary from £2,000 to £12,000. Careful consideration, therefore, needs to be given not only to whether a particular expert is required (and whose use can, therefore, probably be justified on taxation), but also to whether prior authority should be sought from the private client or the Legal Aid Board.

Clearly, no expert should be instructed on behalf of the privately paying client without that client's authority. When such authority is being sought it will be important that the client is given an indication of the anticipated expert fee.

If it is decided that prior authority for the fee shoud be sought from the Legal Aid Board, a form CLA31 should be completed and submitted explaining the need to use the expert and the level of fee to be charged. The benefit is that if the use of the expert either cannot be justified on a party-and-party taxation or the level of fee cannot be sustained, the solicitor will be able to recover the balance of the authorised fee against the fund. However, if this happens, the client will have the unpleasant experience of the unrecovered fees being deducted fom any compensation because of the impact of the Legal Aid Board's statutory charge. For this reason all Legal Aid Board authorities for specific expenditure refer to the case of *Re Solicitors, Re Taxation of Costs* [1982] 2 All ER 683 and emphasise that the client's consent to the step authorised by the Board should be obtained.

Preparing the schedule itself

The relative simplicity or complexity of converting the evidence of financial loss and expense into a schedule will depend both on the complexity of the case and the clarity and detail of the experts' reports.

The format of a schedule of special damages and future loss is to some degree a matter of style. In appendix 6 are included some suggestions for the approach in the preliminary notes to the sample schedules. However, some points need to be mentioned here.

Conference on quantum

In order to finalise the schedule it may be necessary to have a conference with counsel, client and one or more experts. If the claim is sizeable, it will *always* be necessary. With smaller cases, it is a matter of judgment. If there is to be a conference, there should be a full draft of the schedule available for the participants if that is at all possible.

Multipliers

Consideration has to be given to the different multipliers that are going to be applied in the claim. This has been a very vexed question for some time, and at the date of writing it is the subject of comment and proposals from the Law Commission.

Multipliers are dealt with at some length in chapter 14. This chapter also suggests how to maximise the particular multiplier in question. Whether the suggested approach succeeds in the medium to long term will depend on whether there is any change in the law following the Report of the Law Commission of September 1994. It is impossible to say much more at the time of writing.

It should always be borne in mind that if there are particular circumstances which can be used to push up a multiplier, they should be clearly presented in the schedule and supported in the evidence. To take a specific example, if the plaintiff remains systemically particularly fit for his or her age, then it may be worth having a medical report which states or suggests that the plaintiff is likely to live longer than the statistical average. The report can be appended to the schedule and the multiplier can be based on the higher than average life expectancy.

Whatever the assumptions are behind the multiplier placed into the schedule, they should always be made clear and explicit in the text. A multiplier which is higher than usual stands no chance of success unless it is carefully presented and fully supported by argument.

A particular difficulty arises when an overall multiplier must be split between different phases or periods of loss. An example of this is seen in appendix 7, where the schedule in the case of Gary Smith (at p326) grapples with the necessity of splitting up his future loss to reflect the different levels of earnings at different periods of his working life. The calculations are set out in annex 5 to the schedule, the only annex to a schedule reproduced in this book. The method is to:

a) take a point in the middle of each period of time;
b) from the relevant table (the Smith schedule is based on the 4%

tables) calculate the return on money to that point (the 4% figure);

c) multiply the 4% figure by the length of the period to get a proportional 'value' for the period;
d) divide the overall multiplier by the length of the period to get a simple proportion of multiplier for each year; and
e) multiply the simple annual proportion by the value for each period.

The answer may vary considerably from a simple split of the multiplier in proportion to the years in each period of lost earnings. It is recognised that this process is very complex, and reflects some of the difficulties of the schedule in a very large or complex case. It is for such a task that some readers (and the authors) will be tempted to reach for a forensic accountant.

Preamble and text

In any complex case, the court will be helped in understanding the financial claim if a detailed preamble to the schedule is prepared and the various claims are cross-referenced to particular reports or pages of reports. The schedule should be capable of being read as a separate document, without reference to the pleadings. The authors believe there need be no hesitation about repeating information which appears in the pleadings, nor about being fairly discursive in style when drafting the schedule.

CHAPTER 16

The trial

Throw physic to the dogs!

Shakespeare, *Macbeth Act IV Scene 3*

Introduction

The purpose of this chapter is to make suggestions as to the best approach to the conduct of a medical negligence trial. A trial comes about in only a tiny proportion of medical negligence cases. However, it is worth reminding ourselves that the trial is nevertheless the focus and culmination of all the skills and application of the lawyer in the field.

It has been noted elsewhere that the medical case turns remarkably rarely on conflicts of primary fact; that is to say, such conflicts arise frequently in these cases, but the real battleground is usually to be found in the interpretation of primary fact by experts, in the testing of opposing propositions from experts, and in the decision by a (medically) non-expert judge as to which set of opposing propositions is to be preferred. However polite may be the idiom in which these cases are conducted, the system remains adversarial. The essence of advocacy in the medical case is to make the expert propositions for which one is contending seem attractive, coherent and more sensible than those of the other side, so as to prevail.

Immediate pre-trial preparation

Usually, however careful and professional the legal team, many preparatory steps are left until late before the trial. Often the case still seems overwhelmingly likely to settle until the last moment. Sometimes the court listing system will bring a case into the list unexpectedly early, although great effort should be made to avoid this (see chapter 12 on listing). Time must be allowed for last-minute preparations, particularly by the solicitors.

Pre-trial conference

Even in cases which have been well prepared, it is essential to have a full conference with the experts very shortly before the trial. The advocate should think of this as the first stage in the preparation of the opening speech, and indeed it makes sense to have given thought to the opening speech and to the way in which the case is to be put, before this conference takes place. Too often, even the experienced advocate will achieve a really thorough understanding of every relevant point only when faced with the immediate prospect of opening the case to a judge. This level of grasp of the case ought to be achieved at the final pre-trial conference, rather than the night before the case opens.

Another important objective of the last pre-trial conference is to establish the terms which would be acceptable for settlement. Traditionally, this too was only done at the court door. The expense of experts' cancellation fees and wasted legal fees which is involved in court-door settlement of a medical case is so considerable that every effort should be made to reach a final position earlier. The pre-trial conference is the obvious opportunity to do this, where the strengths and weaknesses of the case should be examined under the microscope, with the help of the experts and in the presence of the lay client.

For experts too, the final pre-trial conference should be vital in concentrating the mind. It may in fact be the first conference where every last piece of relevant material will be available for consideration – often all the research material upon which the opposing team of experts rely will have been delivered after any preceding conference.

The lawyers should be unapologetic in taking the experts through their paces in the finest detail, repeating consideration of evidence which the lawyers, and particularly counsel, find complex. The advocate's understanding of the medical points must be so thorough as to be durable; otherwise the presentation of the case will suffer. It is the authors' general belief that medical simplifications designed to help the lawyer are often counter-productive. They run out of steam in the end or lead to confusion. Certainly at this point, any simplification or elision of complexity is dangerous. The advocate must be satisfied that the relevant medicine has been explained in full detail.

Bundles

Delivery of bundles some days before the trial starts will pay dividends with the judge, who will have the opportunity to read them at least sketchily. Good organisation of bundles is vital. This is to some degree a matter of taste. A very useful approach, it is suggested, is to strive for small rather than large bundles. If all the necessary documents are crammed into the smallest practical number of large lever-arch files, then the files become unwieldy, and it is more difficult, for example, to place a relevant GP note beside a relevant hospital note beside a pleading.

A suggested pattern is:

Bundle 1: Pleadings
Bundle 2: Factual witness statements
Bundle 3: Plaintiff's expert reports on liability and causation and supporting material
Bundle 4: Defendant's expert reports on liability and causation and supporting material
Bundle 5: GP notes and correspondence
Bundle 6: Hospital notes and correspondence
Bundle 7: Schedule of loss, counter-schedule and quantum material
Bundle 8: Plaintiff's experts reports on quantum and supporting material
Bundle 9: Defendants' experts reports on quantum and supporting material
Bundle 10: Correspondence between the parties.

Clearly, the size of these bundles will vary from case to case, but in many cases all bundles except no 6 will fit into small and easily manageable files. This also has the virtue that the plaintiff's solicitors can tell the defendant's solicitors that they should prepare bundles 4 and 9 according to the scheme. A disparity in the quality of preparation or the time of delivery to the court can give the plaintiff an important tactical advantage.

It is also suggested that a pagination is adopted which incorporates the number of the bundle − thus Bundle 1 should be paginated p1001 and following. In this way, during the trial a simple note of the page number will bring the note-taker to the right place. Such a scheme also tends to minimise awkward pagination sequences for documents which arise late during the course of the trial – at least the reader knows where pages 8235/1 to 21 can be found and is reminded which side produced it. This scheme also means that if a given bundle becomes too large in the course of the trial, it can simply be transferred to a larger file, instead of having to be split.

It is imperative that copy bundles paginated for use in court are available before the final pre-trial conference and before counsel drafts the opening speech. Annotation of notes which will not in fact be used at trial is fruitless. Drafting the speech without being able to give the proper page references is a waste of effort and irritating.

Very often the legal basis upon which medical notes may be used in court is left unaddressed by the parties. Technically, these notes are hearsay, and require steps under the Civil Evidence Act to admit them. However, in another sense the notes are usually not hearsay – Dr A will have acted as he did because of the fact of Dr B's notes. Any obstructive or pettifogging approach to the use of notes is not recommended. However, it can sometimes be helpful to consider the legal basis for their use, particularly in respect of particular notes which may be heavily challenged or seriously contentious.

Visual aids and graphic material

It will rarely be sensible to try and present a medical case without some graphic illustration – psychiatric cases may be the exception. If anatomy, surgical method, X-rays or scans, interpretation of CTG traces, obstetric manoeuvres, interpretation of slides, interpretation of ECG traces, arteriography videos or charts recording loss of vision are in question, then visual presentation will be important. This list is by no means exhaustive.

It is extremely difficult to convey anatomy, for example, by verbal description alone. Good visual material can make the difference between a judge who is impressed with the accuracy and clarity of presentation of the case, and who achieves a good understanding of the case economically, and on the other hand a judge who is bemused, irritated and prone to error. When the error is revealed in the course of the expert evidence, the judge will be likely to blame the plaintiff's advocate, not his or her own lack of knowledge or failure of comprehension.

Very high quality colour anatomy illustrations are available. Photocopies of an edition of *Gray's Anatomy* bought in a station forecourt are not acceptable. A good anatomical atlas with colour illustrations can complement the more diagrammatic representations of the artist.

Monotone copies of monotone documents are naturally acceptable but special attention must be paid to the quality of copying. ECG and CTG traces can be quite faint. Many cases have turned on the minutiae of such traces. If the working copies are less than optimal, points may be missed or confusion caused. This will almost always rebound against the plaintiff.

It is unwise for the plaintiff's lawyers to assume that documents are monotone merely because the copies are. For example, on occasion the colour of ink in original hospital notes will reveal a change of note-maker which may be vital. In any case where such factors may be of importance, one of the plaintiff's lawyers, and preferably the advocate, should inspect the originals. If there may be any significance in such a point, good quality colour copies need to be made for the trial, in addition to the originals being available.

CTG traces must be prepared for trial in continuous roll copies. This is not excessively expensive. Juggling with a run of A4 sheets with overlaps between the sequences of trace is infuriating.

It would be futile to touch on all the ways of organising good visual aids for the trial. The important point is to ensure that the maximum sensible use is made of visual material. It is also vital that the experts see it before the trial and are happy that it serves their purposes. It is often the case that the experts will obtain or even prepare the material – if it is alleged the wrong drug has been injected, then it will be the experts who can obtain examples of the correct and incorrect ampoules in contemporaneous form. If surgery has failed, then the experts should be asked to prepare diagrams to demonstrate the failure. They should be asked to link the illustrations visually with any diagram in the notes – adopting the same viewpoint and perhaps the same scale, so that the judge can more easily make the visual link between the illustration and the primary documentary evidence. It should be remembered that the experts may need time to prepare such material.

Drafting the opening speech

Naturally, the style of opening speech is a matter for the individual advocate. The authors favour a written Note which can be delivered to the judge with the bundle. The judge will be certain to use the opening note as the introductory document to the case. Experience suggests that the written note of opening and the pleadings will often be all that the judge reads before the trial begins. If the note is clearly drafted and contains a convincing analysis, there is a considerable advantage to be gained for the plaintiff.

It is suggested that the note contains a glossary of relevant medical terms, and that if possible visual material be appended. Usually, a chronology will be necessary. The note must cross-refer to the final pagination of any documentation.

The other advantage of a written note delivered in advance is that the judge tends to become engaged in a more or less informed dialogue about the case with the plaintiff's advocate during the verbal opening in court. The advocate for the defence is powerless to intervene. If handled skilfully, this dialogue can mean that the plaintiff's analysis is set early and firmly in the judge's mind and allows the evidence to become support for a structure already in place, rather than an exercise in construction.

Organisation of evidence

In the non-medical action, the complete case on behalf of the plaintiff is presented and completed, to be followed by the case for the defendant, or defendants. However, this presents problems in the medical negligence action. It means that the experts for the plaintiff give their opinion before having heard the oral evidence of the factual witnesses on the other side. They will have the benefit of the exchanged witness statements, but where the most important factual evidence will be given by professionally qualified witnesses, the developed detail of their evidence is often very important.

Moreover, it is often very difficult to prevent the professionally qualified witnesses from giving expert evidence as well as factual evidence. When an obstetrician is describing why he took certain decisions during the management of labour, he must be permitted to refer to expert matters which *as a matter of fact* informed his decision at the time. It is an extremely fine line between giving that evidence and giving expert evidence which is generally supportive of the defence case. It is very difficult to restrain such witnesses from general expert comment if they come to the witness box after the debate between the experts has begun.

Both of these problems can best be met by rearranging the order of witnesses. If all factual witnesses for both sides give their evidence in the normal sequence, but before any expert opines from the witness box, then:

a) no expert is called on for an opinion before the factual evidence is developed and complete; and
b) it is easier to restrict the professionally qualified factual witness.

This rearrangement has become conventionally accepted in medical actions. It is not a panacea to be applied every time. There are cases when the tactical advantage for the plaintiff will lie in getting the plaintiff's experts to develop their interpretation of the evidence before any professionally qualified witness for the defence has the chance to comment. However, the advocate should consider the order of witnesses in every medical case and make a conscious decision where the advantage lies.

Expert witnesses: theory and practice

The expert witness is not a new animal. The principle of expert witnesses was set out by Saunders J in 1553 in the case of *Buckley v Rice-Thomas* (1554) 1 Plowd 118 at 124. The role of the expert witness is however something which has troubled the courts down the years and particularly the question of preventing the expert spilling over into advocate. In *Davie v Edinburgh Magistrates* 1953 SC 34 at 40, Lord President Cooper gave a succinct account of the way the expert should approach his task:

> Their duty is to furnish the judge or jury with the necessary scientific criteria for testing the accuracy of their conclusions, so as to enable the judge or jury to form their own independent judgment by the application of these criteria to the facts proved in evidence.

Naturally, that duty is easier to state than to perform. However, it should be the aim of every advocate to bring the expert witnesses to that state of readiness. It should be the case that the scientific or medical criteria are capable of agreement. If they are not, the area of disagreement must be defined in conference before the trial and spelt out in the opening. The evidence must be directed at defining the issues as clearly as possible and then assisting the court to decide them. No expert should be taken on trust as to his or her judgment, either by the advocate or the judge. Any expert for the plaintiff should be told before the hearing that the job of the opposing team is to mount a ruthless scrutiny and critique of the premises from which the expert has advanced and the logic by which he has advanced.

In *National Justice Compania Naviera SA v Prudential Assurance Co Ltd (Ikarian Reefer)* [1993] 2 Lloyd's Rep 68, (1993) *Times* 5 March, Cresswell J set out principles governing the giving and receiving of expert evidence (at p 81 in the Lloyd's report):

1   Expert evidence presented to the court should be, and should be seen to be, the independent product of the expert uninfluenced as to form or content by the exigencies of litigation (*Whitehouse v Jordan* [1981] 1 WLR 246 at p256, per Lord Wilberforce).

2   An expert witness should provide independent assistance to the court by way of objective unbiased opinion in relation to matters within his expertise (see *Pollivitte Ltd v Commercial Union Assurance Co plc* [1987] 1 Lloyd's Rep 379 at p386 per Mr Justice Garland and *Re J* [1990] FCR 193 per Mr Justice Cazalet). An expert witness in the High Court should never assume the role of an advocate.

3   An expert witness should state the facts or assumption upon which his opinion is based. He should not omit to consider material facts which could detract from his concluded opinion (*Re J*, supra).

4   An expert witness should make it clear when a particular question or issue falls outside his expertise.

5   If an expert's opinion is not properly researched because he considers that insufficient data is available, then this must be stated with an indication that the opinion is no more than a provisional one (*Re J*, supra). In cases where an expert witness who has prepared a report could not assert that the report contained the truth, the whole truth and nothing but the truth without some qualification, that qualification should be stated in the report (*Derby & Co Ltd and Others v Weldon and Others (No 9)* (1990) *Times* 9 November per Lord Justice Staughton).

6   If, after exchange of reports, an expert witness changes his view on a material matter having read the other side's expert report or

for any other reason, such change of view should be communicated (through legal representatives) to the other side without delay and when appropriate to the Court.

7 Where expert evidence refers to photographs, plans, calculations, analyses, measurements, survey reports, or other or similar documents, these must be provided to the other side at the same time as the exchange of reports (see 15.5 of the *Guide to Commercial Court Practice*).

Although these principles were set out in a judgment in a commercial case, the principles were expressed to be of general application.

It is necessary to say that some parts of these rules are often honoured in the breach rather than the observance. The adversarial system inevitably carries through to some degree to the experts. For example, it is extremely rare for an expert to say anything with which he or she does not fully agree professionally. However, the way the evidence is expressed and presented is inevitably influenced by the 'exigencies of litigation'. Indeed it is established practice for the way things are expressed to be discussed with experts before their reports are placed into final form for exchange. It is also inevitable that an expert witness who genuinely holds a view on a case, and whose view is under attack in the witness box, will to some degree become an 'advocate' for that point of view.

The degree of partisanship is, in the authors' experience, most marked in some of those who appear regularly for the medical defence organisations. One distinguished expert who appears for both sides in this field, has coined the term 'bottom-of-the-barrel *Bolam* boys' for those of his colleagues who repeatedly testify that practice of a very low order would be regarded as acceptable by a reputable section of the profession. Few of these experts would claim that they themselves advocate or adopt such practice; merely that it is (regrettably) within the range of accepted practice.

There are, of course, over-enthusiastic experts who appear for plaintiffs. It has already been stressed that it is most important for the practitioner to recognise and avoid such experts. Once detected in court, their excessive enthusiasm can destroy a whole case, since it destroys the confidence of the judge in any proposition advanced by such an expert.

Having entered something of a caveat, the authors nevertheless feel strongly that the guidelines set out the *Ikarian Reefer* case should be followed, and if they are, will add strength to the position of the expert. Credibility and authority are best established by the expert who meets the difficulties in the case directly, is able to recite all of the relevant data and arguments for both sides, and can then justify his or her support of the claim in the face of all that material.

It is a crucial part of the advocate's job to assist the expert to gain that authority. It was suggested above that the experts should be told that their evidence will be subjected to a full and thorough critique. The best preparation for that experience in the witness box is to have undergone that cross-examination beforehand at the hands of the plaintiff's advocate. The way the expert evidence is led in the witness box should reflect that preparation. The factual premises upon which the expert's logic proceeds must be made crystal clear before any opinion is offered. If there are variants of the factual narrative which the judge might find on the primary evidence, then those should normally be dealt with explicitly and clearly, even if they would lead to an unfavourable conclusion.

It should be remembered that part of the expert's role can be to state why given primary facts are more or less likely. The timing of a manuscript note made by a midwife recording the degree of dilatation of the maternal cervix may be vital. The obstetrician may offer a view on why the timing is likely to be accurate or inaccurate, as well as offering a view on what may be the consequences of that degree of dilatation at that particular time, if the timing is accurate.

The advocate should not fight shy of advising the expert on the basics of giving evidence, if such advice seems to be needed. The injunctions to look at the judge when addressing him, avoid unnecessary and distracting movement or gesture, speak neither too slowly nor too fast, explain technical or scientific terms as the evidence proceeds and remain polite and calm in the face of hostile questioning, may all need to be delivered tactfully by the advocate to the expert; but delivered they should be if needed. The conscientious but inexperienced expert witness should be told these things as a matter of course before going into the box, and can be reassured that a clear and thoughtful discourse based on expert knowledge is rarely met with anything but respect from the court and from opponents.

Cross-examining the defendant's experts

The principles and approach set out above have their corollary when considering how best to cross-examine expert witnesses for the other side. Essentially, it is submitted, this is a matter of content not form, of substance more than style.

The job of the cross-examiner is to remove the factual premises of the opposing expert and/or to expose any weakness in his/her logic. Any direct attack on the authority of the expert will usually backfire unless it arises out of the exposure of poor reasoning or limited knowledge as to the matters in hand.

The *curriculum vitae* and list of publications of an expert should be examined with great care when preparing cross-examination. A little thought and a few polite questions may demonstrate that the witness has little or no practical experience of the precise problem in the case. Sometimes the unwary expert will have produced an overblown CV, or will be found to be the author of a ludicrous number of scientific papers all written in the same year; all actually produced by diligent junior associates. One author is aware of an expert who was revealed never to have held a substantive senior post. Clearly, such cross-examination needs to be handled with extreme delicacy, and perhaps even unctuousness, but it can be devastating in its effect.

It can be very effective to present a written synopsis of propositions towards the end of cross-examination. If the witness has been brought to agree to a sequence of logical propositions, then the concession is often best fixed in a short, typed formulation which can be put directly to the witness in the box. Any quibbles of language can be ironed out and the agreement permanently enshrined in writing, before the opposing advocate has the opportunity to soften and blur the agreement in the course of re-examination and comment. This tactic means that either the expert sticks to the formulation which the cross-examiner wants, or loses authority if he attempts to resile from the document in re-examination.

In conclusion, it is repeated that the essence of the successful cross-examination of the expert is substance, not style. If the cross-examiner has thoroughly grasped the material, and is clear about what is to be put and why; if the scientific and expert material is well-organised and at the cross-examiner's finger-tips, and the advocate is able to use the medical and technical language without solecism; if the cross-examination is logical, well-structured and without unnecessary repetition; and if the tone of the cross-examination is polite or at least appropriate, then the advocate will have done his or her job properly and the issues in the case will be properly addressed. What is more, the authority of the plaintiff's experts will be augmented by an authority granted silently by the court to the advocate, to the credit of the plaintiff's case.

Medical and scientific literature

We have touched on the organisation of bundles above, and on the necessity for the advocate to be fully familiar with this material.

The selection of scientific and medical papers is basically done pre-trial and is dealt with above. However, in most trials the literature continues to grow during the trial as the medical debate develops. In theory this should not happen, but in practice it almost always does.

Organisation of the material is crucial. It should be the task of the advocate and of instructing solicitors, if counsel is acting, to ensure that:

a) fresh literature is disclosed to the other side as early as possible;
b) the index is continually updated;
c) the material is placed sensibly into the existing bundles; and
d) all the experts for the plaintiff see all the material as it emerges, and preferably before the decision is taken to introduce it.

Often the judge gets forgotten. It is very important to remember that the judge's bundle must be updated at the same time as those of the parties, and his additional papers should be paginated and the pagination checked before the material is handed up.

When the medical material is directed to the issue of negligence, it is important to exclude anything which is not contemporaneous, or which the practitioner whose actions are under attack would or should not have seen. This needs to borne in mind as much during the accretion of material during the trial as before the trial. Naturally, when the material is directed to an issue of causation, then it may be as fresh or arcane as may be and still be valuable. Almost always it will be the experts who find the material, but it is important that the lawyers control the flow of evidence and that they ensure the material is understood by them and is really relevant.

It is always helpful to ask that experts produce a digest of any relevant sequence of papers. If there are several cases of a given kind reported in the literature, or several series of research data with comparable but differing results, then a simple table putting the relevant conclusions side by side in very truncated form is most helpful. Once again, the party who makes the judge's task easier in this way will not lose by it.

One cautionary note: it can be unwise to introduce a scientific or medical paper if it is known that the author of the paper has or will take a hostile view of the Plaintiff's case. The danger is that the experts for the plaintiff will comment upon the paper of Dr X, the defence experts will disagree with the proffered interpretation, the court agrees with the suggestion that the matter can only be resolved by asking the author of the paper, and Dr X then gives expert evidence on a broader front than the narrow meaning of the paper or the research, to the detriment of the plaintiff's case. Sometimes the paper will be so important or relevant that it requires to be introduced. However, where there is an element of discretion, it is wise to consider what the author would say if asked about the case.

Handling quantum issues

As the substantive part of the case unfolds, the geography of the case often changes quite radically. The predicted outcome for the plaintiff/patient if he or she had not been treated negligently often looks very different at the end of the trial. This is a strong argument for split trial.

However, assuming a single trial, the legal team must keep a close eye on the implications for quantum issues as the evidence unfolds. This may mean that witnesses should be re-proofed and/ or any accountants instructed should be asked to report again on additional or substituted factual premises. Whether or not an accountant is instructed, the lawyers should be considering whether any review of the schedule of loss is needed as the case unfolds.

Once the quantum issues are directly before the court, then any accountant witnesses instructed should be present to hear the primary evidence presented. In a unified trial, this means that the accountants should hear the plaintiff and his or her lay witnesses who speak on quantum issues. By the same token, any expert witness on quantum must be present to hear their equivalent expert opponent and to hear the evidence of other expert witnesses whose evidence connects with or governs their own. The rehabilitation expert must hear the doctors who are speaking to the plaintiff's expectation of life and future quality of life. The architect dealing with alterations to the family home should hear the doctors and the computer consultant dealing with computer control of the plaintiff's environment. Clearly, the experts will already know in fair detail what their colleagues and opponents from allied disciplines intend to say. However, it is only by hearing the evidence that the risk of differences and conflicts can be minimised. It must be accepted that there will be cost limitations on the attendance of witnesses, but the implications in damages can be very large.

One big advantage of having an accountant on the team, at least in the largest cases, is that a flow of recalculations will emerge as the evidence is heard, which should enable the advocate to outdistance the other side.

It is extremely important that towards the end of the case the plaintiff's lawyers know how their case should be put in the light of the evidence which has actually been given. If additional or even substitute schedules of loss and damage are appropriate, they should be ready. The arguments to be presented on multipliers for future loss should relate directly to the medical evidence actually given, preferably to the medical evidence on both sides. The various multiplicands should be flexed in written form and a decision taken as to whether to present the calculations to the court, or wait to see how the argument proceeds.

Closing speeches

Little needs to be added to the principles set out above governing opening speeches. In closing, it may be even more vital to produce a written note of submissions. Pressure of business will mean that many judges must jump directly from the closing of the case into the next unrelated litigation, leaving their reserved judgments unwritten for some time. When that happens, the advocate who has taken the trouble to write down the arguments deployed will reap an obvious benefit.

Care should be taken to resolve any difficulties or ambiguities in the evidence before the case is closed. If there is any ambiguity about crucial evidence, a part transcript is often a good investment in the larger case. Otherwise a note agreed between the advocates will save scrappy arguments which divert from the main thrust of argument.

The quality of organisation and document-handling throughout the case is important to the quality of closing remarks which can be deployed. The references to additional research papers, extra documents and statements and so forth must be rigorously checked for accuracy before placing them in a speech or a note for the judge.

Receiving judgment and arguing costs

Too often the receiving of judgment is delegated to an advocate who has not been present at the trial. Sometimes scheduling makes this inevitable, but it does leave the party thus represented at a potential disadvantage if any sophisticated argument should arise on costs. For example, if there were two defendants, perhaps a GP and a health authority, and the plaintiff has succeeded against one but not the other, the question of 'Sanderson' or 'Bullock' orders may arise (see White Book notes 62/A4/119 and 120). Detailed knowledge of the case will usually be necessary to obtain such an order, to the benefit of the plaintiff. Where this may arise, a clear effort should be made to get an advocate to court for receiving judgment who has such knowledge.

Conclusion

The medical negligence trial is a very specialised, expensive and challenging piece of litigation. The effects of the alleged negligence have usually touched the life of the plaintiff more closely and more painfully than any mere financial loss could do. On the other side of the case, professional reputations are at stake. In a medical case which reaches trial, the facts are almost always exceedingly complex.

The authors have tried to be as practical as possible in the treatment of the subject. In the end, such a trial should normally only be handled by a committed team of lawyers at least some of whom are experienced in the specialism. Such a case should not normally be handled by an inexperienced advocate, whether solicitor or counsel. Foresight, planning and great care must underpin the approach to trial.

CHAPTER 17

Settlement and structured settlements

My friend Sir Roger heard them both upon a round trot; and after having paused some time, told them, with the air of a man who would not give his judgment rashly, that much might be said on both sides.

Joseph Addison, *Sir Roger de Coverley at the Assizes*

When to negotiate

The vast majority of personal injury claims are settled before trial. Although there are no accurate statistics available, the authors' experience is that the same applies to medical negligence cases. In this chapter are examined the strategy and tactics which the plaintiff's lawyers can use to promote a satisfactory settlement together with the rules which apply in such situations.

The fundamental prerequisite for any settlement is a full and accurate assessment of the strengths and weaknesses of the plaintiff's and the defendant's cases. The modern view is that litigation is to be conducted with each side giving the maximum disclosure of the evidence in support of its case well before trial (see, for example, *Khan v Armaguard* (1994) *Times* 4 March). This is designed to promote settlement, avoid delay and save costs. It has been described as each party putting its cards face up on the table. This is all very well in theory. In practice, it is not until the exchange of witness statements and experts' reports that both sides can begin an accurate assessment of the value of the claim.

Even at this stage, it is usually unwise to think of settlement until the plaintiff's expert witnesses have had the opportunity to consider the defendant's expert evidence and respond to it. Such a response may indicate the need for further interrogatories or other investigation or research. The golden rule is that the plaintiff's team should never enter negotiations over a settlement from a position of ignorance of any aspect of either party's case.

It is not always easy to comply with the golden rule. Pressures to settle before an informed assessment of the case is possible can come from many sources. The client may be anxious, impatient or weary of the apparent delay. The defendant may use tactics such as a payment into court to encourage a premature settlement. The court itself, in the context of case management in interlocutory hearings, may drop heavy hints or at least encouraging remarks as to the hope of an early settlement. The Legal Aid Board may become concerned with the ever-increasing costs of further expert reports. Finally, there is always the personal desire on the part of solicitor to see an end to a difficult and time-consuming case.

All these pressures should be resisted if the plaintiff's lawyers remain unable to make an accurate and informed estimate of the merits and value of the plaintiff's claim. Furthermore, any negotiations when the plaintiff's team remain unsure of key aspects of the defendant's case will be dangerous and a time-wasting diversion from pressing on with the primary goal of preparing the plaintiff's case.

Approach to negotiation

As soon as the expert reports, witness statements, schedules and counter-schedules have been exchanged, assessed and, if necessary, clarified, the negotiations towards settlement can begin. Some practitioners favour a global approach where negotiations are limited to the overall value of the claim without descending into the detail of each and every item in the various schedules. Other practitioners prefer to chip away at every specific head of claim with a view to agreeing as many as possible, leaving the gap between the outstanding issues to be resolved at a later stage. This is usually a matter of style. In practice, the latter approach is likely to emerge in most cases. If the more heroic, global approach fails, the court will not be impressed when asked to try a case where all issues remain outstanding.

Before discussions on settlement begin it is essential that the plaintiff's side has a thorough understanding of the various factors which affect the value of the award to the plaintiff, and the relative negotiating positions of the parties. These may include some or all of the following:

a) Deduction of the value of social security benefits by the defendant, who must pay an equivalent sum to the Compensation Recovery Unit (see Social Security Administration Act 1992 Part IV and the Social Security (Recoupment) Regulations 1990). In cases where the injury occurred before 1 January 1989, the old rules still apply and, depending on the type of social security benefit, either half the benefit over the first five years or all the benefit is simply deducted from the overall award of damages by the defendant.

b) The effect on plaintiffs who are dependent upon means-tested social security benefits (for example, income support or family credit). The receipt of a capital payment of £8,000 or more will extinguish the right to income support. However, if settlement money is paid into a trust fund its capital value is not taken into account and does not affect entitlement to benefit. Note that money held by the plaintiff's solicitor is treated as the plaintiff's money and that it is therefore essential that a trust fund is in existence so that the defendant can pay directly to the trustees. Note further that income from the trust may be taken into account as an income resource.

c) An understanding of the funding arrangements which govern the contributions made to any award by an NHS defendant. This is a complex issue and is discussed below.

In summary, the plaintiff's legal team may enter into sensible negotiations with the defendant where:

a) The chances of success on liability and causation can be accurately assessed from the primary and expert evidence available from both parties;

b) The overall value of the claim can be assessed by comparison of the schedules and counter-schedules of losses and expenditure produced by each party;

c) The value of the likely award to the plaintiff can be assessed having regard to deductions of benefits and the effect of a capital payment to the plaintiff on his or her social security benefit entitlement.

Funding arrangements for awards against NHS defendants

General practitioners

Awards against general medical and general dental practitioners are met by their protection societies, which are not simple insurers. An insurance company can exercise the right of subrogation, take over complete control of litigation on behalf of its insured, and settle the claim or fight it, irrespective of the wishes of the insured. The stance of the protection societies is different.

The societies arose at the end of the last century. They are the Medical Defence Union (MDU), the Medical Protection Society (MPS) and the Medical and Dental Defence Union of Scotland, which occasionally finds itself fighting cases for members who practise in England and Wales. Broadly, they exercise influence but not strict control over cases for their members. They do not override their members' wishes in any ordinary case, and almost always attempt to gain agreement for any move to settlement. No doubt this takes a considerable degree of persuasion behind the scenes on occasion.

Difficulties can arise inhibiting settlement where there is more than one protection society involved. If a patient is suing two general practitioners, each of whom blames each other, the litigation may well be prolonged while the parties on the other side consider their differences. It is always worth finding out which protection societies are involved. Sometimes it is possible to encourage settlement by letting the defendants' representatives know where the plaintiff will lay more stress and more blame, should the matter come to a hearing.

Health authorities

Where hospital medicine is concerned, the arrangements are different. From 1954 until the beginning of 1990, the situation was governed by a government circular HM(54)32, which provided for apportionment of claims between the relevant health authority and the medical defence organisations concerned.

This system was replaced as from 1 January 1990 by 'Crown Indemnity' in the shape of Health Circular 89(34), which is reproduced in appendix 12. This provides that in return for the transfer of ownership of funds held by the three defence

214 Medical negligence litigation/17

organisations, the health service, in the shape of the District Health Authorities (DHAs), would assume financial responsibility for claims against all NHS hospital staff, including doctors. Where the medical element of such claims leads to a liability exceeding £300,000, then there is provision under the circular for DHAs to gain access to the funds held by the medical defence organisations on behalf of the Department of Health. DHAs can recoup 80% of their outgoings in excess of £300,000 in respect of medical cases.

The increased use of structured settlements has meant that at the time of writing there are still such funds available, when it had been anticipated they would have been extinguished by now. DHAs may also take part in regional sharing arrangements, under which districts within an area effectively 'pool' and share their liabilities over a certain limit, which varies between £20,000 and £100,000.

NHS trusts

DHAs retain responsibility for claims arising from pre-trust events. Executive letter 90(195) (which is reproduced in appendix 12) provides that trusts should meet claims from clinical negligence from their own resources, the objective being that costs should be recouped within the internal market through pricing. Trusts cannot get access to either the medical defence organisation funds held under HC 89(34), nor to regional pooling. However, they can gain access to loan funds, the provision of which is governed by Executive Letter 91(19) (also reproduced in appendix 12). Concern about trusts' exposure to large claims has been one of the reasons for proposals for a central fund for trusts, for pooling funds and sharing claims. Proposals are being considered at the time of writing which are likely to be effective from 1 April 1995 and which will apply to claims after that date.

It is impossible to list all the situations when the funding may affect the settlement strategy. Practitioners should have an eye to how this knowledge may assist in a given negotiation.

Negotiations

Discussions on settlement of the claim may take place in a variety of different ways. Open or 'without prejudice' correspondence may be exchanged with a view to pointing out the defects in the other side's quantification of the various heads of claim. A formal telephone conversation on one aspect of the claim may lead to informal and without prejudice discussion by telephone on other aspects of the claim. Sometimes the parties may consider it sensible for a without prejudice round table meeting between the experts and lawyers on one or more aspects of the claim in order to see whether the experts can agree or at least define with certainty the areas of disagreement.

Informal discussion or correspondence between counsel, especially leading counsel, may lead to agreement over particularly difficult outstanding issues. By this stage there should be less scope for the bluffing which is often evident at an earlier stage in negotiation.

Inevitably, some cases do not settle. The interpretation of the evidence by the legal team and the expert witnesses on one side may differ so profoundly from that on the other side that agreement is simply not possible. Simply splitting the difference may be wholly inappropriate. The parties may have to abandon negotiations and proceed to final preparation for trial. If it has not already happened, it is at this stage that the defendant may exert pressure on the plaintiff by making a payment into court.

Payment into court

A well-judged payment in can cause profound problems to the plaintiff and his or her lawyers. It has been mentioned elsewhere how high the costs stakes are in medical cases, where the issues are usually complex and the witnesses very expensive. It is very often the case that the plaintiff's award would be extinguished by an order that the plaintiff pays the defendant's costs after the date of the payment in, or by the Legal Aid Board exercising its statutory charge in respect of the plaintiff's own costs after the date of the payment in.

The response to any serious payment into court should be a rapid and comprehensive reassessment of all the risks involved in the case. The plaintiff should be told of the results of that assessment and should be given an estimate of the minimum value of the claim. It is essential for the plaintiff to be fully advised of the costs risk if the damages finally awarded do not exceed the payment in.

In a legal aid case, it is usually a condition of legal aid that all unaccepted offers of settlement are referred to the Legal Aid Board. Counsel's advice on offers of settlement, including payments into court, is usually required. It is usual to have a conference with counsel and/or with leading counsel where an offer of settlement or a payment into court has been made, so that formal advice to accept or reject the payment in or settlement can be obtained.

Can the plaintiff strike back?

There is no procedural device with the potency of the payment into court. This arises from the rigidity of our costs system. The bite of the payment into court is that the plaintiff will lose all costs from the date of the payment in unless he or she gets the valuation of the claim right. If no offer or payment into court is forthcoming, or if the defendant's offer is too low, and the plaintiff does nothing but win the case, then he or she gets the costs anyway, on a standard basis.

There is one gambit which sometimes brings dividends if used thoughtfully. By RSC Order 22 r14(1) or CCR Order 11 r10 any party to an action may make an offer to the other party which is expressed to be 'without prejudice save as to costs', and cannot be shown to the court until the question of costs falls to be decided. This is a codification of the practice approved in *Calderbank v Calderbank* [1976] Fam 93.

Clearly it is of no force for a plaintiff to say 'settle on my terms or I will seek costs'. If the plaintiff wins, then he or she gets costs anyway. However, depending on the circumstances, it may be possible to say, 'This case will be very expensive indeed to run and you are liable. It is not a high value claim. We will accept £3,000. If you do not agree within 21 days, and the matter has to be tried, we will be seeking costs on the (top scale relevant). We reserve the right to show this letter to the judge . . . ' Another approach is to say, 'This case will be very expensive to run and you are liable. We will accept £20,000. If you do not agree within 21 days, we will show this letter to the judge at the conclusion of the case and ask her or him to note the following for the attention of the taxing master' and then list all the reasons why the case will be long, expensive, requires seven expert witnesses for the plaintiff, etc etc. If there is no settlement, and the matter comes to trial, then the plaintiff will be forearmed for taxation in a very potent way. The authors believe that this is a practice which plaintiffs should develop.

The formation of a compromise settlement

There is nothing about medical cases which is different in this matter – a compromise must simply be a completed contract. Usually, it is extremely simple to achieve if the parties desire it. However, sometimes difficulties arise, particularly in relation to persons under a disability (see below). It is outside the scope of this book to deal with this topic in any depth. The matter is dealt with authoritatively in Foskett: *The Law and Practice of Compromise* (Sweet & Maxwell, 3rd Edn 1991).

Persons under a disability

Where the plaintiff is a minor or a patient, any proposed settlement of the claim requires the approval of the court. A minor is a person under the age of 18 at the time of the proposed settlement. A patient is a person who is incapable of managing and administering his property and affairs because he suffers from a mental disorder (Mental Health Act 1983 s94). 'Mental disorder' is defined by s1(2) of the 1983 Act as 'mental illness, arrested or incomplete development of mind, psychopathic disorder and any other disorder or disability of mind'.

Where the plaintiff is suffering from a mental disorder, before proceedings are formally commenced the plaintiff's solicitor will need to obtain a report from a consultant psychiatrist which deals with the following issues:

a) Is the patient suffering from a mental disorder within the meaning of s1(2) of the 1983 Act?
b) If so, is he incapable of managing and administering his property and affairs because of that mental disorder?

If the proposed settlement arises before proceedings have been commenced, then the medical report must be made available to the court.

The procedure for obtaining court approval of the settlement depends on whether or not proceedings have been commenced.

Where proceedings have not been commenced

The first issue to consider is the correct court. This depends on whether the claim is so large and/or the issues so complex that if proceedings were begun they would be in the High Court. In such a case an originating summons must be issued in one of the forms in Volume 2 of the White Book, Forms 170 to 175. No statement of claim is required. If the proceedings would have been in the county court, then particulars of claim and form N292 must be used.

Procedure after proceedings are commenced

The proper procedure depends upon whether the case has been listed for trial. If it has not been listed, then a summons in the action must be taken out and will normally be dealt with by a master (or district judge outside London). If the case has been listed for trial, then the settlement must be approved by the judge.

Purpose of court approval of a settlement

The purpose of seeking approval of a settlement in cases involving minors or patients is summarised at paras 80/10–11/2 in Volume 1 of the White Book. The court is there to facilitate a settlement and guard against certain risks:

a) The court must protect minors and patients from any lack of skill or experience on the part of their lawyers. The court must be satisfied that the settlement is fair,
b) Settlements are a form of contract. However, infants and patients lack the capacity to enter into such contracts. The approval of the court enables the defendant to settle a case secure in the knowledge that the settlement will not be set aside for lack of capacity on the part of the plaintiff,
c) The plaintiff's solicitors might be tempted to overcharge or even to agree a settlement on less favourable terms if there is an attractive proposal by the defendant to pay the plaintiff's costs. The court is there to ensure that not only the settlement is fair but also that the plaintiff's costs are reasonable,
d) The court ensures that the damages are properly preserved and applied for the benefit of the plaintiff.

Information and material to be put before the court

If the court is to discharge its function of securing a fair settlement, it must have the tools with which to do the job. There is a particular duty on the plaintiff's counsel and solicitors to bring all relevant material before the court. What material is available will depend on what stage the action has reached when a settlement is proposed. For example, if a case is ready for trial, the pleadings and the schedules of damages will be available. Counsel's advice will also need to be prepared for the use of the court. Such advice should always deal with the overall quantum, specific elements which combine to form the total and the elements of risk as to both liability, causation and damages.

Where the settlement is at a much earlier stage, there will be less material to go before the court. Such a settlement is only likely to be reached where the issues as to liability and causation are clear–cut and where the damages are relatively low. For example, it is unlikely that a settlement would be reached in a case of serious brain damage until schedules and counter-schedules have been exchanged. On the other hand, where liability is clear and only general damages are in issue, the plaintiff's medical report and counsel's opinion may be sufficient. The essential factor for the plaintiff's solicitor to consider is whether there is sufficient material to put forward so as to enable the court to reach an informed and proper decision on the fairness of the proposed settlement.

In all cases the court is bound to rely on the experience and integrity of counsel in his or her explanation of the facts and on his or her judgment on the suitability of the settlement.

Structured settlements

There are now a number of specialist texts which deal specifically with structured settlements (Goldrein and de Haas, *Structured Settlements: A Practical Guide* (Butterworths, 1993); Lewis, *Structured Settlements: The Law and Practice* (Sweet & Maxwell, 1993)). The Law Commission's consultation paper no 125, *Structured Settlements and Interim and Provisional Damages*, is also a very helpful background document (HMSO, 1992). This section does not seek to duplicate that work, but rather to look in brief at the question of when and whether a structured settlement should be considered in a medical negligence action and how the possibility of a structure is investigated.

Structured settlements consist of an annuity or series of annuities payable on a monthly or annual basis throughout the plaintiff's life. The annuities are purchased by the defendants or their protection societies, and the annuity payments come from the insurance market and are technically paid to the defendants, who agree to pass them on to the plaintiff. Thus they represent a series of capital payments by the defendants to the plaintiff, and are free of income tax, normally payable on income from annuities (see below).

Sometimes one or more annuities will be deferred and will start at a specified time in the future when it is anticipated that there will be a predictable increase in annual costs. Once settled, a structure cannot be changed. A capital fund (the contingency fund) is, therefore, also usually provided for in order to build in as much flexibility as possible.

In return for agreeing to a structured settlement, the defendants will usually seek a discount on the lump sum otherwise payable. In part, it is argued, this is to cover the costs of administering the settlement.

When to consider a structured settlement

One of the major advantages for the plaintiff of a structured settlement is that as long as it follows the appropriate form which has become known as the Model Agreement (which is set out in the current edition of Kemp and Kemp), the Inland Revenue will treat annuity payments arising from the settlement as capital not income and, therefore, they have a tax-free status. By comparison, investment income from a conventional lump sum award (and the contingency fund of the structure) is treated as income and, therefore, subject to tax.

In the standard personal injury action structured settlements will usually be based on annuities purchased by the defendant's insurers through a life office. Increasingly in medical negligence actions we are seeing what are called 'self-funded' structures. What this means is that rather than being annuity-backed, the defendant health authority or trust makes periodic payments as and when they fall due for the lifetime of the plaintiff. The first such type of structure was that in *O'Toole v Mersey Regional Health Authority* (1992) 136 SJ 880. Since that case there has been much discussion about what long-term guarantees there are for the security of such arrangements. The Department of Health has indicated that legislation may be introduced to enable the Secretary of State to guarantee these arrangements, but until such legislation is in place the guarantee comes in the form of what has become known as the 'comfort letter' from the Department of Health.

Investigating structures

Before final settlement of any sizeable claim, or indeed after success in a trial but before judgment is given, thought should be given to whether a structure would be appropriate. There is no magic figure above which it is always wise to consider a structure. The authors believe that there has been at least one structure set up where the award was less than £100,000. However, structuring such a relatively small award is unusual and is probably not economical. It is more usual to consider a structure when the award is in excess of £250,000 and certainly in cases where the award is in excess of £750,000.

The crucial thing for the practitioner to remember is that the decision to structure or not must be made before the final order. If not, the tax break, which can make a structure more attractive than a lump sum, will be lost.

Potential advantages for the plaintiff

There are two potential advantages for the plaintiff of a structured settlement. These are (a) the way in which periodic payments are treated for tax and (b) long-term security.

The tax advantages of structured settlements have already been mentioned above.

Anyone with any experience of personal injury litigation will be familiar with the worries of a plaintiff that the damages may not last his lifetime. With improvements in medical science and the impact that this has on longevity, there is an increased prospect that the plaintiff will outlive the predicted life-expectancy on which damages have been calculated. The fact that payments under a structured settlement will last for the lifetime of the plaintiff can be a determining factor in deciding whether or not to go for a structure.

Potential disadvantages for a plaintiff

There are probably three potential disadvantages of a structured settlement for a plaintiff of general application. These relate to flexibility, financial benefit and the length of time for which payments last.

Lack of flexibility

Once a structure has been set up, it cannot be changed. Careful thought needs to be given to what the annual costs of care might be if the currently proposed care arrangements should break down. For example, if a person who is currently cared for at home has to be moved into residential care, it may be that the annual payments payable under the structure will be insufficient. Some flexibility can be built in by creating a sizeable contingency fund. However, income generated by the capital in such a fund will be chargeable to income tax. The larger the percentage of the award that needs to be placed in the contingency fund, the weaker the tax benefit argument for a structure becomes.

Dubious financial benefits

When the first awards were structured in this country, there was a tendency to assume that such settlements were self-evidently a better financial option than lump-sum settlements, in terms of investment return. Doubts about that assumption have been expressed cogently elsewhere and it is not intended to repeat the arguments here (see Carol Ellison, 'Unsafe Structures?' *Law Society's Gazette* 8 September 1993). The lawyers advising the plaintiff must give careful consideration to whether the structured settlement or the lump sum award will most benefit the client.

Length of time payments last

Sadly, it is a fact of life that some clients die very soon after receiving an award of damages. In such cases, the traditional lump-sum award is a windfall for those benefiting under the plaintiff's estate. This is one reason why defendants favour structured settlements. For some plaintiffs, however, the potential benefit to those who have carried the burden of caring for them will be a factor in deciding against a structured settlement.

How to investigate

No practitioner should consider advising a plaintiff about an offer of a structured award without the benefit of advice from a forensic accountant.

There are now a number of firms of accountants who have acquired experience in advising on the relative merits of a structure as against a lump-sum award. There are many more who would like to acquire such experience. The authors consider that the inexperienced solicitor should only use a firm of accountants with proven experience.

Accountants' fees are high. It is not unusual to receive a fee note for several thousands of pounds, sometimes well in excess of £10,000. The prudent solicitor will always obtain estimates from a number of firms before selecting the accountant. Whether acting for a private or a legally aided client, he or she must obtain the client's authority to incur fees of this magnitude. In the case of the legally aided client the prudent solicitor will also obtain prior authority for the accountant's fee from the Legal Aid Board in order to ensure recovery of the fees against the fund on taxation, if not against the defendants. Where such authority is sought, the Legal Aid Board will almost certainly require several estimates.

The basis of the investigation

Every case will be different because of the age of the plaintiff, the nature of his or her disabilities, his or her life expectancy and the circumstances in which he or she will be cared for. Any investigation into the relative merits of a structure against a lump-sum award will have to be carried out within the individual context. The accountant must be made fully aware of the background and of the advice on any future care and equipment needs received from other experts, including their cost. It will probably be necessary for the accountant to meet the plaintiff and/or the plaintiff's carers.

Set out below are some general points which must be considered by the accountant and, in turn, by the lawyers once the accountant's advice has been received. The list is not intended to be exhaustive but to be indicative of the sort of issues that must be addressed if there is to be a real balancing of the relative merits.

Reference is made in these notes to guidelines from the Court of Protection. Any practitioner advising a plaintiff will be well advised to ask the court for the current guidelines.

a) What justification is there for *any* discount sought by the defendant?
b) If there is justification for any discount, what should it be?
c) What is the net first year return:
   (i) from a lump sum?
   (ii) from three different levels of contingency fund with linked structured settlement?
d) Assuming three different life expectancies, what returns for each of those periods of equal annual size in today's money can be expected from:
   (i) a lump sum?
   (ii) a contingency fund and structured settlement?
e) Assuming periodic annual needs in three different amounts in today's money, how long would:
   (i) a lump sum, and
   (ii) the three different contingency funds or structured settlement splits,
   actually last?
f) It has been said that care costs rise by 2% per annum over RPI. How would such an assumption affect the answers to the previous question?
g) What difference would be made by direct tax increases to (say) 27% and 40%?
h) How much below the established multiplicands can actually be saved in the early years?
i) The answers to the questions above should take into account the current guidance from the Court of Protection.

Once the accountant's opinion has been received, a conference should be arranged with counsel so that counsel can advise:

a) whether or not it will benefit the plaintiff more to have the award structured; and
b) whether the current structure offer should be accepted.

In considering his or her advice, counsel must take account of all the factors in the individual case, and in particular:

— likely life-expectancy
— likely risks of the care regime breaking down or needing to be varied;

— relative financial benefits and disadvantages identified by the accountant; and
— views of the plaintiff (or plaintiff's next friend).

The decision about the form of settlement will be crucial for the plaintiff and for this reason alone it should not be difficult to justify the conference or the accountant's attendance on taxation.

Procedure for approval

The *Practice Direction* [1992] 1 WLR 328 sets out the procedure to be followed where approval for a structured settlement is sought. It is reproduced in appendix 9. As this book does not seek to be a specialist text on structured settlements, it does not reproduce the model agreement. However, in appendices 10 and 11 are precedents for the initial documents which will enable the process of investigation of a structure to proceed. They are the 'holding order', which preserves the position, with the agreement of the court, following agreement between the sides as to the valuation of the claim on a traditional basis, and the first letter of instruction to a forensic accountant. For further precedents, the practitioner is referred to the specialist texts.

If there is a decision in favour of a structured award in a case requiring the court's approval of the settlement, counsel's written opinion will have to have been lodged at court. In cases where the plaintiff's affairs will come within the jurisdiction of the Court of Protection, the court will also want to know that approval of the Court of Protection has been given. Before giving such consent, the Master of the Court of Protection will require counsel's written advice in order to be able confirm that the court would be prepared to approve the form of settlement.

As already indicated, if a structured settlement is to benefit from the tax break, the agreement must follow what has become known as the model agreement.

The future

At the time of going to press the Law Commission had just published its report following consultation. It has recommended the creation of a statutory scheme to rationalise and simplify the procedures for making a structured settlement (*Structured Settlements and Interim and Provisional Damages*, Law Com No 224,

HMSO 1994). Even if these recommendations are put into place, it is unclear whether they will have any practical impact on structured settlements in medical negligence cases, which are generally what are called self-funded structures rather than structures based upon annuities purchased through a life office.

At the time of writing, interest rates are beginning to show signs of rising once more, which will mean that the achievable gross return on structured settlements will improve. It may be that the tide will now turn once more in favour of structures, as a means of providing life-time security for the seriously injured plaintiff.

CHAPTER 18
The end of the client's case

Nevertheless, there can be no doubt that Lord Eldon was guilty of unjustifiable delays. . . . Another example is Collis v Nott, *which was argued in 1817. When in 1823 Lord Eldon was pressed for a decision in the case, it was found 'he had entirely forgotten it' and it had to be re-argued.*

Sir Robert Megarry, *A Second Miscellany-at-Law*

As we have seen in the preceding chapters, there are various ways in which a case may end. It may end at the conclusion of the investigation either because the lawyers advise that there is no reasonable prospect of succeeding or because the client decides that he or she does not wish to take the risk of pursuing the case. It may end during the case because, for example, after disclosure of witness or expert witness evidence the lawyers advise that there is no longer a reasonable prospect of the claim succeeding. It may end because an offer of settlement is accepted. It may end after judgment at trial.

However the case ends, the question of costs will have to be resolved. In addition, both the clients who successfully recover damages and those who do not may be in need of advice on a number of matters. It is too easy for lawyers to forget what may be the implications of the case ending. We believe that a professional approach requires the lawyers to consider and address the issues and problems which may arise, both for the client and the lawyers, on conclusion of the case.

Costs

When costs are not recoverable from the defendant
Legal aid cases
Costs will be paid by the legal aid fund in those cases where no substantive proceedings have been issued against the defendant or 207

where the plaintiff has been unsuccessful in proceedings. If costs are to be paid by the legal aid fund, there will have to be an assessment or taxation of costs before the lawyers can be paid. If no proceedings have been issued, the certificate of discharge of legal aid (see below) is the authority to assess costs. It will also be the authority to tax in a medical negligence action where a pre-action application has been issued, but no substantive proceedings have been commenced.

When the lawyer advises the client following investigation that there is no reasonable prospect of success on a claim, he or she should then report this advice to the Legal Aid Board. The Board will send the client what is called a 'show cause' letter and unless the client is able to show that there are reasonable grounds for continuing the action, the certificate will be discharged (Civil Legal Aid (General) Regulations 1989 reg 81).

Despite the Board's attempts to speed up administration, the 'show cause' procedure can be very slow. Where the client accepts the lawyer's advice, the most efficient way of getting a certificate discharged is to ask the client to sign a form consenting to discharge of the certificate and for this form to be sent to the Board with a completed request for discharge form.

Where no substantive action has been commenced, but an application for pre-action discovery has been made prior to the investigation, costs will have to be taxed unless they amount to less than £500, in which case they must be assessed (Civil Legal Aid (General) Regulations 1989 reg 105(2A)).

Where substantive proceedings have been commenced, the legal aid costs will have to be taxed unless the costs amount to less than £1,000 (Civil Legal Aid (General) Regulations 1989 reg 105(3)(a)).

Privately funded cases

In the private case all that will need to be done is to render the client (or in cases where funding is being provided by a legal insurer or trade union, the funder) a final bill for all unbilled work.

The client has the right to ask for the solicitor-client costs to be taxed (Solicitors' Act 1974 s70).

Where costs are recoverable from the defendant

Legal aid cases

It is frequently possible to agree costs with the defendants without the need for taxation. If this is done and no claim is to be made on the legal aid fund, then, following payment of the agreed costs, legal aid form CLA26 will have to be sent to the Legal Aid Board.

In cases where party and party costs are agreed and the certificate was granted on or after 25 February 1994, the plaintiff's solicitor can apply for an assessment of legal aid costs if it is believed that they amount to less than £1,000 (Civil Legal Aid (General) Regulations 1989 reg 106A). Where the legal aid costs will exceed £1,000, he or she may apply for taxation of legal aid costs only (reg 107A(2)).

Privately funded cases

If costs are not agreed in full, but a compromise agreement on costs can be agreed with the defendants, this will have to be approved by the client or funding body because those costs not recovered from the defendant will, inevitably, increase the costs payable by the client. If costs are not agreed, it will be necessary to have them taxed. The client has the right to have the solicitor–client costs taxed (Solicitors' Act 1974 s70).

Where plaintiff is a minor or under a disability

RSC Order 62 r16 requires the taxation of costs in all cases involving minors and those acting under a disability unless the court orders otherwise. The normal order when a settlement is approved by the court is for party–and–party costs to be taxed if not agreed and with the plaintiff's solicitor waiving any further costs.

Justifying costs on taxation

We have referred elsewhere to the importance of detailed attendance notes on the solicitor's file and of counsel preparing notes to justify costs and fees on taxation, whether that taxation relates to party–and–party, solicitor-client or legal aid costs.

The award

Release of compensation to client

In a case where the client received legal aid, the compensation cannot be released to her or him until the costs have been recovered and any statutory charge has been calculated and deducted (Civil Legal Aid (General) Regulations 1989 reg 90). Receipt of compensation by the client can often be delayed by many months or even a year or more in those cases where costs have to be taxed. This delay is something about which it is essential the client is given prior warning. It is something that clients find hard to understand and hard to bear following the stresses of the litigation.

It is possible for the impact on the client of the delay to be eased if the solicitor is able to give an undertaking to the Legal Aid Board that costs will not exceed a specified amount and that if they do, no claim above the specified amount will be made on the fund. If the solicitor is able to do this, then the Board will authorise release to the client of any compensation in excess of the specified amount (General Regulations reg 90).

Advice on handling the award

Many clients will not have managed sums of money of the size of their award before. For some plaintiffs an award of compensation is the source of much anxiety.

Advising clients on how to invest compensation is not something which any lawyer should enter into without appropriate experience and expertise. However, it is the authors' view that when a client is sent a cheque for his or her damages the lawyer should point out that the award is intended to cover both past and future expenditure, indicate the wisdom of obtaining investment advice and suggest several potential sources of such advice. Where there is a substantial award the lawyer should also remind the client of the importance of making a will.

Impact on social security entitlement

The plaintiff may have been relying on means-tested social security benefits such as income support or family credit. The award or settlement will usually mean that a substantial capital sum is received by way of damages. Capital of £8,000 or more will mean that the client will cease to be entitled to income support (Income Support (General) Regulations 1987 reg 45). However, if the capital sum is paid into a discretionary trust, the plaintiff may still be entitled to income support (see Sch 10 para 12 of the Regulations). Care should be taken to ensure that the trust is in place before any money is paid out of court or by the defendant. The money must be paid directly to the trustees. If money is paid to the plaintiff's solicitor, it is treated as the plaintiff's capital (*Thomas v Chief Adjudication Officer, R(SB) 17/87*). However, the income from the trust fund is then taken into account as income for the purposes of calculating income support (Income Support (General) Regulations 1987 Sch 9 para 22).

Those under a disability

Where the plaintiff is under a disability because of mental disorder, the Court of Protection will have jurisdiction over his or her affairs and a receiver will have to be appointed. Their responsibilities often weigh heavily on receivers despite the involvement of the Court of Protection. It is important that the lawyer recognises this. The lawyer acting in cases in which the Court of Protection is involved should ensure that he or she is familiar with the procedure for the appointment of a receiver and what happens following that appointment. If the family is well informed, it will have less cause for anxiety.

Where the plaintiff is under a disability because of age but will be competent on reaching majority, a trust will have to be set up under RSC Order 80 r12.

Information about Court of Protection procedure can be obtained from the Public Trust Office.

Counselling, support and equipment advice

Regardless of the stage at which a case ends, the client or client's family may be in great need of emotional or practical support. The end of the case is often a time of conflicting and powerful emotions for the client and family.

In those cases in which the legal advice has been that there is no claim which can be pursued, the client may feel that all that should have been done was done. If, however, the legal advice has been that, although there is evidence of negligence, the prospects of success and/or potential compensation are low, the client and family may feel bitter and disappointed by yet another system or profession. The client who loses at trial will, obviously, be extremely disappointed, but having witnessed and been part of a rigorous and public examination of the quality of care provided, that disappointment may be tempered by the sense of a battle well fought.

It is not only in an unsuccessful case that the client may experience an emotional 'crisis' at the conclusion of the case. During the litigation any one of a number of concerns and emotions may have been the motivating force for the client: anger, concern to prevent a recurrence, or a pressing need to provide a certain future in the form of financial security for a disabled child or surviving family. It is often only at the point of settlement that the client or family will experience fully the harsh reality that no money (let alone the size of awards made within our system) can compensate for injury and the consequent months and years of physical and psychological pain; for disfigurement, disability and associated practical and financial problems. Where medical negligence has led to the death of a loved one, it is not uncommon for clients to experience the process of settlement as that of a price being placed on the life of that loved one. Thus at this stage the client who has apparently come to terms with what has occurred may once again experience great anguish.

Problems of disengagement

The end of the case is also the point at which the lawyer/client relationship comes to an end. Where the client has found the relationship with the lawyer (or the whole medico-legal team) very supportive, this change will need to be prepared for. The lawyer must be able to disengage if other cases are to get the attention they require. At the same time, the practitioner must recognise that the client who has received advice throughout the lifetime of the case may demonstrate a desire for continuing advice. There may be a period of adjustment when what appear to the lawyer to be simple queries, or queries better addressed elsewhere, are presented for answer. For example, the family carers of someone for whom an official receiver has been appointed, may telephone the lawyer with queries which should be referred to the receiver.

Other problems and referral to other agencies

The end of the case may reveal other problems. Some of these will require advice from the lawyer, others will require referral to other agencies. Some examples are set out below:

a) Where a family has become divided by divorce or separation the lawyers may be asked to advise on what proportion of an agreed settlement reflects the past care or loss of earnings provided by one family carer. The lawyers will need to have in mind the House of Lords' judgment in *Hunt v Severs* [1994] 2 WLR 602, HL, in which it was indicated that damages paid in respect of past care provided by a member of the family were held on trust for that person by the plaintiff.

b) Where the negligently caused disability has affected a child's educational needs, advice may be needed about how to ensure that appropriate provision is provided.

c) The client who has had a stillbirth may want and need support from either an individual counsellor or from an agency such as the Stillbirth and Neonatal Death Society (SANDS). The addresses of this and similar organisations are in appendix 13.

d) The client with a disability may need advice about equipment, care facilities and opportunities for those with that particular disability. Organisations which may prove to be a useful starting-point are the Disability Law Service and the national organisations campaigining for and specialising in the provision of services to those with a particular disability, eg, Scope (formerly known as the Spastics Society), which works for and with those with cerebral palsy.

Both during and after a case (and perhaps especially in unsuccessful cases), a client may need advice on what benefits she will be eligible for. If the lawyer is unable to provide this s/he should be able to provide the name of a local agency who can help (this will be a requirement for those lawyers with a legal aid franchise).

Lawyers acting for plaintiffs in medical negligence claims should be familiar with what agencies exist both nationally and locally which may be capable of providing invaluable advice or practical help to the client. In appendix 13 are listed some agencies which may be able to provide such help. Knowing how to access that information may be just as important for the client who has recovered in excess of £1,000,000 as it is for the client who has recovered considerably less or who is unable to proceed with a claim.

CHAPTER 19
The medical inquest

Here's a corpse in the case with a sad swell'd face,
And a Medical Crowner's a queer sort of thing!

Rev Richard Harris Barham, *The Ingoldsby Legends*

Introduction

An inquest involving technical medical issues which may have caused or contributed to the death presents particular problems of preparation and of advocacy. Since most inquests still happen within a relatively short time of the death, families are often acutely distressed when giving instructions. Frequently, lawyers are not instructed until the eleventh hour before the hearing. There is no legal aid funding available. Information is at a premium. Coroners gather information to themselves before the hearing, including relevant witness statements, but very little of this information is released to interested parties before the hearing. Medical and nursing witnesses are usually very frightened of the inquest and are often more than usually reticent as a consequence. In the past, families have not normally had access to the medical notes before the hearing, although this situation is now changing.

The nature and limitations of the inquiry can lead to bafflement and confusion. To the lay mind, all courts are adversarial. Clients often fail to grasp that the issues of liability and blame are outside the jurisdiction of the coroner, although blame is usually at the forefront of all parties' minds during the hearing. For the advocate, trying to avoid the imputation of blame makes cross-examination difficult, sometimes tortuous and artificial. Yet questioning is the only vehicle available for suggesting the facts, since no address on the facts is permitted. Perhaps most of all, the very individual way in which a number of coroners' courts are run can make the procedure troublesome, even for the experienced lawyer. This last point applies particularly to a case that turns upon medical issues, since so many coroners are medically qualified, and have taken a medical view of the case themselves before the inquest resumes for a full hearing.

In this chapter are addressed some of the practical problems special to the medical inquest from the point of view of those representing the family or others close to the deceased. There is no attempt at a comprehensive review of the law on coroners, and it will be wise for any practitioner to look at one of the authoritative textbooks on the subject if a substantive point of coroner's law or procedure arises.

Taking initial instructions

Most clients will recently have gone through the very painful experience of witnessing the death and perhaps preceding illness of someone they love. Grief, guilt and anger almost always surface early in their contact with lawyers, yet those emotions will frequently be unfocussed. In contrast to deaths caused by accidents on the road or in the workplace, relatives will often have only the haziest idea of what led to the death.

However, the key to the cause of death will frequently be found in what they have to say. Very often some explanation will have been given to them by treating doctors. That explanation may have been very guarded or may have consisted of a series of euphemisms, but the solicitor or independent medical experts retained for the family must attempt to decode what has been said to gain an initial 'line' on the case. That 'line' may in the end prove to be wrong, but it is all there is by way of first guidance for the preparation of the case.

For these reasons, it is doubly important to proof clients with care. It may be very harrowing and exhausting for the clients, and they must be told how important it is and why. It will be very dispiriting for the informant if the process appears pointless, and less information will emerge. Witnesses must be encouraged to recall every detail and the matter must be pieced together in as close to chronological order as possible. Hearsay is admissible before a coroner (*R v HM Coroner for Greater Manchester ex p Tal and Another* (1984) 22 May QBD (unreported)) and thus may be included even in a statement which will eventually go to the coroner, with a view to the witness being called. A suitable qualification in the text may be useful to protect the witness against any comment later.

Preparing the client

It is wise, early in the process of taking instructions, to get across to the client or clients the limitations of the inquest. The essential principle to be explained is that the purpose of the inquest is to establish who the deceased was and how, when and where he or she came to die (Coroners Act 1988 s11(5)(b)). The Coroners Rules 1984 r36(2) prohibit the coroner and the jury from expressing an opinion on any other matter. There must be a full and proper inquiry into the death (Coroners Act 1988 s13(1)(b)); however, this is nowhere satisfactorily defined.

The Coroners Rules 1984 r22 stipulate that no witness shall be obliged to answer any question tending to incriminate himself, a point which may arise in cases of gross negligence leading to death. Rule 42 states that:

> No verdict shall be framed in such a way as to appear to determine any question of –
> (a) criminal liability on the part of a named person, or
> (b) civil liability.

Rule 20 recites that any 'properly interested person', a term which expressly includes the family of the deceased, may ask questions of a witness at an inquest, but 'the coroner shall disallow any question which in his opinion is not relevant or is otherwise not a proper question.' What is or is not a 'proper question' is not defined, but any question designed to establish criminal or civil liability will almost always be disallowed under this rule.

The conjunction of these rules can lead to artificiality, and this is one reason why a full explanation to clients at an early stage is imperative. A hypothetical example can be useful in making the practice as clear as it can be. Let us suppose it emerges that a surgeon has accidentally lacerated a major artery, and the patient has bled to death. The question 'Was it the perforation of this artery which led to the fatal bleed?' is certainly proper. Questions as to the precise moment and manner in which the artery was perforated will be proper. The question, 'Did you intend to perforate this artery?' is also proper, but many coroners would interrupt at that point, for fear of the questions which may follow. The question, 'Was perforation of this artery part of the planned approach to this operation?' will be more likely to be allowed, by reason of its neutral tone. The question, 'Was it not a mistake to perforate this artery?' is certainly improper.

It would be inappropriate here to enter into the debate as to whether these rules are on balance beneficial. However, it is often the case that everyone involved in an inquest is aware that there are in fact 'two sides', and the artificial pretence that there are not frustrates many families (and advocates). Furthermore, the limitation on questioning does on occasion operate so as to inhibit clear and direct cross-examination.

Despite these difficulties, it is usually possible, without infringing the rules, to bring out the central evidence upon which a reasonably well-informed judgment may later be made on the prospects for civil action. The client should be told that. It is sometimes the case that everyone in court is fully aware that the medical treatment described has been deficient, and an elaborate forensic gavotte ensues to avoid stating that conclusion baldly. Provided the clients are aware that the facts are the objective of an inquest, rather than the conclusion based upon those facts, most inquests will be valuable for them. If the rules and their effect are not properly explained, then the lay client may come away seething at what appears to be a whitewash.

It is helpful to deal directly with the question of verdicts. While this is discussed in more detail below, it is usually enough to emphasise that the verdict is merely the 'label' stuck upon the file, by the jury or coroner, at the end of the case. The client should be warned that the advocate cannot argue for a particular verdict. It should be made plain that the verdicts are sometimes difficult to follow, and are always more or less crude categories. The client will know that the verdict is normally given great prominence in the reporting of a case, and thus the verdict inevitably assumes importance. However, it is usually wise to attempt to reduce the degree of significance the client gives to it.

In a case where civil proceedings are in contemplation at all, it is likely to be the facts revealed by the inquiry, rather than the view of those facts expressed by a given coroner or jury, which will decide the approach of the defendants to an action. A verdict which suggests neglect is no guarantee of a settlement and a verdict of death by natural causes is no bar to successful proceedings. This is particularly so in medical cases, where liability will turn upon an expert view of the facts. Such expertise may not be possessed by or be available to the coroner (see below). The case is different in a road accident or an accident at work, where the judgments made by the coroner are more likely to foreshadow those of a judge.

Legal aid

Legal aid is not available for representation at an inquest, but preparation for an inquest can be undertaken under a legal aid green form. The costs of instructing counsel will not be covered by the green form.

Costs

If a medical negligence claim is successful, then so long as a taxing master can be satisfied that the preparation for and representation at the inquest was an essential part of the pre-action investigation, the costs should be recoverable against the defendant in the same way that other pre-action investigation costs are. Support for this may be gained from the case of *Stobart v Nottinghamshire Health Authority* (1992) 3 Med LR 284, discussed below.

Preparation after first interview

The first step after initial interview is to make contact with the relevant coroner's officer. A great deal may be achieved as a result of good professional relations in this quarter. It is essential that the coroner is aware that lawyers are acting for the family. It is usually possible to get some indication of how the coroner intends to approach the inquest, whether he or she intends to convene a jury, what witnesses he or she has it in mind to call, how soon he or she envisages a hearing. It will always be of assistance if the coroner is aware that the lawyer intends to approach the hearing with the rules as to the limitations of an inquest in mind.

It may emerge that the coroner considers that no full inquest is necessary, since he or she believes that the post-mortem examination demonstrates that the death was natural, and that none of the other circumstances apply which mean there must be an inquest. It sometimes even arises that the death has not been reported to him or her. In the latter case, the solicitor must lay before the coroner such facts as will alert him or her to the fact and general circumstances of the death, and do so in writing.

If the coroner believes the death to have been clearly from natural causes, and the clients disagree, the solicitor must write setting out all the circumstances which may persuade him or her otherwise, and do so immediately. If the coroner then maintains the position that the death was natural, depriving the court of jurisdiction, that conclusion may be tested in the Divisional Court, if it can be argued that it was unreasonable (Coroners Act 1988 s13(1)(a)).

Post mortem examination

The Coroners Rules 1984 r7 stipulate that the coroner must inform the relatives of the deceased (and some other persons) of the time and place at which examination is to be made, and the relatives have the right to be represented at the examination by a medical practitioner. This should be considered by the family if the medical cause of death is in issue and their financial means permit. The relatives have no right to a copy of the post-mortem report made to the coroner, despite recommendation 74 of the Brodrick Committee published in 1971 (Cmd 4810), but it is the practice of most coroners to release it. If a given coroner states an intention not to do so, it may be effective to quote the Brodrick Committee recommendation and ask for reconsideration. If there is a refusal to release the report in a case where it is still intended not to hold an inquest, the coroner should be asked to state reasons in writing. Speedy recourse to counsel is then recommended with a view to action in the Divisional Court with the *fiat* of the Attorney-General under the Coroners Act 1988 s13.

Record of proceedings

It may also be of great importance to establish early on whether an adequate record will be taken of proceedings in the court. Arrangements differ from court to court. Very often there will be a tape recording of the proceedings, which will enable the detail of answers given in evidence to be reconstructed accurately. The potential importance of this will be obvious to the reader. However, some courts have no recording facilities at all, and any official 'transcript' will merely be a résumé of the evidence and conclusions prepared by the coroner. This will usually be very unsatisfactory as to the medical detail. If those representing the family are forewarned of this, then preparation of full notes can be made a priority, with a view to analysis after the event.

Summoning a jury

Another point to check with the coroner is the question of whether he or she intends to swear a jury in the inquest. A jury is required in various circumstances set out in Coroners Act 1988 s8(3). The most pertinent to the 'medical' inquest are a death which occurs in custody, where medical treatment in prison is in issue, where the death arose from a notifiable incident or disease or where '. . . the death occurred in circumstances the continuance or possible recurrence of which is prejudicial to the health or safety of the public or any section of the public'. The last test is the most elastic. On one view, any breakdown of a system within a hospital which leads to a death might reasonably be thought to be within the test, given the implications for future patients. Once again, there is no firm precedent on the point, and coroners have tended to be more restrictive in their approach to this section.

If those representing the family find out well in advance what the coroner's thinking is, then it should be possible to make representations for (or against) a jury in time for the application to have the maximum chance of success. That can be done informally, by letter or in court. If there is a prospect that the family will wish to challenge a refusal to convene a jury by seeking judicial review of the coroner's decision, then an early application in court is advised, so as to have a formal decision recorded. An application at the beginning of the resumed hearing has much less prospect of success, since the witnesses have been gathered and time set aside. However, the application must be made even then if it is appropriate.

Access to medical records

At the same time as approaches are made to the coroner and the coroner's officer, it is necessary to seek information directly by obtaining the medical records. This matter is dealt with elsewhere but it is so important that it bears some restatement here.

In almost every case in future, the death leading to an inquest will have taken place after the Access to Health Records Act 1990 came into force on 1 November 1991. By s3 of that Act, the 'patient's personal representative and any person who may have a claim arising out of the patient's death' may apply for access to any records which were brought into being after the commencement of the Act. They should be supplied as of right, subject to some qualifications which are unlikely to apply in the case of a patient who has died. If all the records have been brought into being within the 40 days preceding the application, they must be supplied within 21 days. In other cases, they should be supplied within 40 days. It should be noted, however, that if the deceased requested that the records should not be supplied after his or her death, then access should not be given (s4(3) of the Act).

Timing of the obtaining of the records is obviously crucial, and this point was considered in the case of *Stobart v Nottinghamshire Health Authority* (1992) 3 Med LR 284, of which a short account appears in the *AVMA Medical and Legal Journal* of April 1992. There, the defendant health authority refused discovery of the deceased's health records under Supreme Court Act 1981 s33 until the inquest was complete. Rougier J decided this was wrong, since the obtaining and use of the records explicitly for the inquest was well within the purposes for which pre-action discovery should be granted.

Although there is no further case on the point, this decision makes it easier to argue that the family should have access to the medical records before the inquest. This case, in conjunction with the tight timetables in the legislation, should make it easier to persuade coroners not to list inquests before the records have been obtained. In time, the practice may change and coroners may supply the records which they have obtained to interested parties for the purposes of the inquest. At the time of writing, the practice remains not to do so.

The Access to Health Records Act 1990 is not retrospective. It only applies to records brought into being after the commencement of the Act. In most cases, these records will encompass all that is central to the death. In most cases, the supplier of records will not take the trouble to sift out earlier records, but will simply supply the whole bundle. However, lawyers should be vigilant for the case where this point is of significance and consider whether an application for voluntary discovery or application to the Court under Supreme Court Act 1981 ss33 or 34 is appropriate.

It is also necessary to consider whether the family doctor of the deceased can provide useful information as well as records. Often GPs will speak informally about events before a death, once they are assured that there is no potential criticism of them or of their partners, and when the request is made by the family of the deceased.

Instructing experts

At the same time as the other steps outlined above, thought must be given to instructing an expert or experts to assist in the case. Choosing experts is dealt with elsewhere in this book. However, slightly different criteria may apply in the preparation for an inquest. It is not always necessary to contemplate calling the expert in the inquest itself. The principal purpose of the expert may often be to equip the advocate to ask the correct questions of a medical witness and to understand the evidence and the information which is available before the hearing. As previously observed, funding is often very difficult in preparing for an inquest. Naturally, appropriate expertise is necessary, but in a case where the principal function of the expert will probably be to advise rather than give evidence to the coroner, it is often acceptable to involve an expert who is relatively junior. Certainly, such help is better than none.

The Coroners Act 1988 s26(1)(a) provides that the coroner shall pay the fees of every medical witness. Thus, if a medical witness has been retained by the family but is called by the coroner at the hearing, application should be made by the advocate at the close of the hearing to ensure that the coroner will defray the fees.

In cases where drugs may be of importance, it is always worth identifying the drugs and checking the entries in a recent edition of the *British National Formulary* (BNF), which is jointly published by the BMA and the Royal Pharmaceutical Society at modest price, and is easily available. In all cases, it is helpful to see relevant medical texts in advance of the hearing, if the medical issues are clear enough for the reading to be reasonably well directed.

Instructing counsel

If counsel is to be instructed for the hearing, then it is wise to have a conference in advance of the hearing, even if relatively little hard information is as yet available. Obviously the best time for such a conference is when the notes, post-mortem report and any statements are all available to be considered and discussed. However, even in a case where for one reason or another that material will not be available in advance of the hearing, it is always advisable (if funding permits) for the lay clients to meet the advocate who will represent them before assembling at the court door.

At any such conference, the line of enquiry to be followed must be thoroughly gone through with the clients. The limitations and difficulties of the procedure should be discussed fully once more. Any expert advice which has been received on the records should be discussed, and usually the expert should be present at the conference.

Preparation for the hearing

There is likely to be almost no written material before the hearing which is held by all parties. The coroner will have copies of some notes, perhaps all notes, and will have statements from a number of witnesses. Apart from the report from the pathologist, the family are likely to have nothing from the court. Those representing the doctors or health authority will be better positioned, since they will have automatic access to the notes they hold, and will have copies of the statements given to the coroner by their personnel. However, if two or more 'medical' parties are involved, such as a general practice and a hospital, they may very well not have each other's material.

This can lead to slow, muddled and ineffective questioning at the hearing, while the advocate struggles to make a sensible shape out of a morass of unfamiliar notes held in different form by different witnesses, or indeed missing altogether.

By far the best answer to this problem (although undoubtedly an expensive one) is for the family's solicitors to sort, paginate and place the records into a bundle, copied in sufficient numbers so that the coroner, a witness, the family's advocate and other advocates all have the same body of records in the same sequence.

If this act of seeming altruism can be afforded, it very often pays considerable dividends, since the efficiency and commitment of the family's representatives will be beyond doubt, points can be developed economically and with minimum distraction, and witnesses will be less tempted to resort to bluster.

Whether or not the court will prepare a verbatim record, it is wise to ensure someone will be at court whose main job will be to note the proceedings. Full transcripts are very expensive. It is a very exceptional advocate who can cross-examine adequately and note well at the same time.

Even if there has been a conference in advance of the hearing, it is wise for the advocate to meet the family again at court with time for discussion before the hearing. Other family members, who can properly be regarded as clients, may very likely come to court who were unable to come earlier. A recapitulation of the approach to and limitations of the inquest is almost always helpful.

The hearing

Enough has been said above about the general manner in which the medical inquest is most profitably approached. The reader must have resort to one of the leading texts on coroners' courts for a full account of substantive law and procedure.

Since the coroner has more licence than the president of almost any other judicial tribunal in the way the court proceeds, and in the way evidence is admitted or excluded, it is wise for the advocate to know as much as possible about the individual coroner concerned. Is he or she medically or legally qualified or both? If medically qualified, what is or was his or her practice and expertise? Is he or she full-time or part-time? Will he or she know any of the witnesses to be called? Usually someone will know the answer to these questions and they will give the advocate the opportunity to approach the case in the way which will be most effective with the individual coroner concerned.

If there is a jury in the case, the advocate should try to ensure that the jurors are supplied with pen and paper to make notes and are informed of their right to ask questions.

The order of witnesses is a matter for the coroner, but he or she will usually be prepared to discuss that with the advocates. It is often sensible to take the pathological evidence early. If questions of the detail of the cause of death are hammered out first, then it is often possible to avoid blind alleys. However, it is rarely satisfactory to permit the pathologist to depart after giving evidence, although he will often wish to do so. If that happens, and subsequently a point arises which calls for pathological interpretation, a hiatus may develop in the case which can be very unsatisfactory. It is much better in all but the clearest cases to attempt to keep the pathologist present until the end.

Pathological evidence can be profoundly distressing for family members, particularly for the parents of a dead child. It is usually helpful to raise this with the clients before the hearing and explain that any member of the family who wishes to leave the court while the pathologist gives evidence may do so.

Role of the family's advocate

Coroners often appear to be ambiguous about lawyers appearing in front of them, particularly for families. The advocate should always introduce himself at the beginning of the hearing, particularly if there is a jury. The coroner may otherwise ignore the lawyers at that point, leaving the jury taken aback when later an unknown figure stands up to intervene.

The family's advocate will almost certainly be the only advocate making the running in questioning: those who act for the professionals see their role as purely defensive, and may very often remain silent throughout. No effort is likely to be made by any other lawyer to piece things together in any positive way. The order of questioning by advocates is also a matter for the coroner, who will usually require the family's advocate to go first in any questioning except when a member of the family is giving evidence. The evidence-in-chief of any witness is taken by the coroner.

Since the main usefulness of an inquest is as a fact-gathering exercise, the advocate for a family may well want to range widely. Most coroners will give a good deal of licence as to the breadth of enquiry, provided questioning does not become hostile or seem to be geared to establishing blame. However, the wise advocate will anticipate an enquiry from the coroner as to the point of each line of questioning. It is useful to have an answer ready which will allow the questioning to continue without spelling things out to the witness in a way which will enable the evidence to be tailored. That is not always easy.

It is always right to ask medical witnesses to express their evidence in language which the family and public will understand. Many coroners will do this, but if they do not, or if the medics forget the injunction, it is essential for the advocate to remind the witness. Nothing is more unsatisfactory than a conversation in impenetrable medical jargon which excludes the family. Often the jargon will need to be employed, but the advocate should insist on clarification as the evidence proceeds, if necessary offering his own understanding of each segment of technical evidence for agreement or correction.

Submissions

As mentioned earlier, the advocate is not permitted to address the coroner on the facts. His right of address to the court is confined to matters of law, but this can often be extended to mean mixed law and fact. Coroners differ on what they will permit. Some will launch into a verdict or a summing up to the jury without asking if there are any submissions. It makes sense to anticipate this where the tribunal is unknown to the advocate by announcing that there are submissions at the close of the evidence.

Many coroners will allow what amounts to a submission of 'no case': argument suggesting that there is insufficient evidence to permit a given verdict, or to allow a given verdict to go to the jury for consideration; or alternatively argument suggesting that there is sufficient evidence so as to mean that a particular verdict must be considered. In the course of a satisfactory submission of that kind, however, the facts must be rehearsed in order to see what interpretation may reasonably be placed upon them. Advocates who face this problem may remind the coroner of the remarks of the Divisional Court in *R v East Berkshire Coroner ex p Buckley* (1992) 157 JP 425, where the court recognised that there must be allusion to fact in order to make sense of such submissions. However, many coroners will simply not permit this and will confine the advocate to a series of assertions or propositions about what conclusion may reasonably be reached. This is yet another unsatisfactory consequence of the 'non-adversarial' convention.

The verdict

Two verdicts (misadventure or accidental death and death by natural causes) are frequent in medical inquests; others arise for consideration less frequently, but still need to be considered.

Natural causes

The conclusion may be that the deceased died from natural causes. This is appropriate where the facts show the actions of medical and para-medical staff played no significant part in the death, which arose simply from the underlying disease.

Accidental death

The interchangeable verdicts of accidental death and misadventure are the appropriate verdict where the treatment or a consequence of the treatment has caused the death. This is the case even where there is no suggestion by anyone that the treatment was other than of a very high standard. Thus if a patient dies from a rare idiosyncratic reaction to a properly administered and suitable drug, the proper verdict is misadventure or accidental death.

Lack of care or neglect

Until very recently, the verdict or additional part verdict of 'lack of care' was often regarded as a potential outcome of medical inquests. This verdict by implication carried criticism of those who had care of the deceased. There was an inherent conflict between this verdict and Coroners Rules 1984 r42: how can a verdict of lack of care be made without carrying the implication of a 'determination' of at least civil liability? This conundrum led the courts into some fairly tortuous reasoning (see *R v Surrey Coroner ex p Campbell* [1982] QB 661; *R v HM Coroner for East London ex p Rubinstein*, (1982) *Times* 19 February; *R v Portsmouth Coroner ex p Anderson* [1987] 1 WLR 1640; and *R v Southwark Coroner ex p Hicks* [1987] 1 WLR 1624).

In the case of *R v HM Coroner for North Humberside and Scunthorpe, ex p Jamieson* [1994] 3 WLR 82, the Court of Appeal considered the verdict of lack of care and changed the law considerably. This case is required reading in full for any advocate faced with an inquest where a failure of medical care is thought to have contributed to the death.

The facts of the case are material. The deceased was serving a long custodial sentence and hanged himself in a prison hospital. It was clearly the view of those representing the family that if a minimum degree of care and supervision had been offered to the deceased he would not have succeeded in killing himself.

The central points which emerge from the judgment are as follows:

a) Lack of care, which was more appropriately described as 'neglect', was the obverse of self-neglect and connoted a gross failure to provide adequate sustenance, medical attention or shelter for a person in a position of dependency, whether by reason of a mental or physical condition.

b) Neglect could rarely if ever be a free-standing verdict, and was only appropriate as ancillary to any verdict where there was a direct causal connection between the relevant conduct and the death.

c) Where the deceased had killed himself, suicide had to be the verdict, and neglect could not be said to have contributed to that cause of death.

There are various dicta throughout the judgment which may be seized upon and applied in future efforts to tease out the implications of the case. Broadly, it appears that the Court of Appeal wished to restrict greatly the ambit of what was 'lack of care' and is now termed neglect. The sense of the case is that it is only if the central or principal cause of death, as in the case of starvation, was the result of the failure of the hospital or prison to feed him or treat him, that neglect will arise.

This case is likely to be the subject of much attention and argument. There is an inevitable tension between the limits set on the inquest on the one hand and on the other hand the human desire to understand not merely what went wrong, but why it went wrong and whose fault it was. In truth it is impossible fully to understand why something went wrong without illuminating whose fault it was, if fault there was. Whatever formulations are offered by the courts, that tension will continue to be felt in the way inquests are conducted.

Self-neglect and suicide

From time to time, the verdicts of want of attention at birth, self-neglect, suicide, and death as a result of attempted or self-induced abortion will arise in the context of a medical inquest. There is little that is legally controversial about such verdicts.

Unlawful killing

What is more problematic is the verdict of unlawful killing. This may arise where the care offered by medical or para-medical staff is of such a very low standard that recklessness or gross negligence sufficient to constitute the basis of a manslaughter charge may be in question. Alternatively, if the evidence seems to suggest that a murder or infanticide charge may be in question, as for example following a 'mercy killing' of a terminally ill patient suffering extreme pain, in such circumstances, unless he or she has been informed that there is no need to do so by the Director of Public Prosecutions, the coroner has a duty to adjourn the inquest and send particulars of the evidence to the Director for consideration of charges (see Coroners Rules 1984 r28(1))

It is usual in such cases for the Director to require an adjournment for long enough to consider criminal proceedings, and if such proceedings are initiated, then the inquest is normally adjourned until after the end of those proceedings. It follows that in most such cases the essential issues are decided elsewhere, before any closing of the inquest.

After the inquest

The central notion of this chapter has been that the main achievable benefit of an inquest lies in the knowledge gained about what happened in the time leading up to the death. It follows that part of the process of assisting a family through an inquest is to debrief them adequately at the end. Many families will not intend to take any further legal action, whatever the outcome. Some who do, will find that it is wholly uneconomic to do so, even if there are good legal grounds. Whether or not there is an intention to go farther, we regard it as essential to good practice to go through the main points of the

230 Medical negligence litigation/19

evidence again, ensuring that the family have properly and thoroughly understood what has been said.

If an expert has been present at court, then he should be invited to take part in the debriefing conference, but experience suggests it will be more effective if the lawyer or lawyers lead that discussion.

Naturally, if there is any prospect of a fatal accident action, that must be discussed then in outline. However, it is wise for the family to be advised to pause and consider the question of civil action for a period before committing themselves to that course. This is particularly important since instructions to commence a fatal claim must be taken by a defined category of client, very often a narrower segment of the family than those represented by the lawyers at the inquest. If a decision is taken immediately at the conclusion of the inquest, there is a real risk that a decision to initiate action in principle will be taken for emotional reasons rather than with an adequate eye to the likely costs and benefits of legal action. An added risk is that the representatives of the estate and dependants will be swept into a commitment to action by other members of the family, without proper time to think.

Statements to the press

It often happens that the press wish for comments following a medical inquest. The decision whether to make any comment to the press remains naturally one for the family. The lawyers should be prepared to discuss this immediately after the close of the proceedings, and should be prepared to advise on what may accurately and safely be said. If the family wish it, there is now no professional objection to either solicitors or barristers discussing the case with the press.

CHAPTER 20

The future

You can never plan the future by the past.

Edmund Burke, *Letter to a Member of the National Assembly*

Lawyers are called upon to do many things on behalf of clients, not the least of which is to predict the outcome of litigation. The ability to predict the future is supposedly based on judgment and experience – the more you do it, the more accurate you become. The authors have not written about the future before, so in this exercise their conclusions are not improved by experience. (At least they are experienced enough to begin with a typical lawyer's disclaimer.)

Medical mistakes

Medical mistakes will go on happening. Indeed, as medical techniques advance, extending the potential for cure and palliation of disease and injury, mistakes are easier to make. This strikes people as paradoxical, but is in fact easy to understand. Physicians are faced with more rapid change in medical techniques and technology than ever before. One distinguished surgical expert has suggested recently that medicine today has a half-life of five years and diminishing. A doctor trained at the beginning of this century and ending his or her career in 1940 would have many techniques and drugs in the armamentarium throughout that career. A doctor trained in 1950 and ending his or her career in 1990 will still use aspirin and will still profit from the ability to communicate well with the patient. Most of the rest of the drugs and equipment will have changed, perhaps four or five times over. This process is likely to speed up rather than slow down.

The authors believe this cyclical revolution in medical practice will serve to sustain the *Bolam* test. Change happens so rapidly that litigation is ever more often an exercise in medical archaeology. In many cases all parties are keenly aware that they 'would not do that now'. That consciousness reinforces the notion that the only just approach is to examine the conduct of the doctor by the standards of the day, and having regard to the variation of practice at the time, with an underlying requirement that the practice must not be unreasonable or obviously stupid.

The speed and extent of change means much better medicine overall, but also means that more practitioners will fail to keep up with change. The financial stresses of the current organisational revolution in British medicine will not go away. These pressures add to the number of mistakes, as corners are cut to save money.

A good current example is the surgical 'day case' and in particular the various 'keyhole' techniques in surgery. 'Keyhole' surgery is long-established in some procedures but is now spreading rapidly into other areas. The keyhole approach is sold to patients as permitting surgery with smaller scars and a quicker recovery period. Depending on the particular operation involved, there may or may not be clear advantages in the technique. For example, for surgery to the gall-bladder there probably is a balance in favour of the 'keyhole' technique, although it appears the complication rate is higher. For surgery to a direct inguinal hernia, the advantages are distinctly unproven.

However, the main reason for 'keyhole' surgery is that it carries advantages for what Americans term the 'medical-industrial complex', which are not described to patients. Many more patients can be processed, since their stay in hospital is for a matter of hours or very much shorter than with the traditional 'open' procedure. Whether in private medicine or in the context of the new NHS market reforms, this means more profit for surgeons and hospitals. Secondly, many more expensive disposables are used in the keyhole technique. This means more profit for the manufacturing companies. Naturally there can be no objection to increased efficiency and profit, or saving of NHS funds, if they go hand-in-hand with better results for patients. There must be more concern where the change happens rapidly for financial or political reasons and there is no demonstrated advantage for patients. That kind of process is likely to lead to mistakes and thus to litigation. We fear change for that kind of reason may happen more often in the future rather than less.

The future of the legal system

Victims of medical accidents will expect – and should receive – an honest and full explanation of what went wrong and fair compensation for damages suffered and losses sustained. The major questions for the future of this part of the legal system concern the rights of victims to obtain a full explanation and fair compensation. An important element in these concerns is the role to be played by lawyers in enforcing the victim's rights.

In a fascinating editorial in the *AVMA Journal* for Spring 1994, Arnold Simanowitz analysed five government reviews in progress, all of which have an impact on the rights and expectations of the victims of medical accidents.

The Wilson Committee review of the NHS complaints procedure is likely to improve the chances of securing for the victims of medical accidents the right to an honest and full explanation of what went wrong. The second review touched on by Simanowitz was an enquiry by the Department of Health into financial arrangements for meeting the costs of claims made against NHS trusts and other NHS providers of health services. It includes the proposal that claims against trusts must be handled on their behalf by an approved panel of lawyers (very similar to the Law Society medical negligence panel).

The Lord Chancellor's review of personal injury litigation considered no-fault liability. We return to this below.

The fourth review in question was carried out by the Legal Aid Advisory Committee into the cost of personal injury litigation. The Association of Personal Injuries Lawyers (APIL) carried out research which demonstrated that the perceived costs to the legal aid fund were exaggerated. More research into this area needs to be done, but it is interesting to note that the APIL survey showed that costs and/or damages were recovered by plaintiffs in medical negligence claims in 66% of all cases. The full research results are to be found in (1994) *Journal of Personal Injury Litigation* 30.

Finally, Arnold Simanowitz considered Lord Woolf's review of civil procedure. No results have yet been published, but some indication of the thinking being done has surfaced in public. In an extended article in the *London Review of Books* of 20 October 1994, that most literate of judges, Sir Stephen Sedley, reviewed the field of medical litigation. The article is written in the guise of a review of the second edition of *Medical Negligence* edited by Powers and Harris, but is in truth a wide-ranging look at this field of litigation and its future. He writes, *inter alia*, as follows:

> . . . the family courts in child-care cases have now put a stop to the use of litigation as the continuance of domestic disputes by other means. They do not allow parties to pick and choose which experts' reports they will show the court and which they will not; and they require to see how the expert has been instructed. They have been able to do this because of their supervisory role in child protection, a role which the courts that try medical negligence cases do not – in current legal theory – possess. It is for this reason that the trench warfare which now characterises much civil litigation . . . may have to yield to a system in which the parties define the issues and the court then takes charge of the means by which they are to be canvassed.
>
> Lord Woolf, who is reviewing the whole of civil procedure for the Lord Chancellor, is known to be thinking about such a move. . . . If [the limitation on the court's power to appoint its own expert] is removed, the way will be clear for the court, having seen the issues defined by the parties, to appoint an expert from an agreed list to give an informed opinion. The expert will of course be open to questioning and challenge by each side; and so each side will want its own specialist adviser to brief it on what challenges to raise. This is entirely acceptable . . . but it will have to stop at the point where a party tries to back its challenge by putting in front of the court's expert the contradictory report of another leading practitioner in the field. To allow this would be to readmit the whole stage army to the courtroom, for if one side can do it, so can the other, and if each can proffer one contrary expert's report, each can proffer half a dozen . . .

One imagines that Sir Stephen Sedley would be unlikely to write after that fashion unless these thoughts were being seriously considered by Lord Woolf. Therefore it seems very likely that a result of the Woolf recommendations, if adopted, will at least be that the judiciary, from district judge upwards, will be exerting much greater control over medical negligence cases, with particular emphasis on full and early disclosure of evidence, including expert evidence, together with strict compliance with very tight timetables.

There is no place within the confines of this chapter for a full debate on the merits of the ideas exposed in Sir Stephen Sedley's article. The authors record their strong feeling that such a *dirigiste* system could be likely to lead to great injustice to plaintiffs. One has only to consider the kind of expert who would apply for the judicial panel to realise how conservative would be the general approach which emerged. The advice of the court's experts would be given enormous weight by the judges, and could never be challenged by the oral evidence of opposing experts – only by their propositions filtered through questions from an advocate. It would be inevitable that a semi-proprietorial or at least collegiate feeling would develop between the judge and 'his' expert, which at least in some cases and with some judges would stifle debate. The closest parallel currently to be observed is between coroners and the local consultants frequently called upon to advise them, and the precedent is not cheering. The selection of witnesses and of specialist issues to be examined would in the last analysis rest with the generalist judge rather than the specialist lawyer, surely a retrograde step.

In summary, it is one thing to achieve and maintain a true independence of mind as an umpire. It is quite another as an examining magistrate, pursuing your own line of thought with the assistance of your own expert, irritated by the parties' lawyers' interruptions and objections from the sidelines. The authors are very concerned as to how such a system would work in practice.

In the end, medical litigation will always be relatively slow, cumbersome and difficult because of the inherent complexity of the issues involved and for administrative reasons, derived from the fact that it *should* be based on close sustained attention and advice by the most senior medical practitioners. There is no help for that. The only way medical justice can be made radically cheaper and quicker is by diminishing its quality.

The authors' view of the future is that the medical negligence lawyer is bound to be made the subject of more external control over the conduct of cases. The Law Society's medical negligence solicitors panel is now coming into being, the criteria for the grant of legal aid will be more restricted, the rates payable will never be generous and the conduct of the case will be subject to a greater judicial intervention, especially in terms of strict time-tables. The use of interrogatories, meetings of opposing expert witnesses and meetings of opposing counsel will be encouraged so as to define and, if possible, agree issues. Solicitors and counsel on both sides will be obliged to justify why issues have not been agreed before trial and if they cannot do so, will be penalised in costs. Provided change is pragmatic and introduced with care, things will improve, but no amount of changing the system will make this litigation easy or cheap.

It remains to be seen whether as a consequence of any change, the overall time table from medical accident through to trial will be any shorter than it has been in the past. It is interesting to look back at the case of *Bolam* (see p240) yet again. On 23 August 1954, Dr Allfrey administered electro-convulsive therapy to Mr Bolam. It was on 20 February 1957 that Mr NR Fox-Andrews QC opened the case before Mr Justice McNair and a jury at the Royal Courts of Justice. Most practitioners today would regard a two-and-a-half-year period from medical accident to trial as fairly expeditious.

Law Society's medical negligence panel

At the time of going to press the various solicitors who have expressed an interest in the panel have been sent their application forms for applying to go on it. It is unlikely that many of those applications will have been processed by the time of publication.

Clearly, the benefit to the client of such a panel will be that clients will be able to enquire whether or not the solicitor they propose instructing has been recognised as having sufficient experience in the field of medical negligence litigation to qualify for the panel.

At this stage there is no likelihood that the right to conduct medical negligence litigation will be limited to those on the panel. There has, however, been speculation amongst practitioners about whether there will be any attempt to link panel membership to legal aid by the introduction of a requirement that the nominated solicitor on a legal aid certificate be a solicitor on the specialist panel. It remains to be seen whether any such 'quality control' regulation is introduced. Those clients seeking a solicitor via the Law Society's Accident Line will be referred to a panel solicitor.

Funding

Funding of legal aid litigation is clearly going to be of even more concern to practitioners and clients alike in the future. The combination of the high cost of medical negligence litigation, the need for a thorough pre-action investigation, for which costs are not recoverable against the opponent if the claim is not pursued, the reduction in eligibility for legal aid, the requirement that legal aid contributions be paid throughout the lifetime of a certificate; all these mean increasing costs pressure on clients.

The extent to which the introduction of conditional fee arrangements will ease the pressure is far from certain. At the time of going to press, it is understood that insurance to cover the risk of paying defendants' costs, which will reduce the financial risks for the unsuccessful plaintiff, will not initially extend to medical negligence litigation. Without such cover, it is unlikely that plaintiffs will feel confident about entering into a conditional fee arrangement. However, the successful plaintiff may well find damages are substantially reduced by the impact of the additional level of fees payable under the conditional fee arrangement.

Franchising of legal aid

At the time of going to press many firms of solicitors across the country have applied for a legal aid franchise for personal injury and medical negligence work. Auditing has been carried out and after vigorous (but not wholly successful) campaigning by legal aid practitioners to amend the provisions of the franchising contract, there will be a significant number of firms with a legal aid franchise by the time of publication.

In the short term, franchising is likely to benefit the medical negligence practitioner because of the right of franchised firms to apply for legal aid interim payments at an enhanced rate rather than the standard rate. There are, however, fears that in the long term franchising will significantly affect the income of legal aid practices. Two ways in which income may be reduced are:

a) the amount of fee-earning time that will be spent by individual practitioners and by franchising and supervising partners in fulfilling the administrative requirements of franchising (much of which will not be recoverable chargeable time); and

b) the possibility of competitive tendering, about which there has been much speculation and comment but no confirmation.

No-fault liability

The authors doubt that a system of no-fault liability with standardised awards will be introduced. The Criminal Injuries Compensation Board scheme has been so discredited that it cannot be held out as a rational model for the future. In addition, the medical establishment will eventually realise that a 'no-fault' system would be a disaster for them, rather than a blessing, for the same reason that would make such a system extremely expensive.

Any such system, which avoided the necessity of proving fault, would immediately bring into the system a huge number of extra cases, where injury had been sustained as a result of medical care which was not negligent. The number of cases in such a system would be many times greater than the caseload produced by the tort system. And in each case, the question of causation would still have to be argued as now. If any attempt was made to create a specialised bureaucracy and tribunal system, it would be bound to be chronically underfunded from the start. The caseload would not be lightened by specialist lawyers weeding out the pointless and hopeless cases. Such a prospect is disastrous for doctors and those who fund awards of compensation to patients.

Moreover, there would be constitutional objection to the establishment of special protection from legal action for one profession, which would make it unlikely that the 'no-fault' system could be other than voluntary. Damaged patients would have to choose whether to litigate or invoke the 'no-fault' system. By reason of the attendant problems we have touched upon, we believe that any 'no-fault' system would in the main *only* be used by those unable to sue, either because they had no case in negligence or for financial reasons. It would thus be an add-on system, costing extra in time and money to the medical profession and to medical institutions. Naturally, it would be a field day for the lawyers.

Expertise

The most noticeable change in this field of litigation over the last decade is the development of expertise, legal and medical, available to the medically injured patient. This was long overdue. If one thing can be predicted with certainty, it is that this process is irreversible, so long as a tort system remains available to the injured patient. One need feel no sort of hostility whatever to the medical profession in order to feel that this is a positive process. The better the lawyers and the better their advisers, the fewer will be the poor or unmeritorious cases pursued.

This book has been the authors' best effort to contribute to that process. They hope that it will prove to be of some use.

Postscript
Bolam v Friern Hospital Management Committee
(The Times 20–26 February 1957, QBD)

Before Mr Justice McNair and a jury

The hearing was of an action by Mr John Hector Bolam against Friern Hospital Management Committee claiming damages for negligence in electro-convulsive therapy treatment administered to the plaintiff on August 23, 1954. The defendants denied negligence.

Mr N R Fox-Andrews, QC and Mr Roger Ormrod appeared for the plaintiff; Mr James Stirling, QC and Mr E Sutcliffe for the defendants.

20 February 1957

Mr Fox-Andrews, opening the case for the plaintiff, said that he was now a helpless cripple and would be so for the rest of his life. Before 1939 he was a salesman in the motor industry, earning about £1,000 a year. He was an officer in the Royal Engineers in the early part of the war and was discharged in 1942 suffering from nervous debility and depression of a very serious character. After the war he had a series of jobs but early in 1954, although physically fit, he suffered attacks of depression to such an extent that in the spring of that year he tried to take his own life. He went to the defendant hospital, a mental institution, on April 29, 1954, as a voluntary patient and stayed there until July 30. During that period he did not have any special treatment except rest and made a good recovery and was able to go back to work.

His depression returned, and on August 16 he went back to the hospital as a voluntary patient. On August 23, 1954, he was given a form of electrical treatment in the course of which, while he was unconscious, both his thigh bones were forced through their sockets, which were smashed, and as a result he would never walk properly again.

240

Electro-convulsive therapy was a form of treatment given to relieve and cure, if possible, serious depression. It was a comparatively modern discovery, first used in this country about 1939. The patient was put on his back. Two electrodes or terminals were placed one on each temple and the switch pressed. What happened then was dramatic in the extreme: an electric current was passed through the patient's brain and he became utterly, instantly, totally and helplessly unconscious. If no precautions were taken his limbs and body began to jerk in the most violent manner, because the electric current caused terrrific – and he used the word purposely – muscular spasms all over the body. Every trained medical man realised that if no precautions were taken there was a grave danger that those terrific muscular contractions might cause very serious injury. The treatment when given without any form of precaution was a ghastly thing to watch. The patient was to all intents and purposes having an epileptic fit of the worst possible type – and that was the whole object of the treatment.

In the early days injuries were caused in a pretty high percentage of cases but there were now two recognised types of precautions. One was physical restraint, either by a restraining sheet being placed over the patient so that he could not leap up, or, sometimes at the same time, by nurses pressing down on the patient's pelvis and holding his shoulders down. Whilst not a guarantee against injury, it minimised the risk, and the more it was used the smaller the incidence of fractures. The other precaution now widely taken in this country was the administration of a relaxant drug which had the effect of making the muscles of the patient not react at all, so that he could not hurt himself. The giving of that drug caused an unpleasant experience, because before becoming unconscious the patient felt as if he were dead, and therefore it was often accompanied by the giving of an anaesthetic. There were people who criticised the use of the drug on the ground that there was some risk in the giving of an anaesthetic, but thousands of anaesthetics were given every day, and there was no suggestion that the plaintiff was the sort of person whom it would have been inadvisable to give the drug and anaesthetic to.

The plaintiff's main case would be that the hospital's negligence was that they caused his injuries by failing to take any precautions either to prevent, or to try to minimise, the risk of injury.

The hospital had admitted that they did not take any precautions at all except to support the patient's jaw, so that he could not gnash his teeth, and put a pillow under his back. Correspondence showed that the hospital had had other cases of similar fractures, though not, as with the plaintiff, bi-lateral cases, during the previous seven years. He suggested that that was one of the most important factors in the case. Not only did the defendants know of the danger to a man whom they were going to put into an epileptic fit, not only did they not warn him, not only did they not take precautions, but they did, or failed to do, all these things, when the same thing had happened five times before. Was that not really rather shocking?

21 February 1957
Evidence was then called on behalf of the plaintiff.

John Bulmer Randall, consultant psychiatrist, of Harley Street, giving evidence for the plaintiff, demonstrated two of the machines used in giving ECT treatment, and described the convulsive reactions of a patient. The witness said that when a relaxant drug was given the movements should be very slight indeed. What he liked to achieve was sufficient to give the slightest movement – for example, a very slight movement of the feet as was demonstrated in the television series 'The Hurt Mind'. In a modified convulsion, that was, when a relaxant was used, it was sometimes difficult to know when the first phase had taken place. Relaxant drugs were not commonly used until 1946 or 1947 for ECT purposes; the drugs then available were dangerous and unpredictable.

In his experience, fractures did occur before the use of relaxant restraints, but he knew of only one fracture among the cases under his supervision when a restraining sheet was used, and none when relaxant drugs had been used. They were not in as common general use in 1954 as they were today. He always advocated the use of an anaesthetic when a relaxant drug was used. In 1954 he would not have carried out ECT without any form of restraint. There was a school of thought which would give ECT without any restraint, but the witness would not do so.

Cross-examined by Mr Stirling, the witness said that relaxant drugs were given without an anaesthetic, but he disapproved of the practice because of the terrifying effect on the patient.

Counsel: You know the risks in the use of relaxant drugs is a real one? – It is an anaesthetic one.

Is it not debatable in medical circles what it is that causes the fatalities that do occur? – There appear to be two; prolonged loss of breath, and the risk of relaxation of muscles of the gut causing a reflux of the stomach contents and asphyxia. That is why there must always be an anaesthetist skilled in resuscitation.

Is there any known antidote to Scoline? – No.

His Lordship: If there is no antidote are there any steps which you can take to remedy the effects? – You can apply continual oxygen, in an artificial lung, if necessary.

Is it your view that deaths due to relaxant drugs, particularly curare-like drugs, might not be due to depressed breathing but to some toxic effect acting centrally? – I would not like to express any opinion. The drugs act differently. Scoline acts on the spinal cord. Curare acts on the muscle itself.

Answering further questions the witness said that he had experience of about 6,000 to 10,000 cases in which relaxant drugs were used. He had never had a death. He had used the drugs tentatively at first. He agreed that the dangers were real, but said that experience showed that they were not great using a skilled technique and anaesthetics. He had used the drugs tentatively until about four years ago. He agreed with a citation from a medical book that mental suffering could be the greatest ill that man was heir to and that shock therapy might often be the only relief for it.

The patient should be aware of the nature of the treatment. Some patients, in very severe depressions, were not affected one way or the other by a warning, but he thought that it might be helpful to others. Other people might take a contrary view.

Counsel: Is there, even today, a vast body of medical opinion who prefer and think it wiser to give ECT straight? – There is a large body of opinion today which thinks that ECT should be given unmodified.

In 1954 there was an even larger body of opinon? – Using restraint instead of a relaxant, yes.

Persons whose opinion you would respect although you might not agree with them? – Indeed.

Regarding the use of manual restraint, the witness said that he knew that some doctors were of opinion that the more restraint there was the more likelihood there was of fracture.

His Lordship: Have you any idea what the majority view is? I learnt with surprise that restraint is not used as often as I had expected.

The witness said that he was aware that different practitioners adopted a variety of positions for putting their patients into, and that there was a body of opinion that the less restraint that was applied, except for the chin, the better.

Is what is called a 'sub-shock' a very bad thing for the patient – that is, an electric current passing through which does not produce convulsion? – It is inadequate. It does not do any harm unless practitioners have given many in an attempt to produce a convulsion when it would produce confusion and headache.

Mr Stirling, opening the case for the defence, said that negligence was not established by showing that some other doctors would disapprove of a particular practice. It was probably apparent here that there were at least two schools of thought, each entitled to their own opinion; it was not for the jury to decide between them.

Dr J de Bastarrechea, consultant psychiatrist attached to the defendant hospital, gave evidence. He said that he was opposed to the use of relaxants. There was an inherent mortality risk, and a proportion must inevitably die if enough cases were given relaxant drugs. He had not been able to find English figures but a survey carried out in the United States for the five years between 1948 and 1953 showed one in 370. If the figures were broken down one in 2,000 would be acceptable. The witness had decided against the use of relaxant drugs before learning of the survey results on his impression from the general theory of medicine that there must be a risk involved in anything which paralysed respiration. That was confirmed by the survey.

His Lordship: Do you ever give relaxants now that you have these figures? – Where the patient's life might be risked by straight ECT. I worry about it more but I have to consider other risks.

The witness said that whether a relaxant should be given was in each case considered from every aspect. He had always stayed on the technique of non-restraint.

Cross-examined by Mr Fox-Andrews, the witness, referring to the five other fractures occurring at the hospital during the past seven years, said that he did not know how many of these patients were still there. They were not his cases. A fracture of this type was rare in the course of ECT. Six in seven years meant six in roughly 70,000 cases.

Do you know of any other institution or hospital in this

country where ECT is given, which has had six similar fractures? – No, because I have not had access to their records.

Counsel asked for the production of the records of the five other fractures on the grounds that they were relevant and that the witness had sought to distinguish them. His Lordship ordered that the records be produced.

About 10 people, the witness said, administered ECT at the hospital. There had been deaths during ECT there, but none among his cases. There were two schools of thought there: those who always gave relaxants and those who gave them in selected cases. He (the witness) would not exclude their use. One of his juniors always gave them and he would not think of telling him not to. For the most part they had all stopped using manual restraint at about the same time; his team had been taught not to use it.

Counsel: Do you agree that manual restraint seems to be in accordance with common sense? – Yes, but not necessarily in accordance with medical sense because experience shows that you still get fractures. When restraint has stopped at least the fractures did not increase.

His Lordship: Common sense is a phrase we often use to describe our own sense.

22 February 1957

Dr Bastarrechea, further cross-examined, said that he did not warn his patients of all the risks of ECT treatment; he indicated that there were some slight risks. There was the risk of fractures and the risk to life.

Mr Fox-Andrews: Is there not every reason to believe that if the plaintiff had been given a relaxant drug he would never have suffered this disaster? – Every reason to believe that he would not have suffered this disaster, but he might have suffered a worse one.

You have not yet suggested any reason why the plaintiff should not have been given a relaxant drug. – I approach the matter from the other angle: I find out if there is any reason why a patient should be given a drug, not why he should not be given one.

The cases of six other patients who had suffered fractures of the acetabulum (hip socket), the witness said, could not be compared with the plaintiff's case. The degree of injury was much less in the other cases; the resulting disability was practically nil. Even two months in bed was better than an infinity in the grave.

Asked whether he could produce in any work known to him any statement that it was ever right to take no precautions, the witness mentioned the leading textbook of Kalinowsky and Hoch. He did not know of any precise statement that neither relaxants nor restraint should be given, but it was stated in *Clinical Psychology: Introduction to Physical Methods* by Drs Sargant and Slater, that there was no general consensus of opinion. He could not find any statement which said that anyone undergoing ECT should not receive relaxants or manual restraint. Absence of manual restraint in itself was a precaution in his experience.

Dr Colin Forbes Allfrey gave evidence that for the past four years he had been senior registrar at Friern Hospital. Between 1946 and 1954 he had given approximately 8,000 single treatments; each patient would receive an average of five treatments. He had been taught not to use restraint as it had been described in this court, other than holding the chin and a pillow under the back. About 1949 or 1950 he had started to use relaxants in a very small number of selected cases, following the general practice of the hospital, as where there had been a recent fracture or a patient was known to have a hernia or an ulcer or tuberculosis.

He (the witness) took over the plaintiff's case when Dr de Bastarrechea went on holiday. There was nothing in the plaintiff's history or which physical examination revealed which suggested that a relaxant should be used. If a nurse had been lying across his pelvis or two nurses pressing it down, it would have had no effect on the injuries the plaintiff sustained.

The technique he (the witness) adopted on that occasion was the one he had used on other occasions. In his view there was nothing in the technique which would increase the risk of fracture. He had realised that something untoward had happened a few minutes later when the plaintiff began to recover consciousness and complained of pain in the legs.

He (the witness) was now using relaxants to a greater extent, because a new one, Brevidil, was considered safer. He had left neither the non-relaxant camp nor the non-restraining camp.

Mr Fox-Andrews, cross-examining: Do you know that the ECT register of the hospital shows that in the case of every patient to whom you gave this treatment over the next seven days after you had treated the plaintiff you gave every one a relaxing drug? – Yes. That was because, until I had become certain in my own mind that there was nothing wrong with my technique, I thought that for the next week or two I should not take the added risk of other fractures, at least until Dr de Bastarrechea returned and I was able to discuss the case with him.

Did you have an anaesthetist to give the anaesthetic to those patients? – I think that the Brevidil was given without anaesthetic.

23 February 1957

Dr Bastarrechea, recalled, gave figures from the defendant hospital's records of deaths associated with ECT; there had been four recorded deaths associated with ECT and Scoline and two associated with ECT straight, although in one of those two a coroner's jury had returned a verdict of death through natural causes.

Leonard Gilbert Page, deputy medical officer at the Three Counties Hospital, Bedfordshire, author of a number of works on psychiatry, gave evidence. He spoke of treatment in an ordinary hospital bed with ordinary coverings, sheets, blanket and counterpane, tucked in in the normal way. Most patients, he said, were already in bed before treatment and it was convenient to have them comfortably covered and, if possible, asleep. Some would have had a sedative.

Cross-examined, he said that he would think that the technique of treating his patients in bed was comparable to the use of a restraining sheet.

Alex Anthony Baker, consultant psychiatrist and deputy superintendant at Banstead Hospital, said that since 1953 he had adopted the method of treating patients in bed: they were not always tucked in, and in the summer months they were lyng on top of the bed.

Mr Stirling, addressing the jury for the defendants, said that the plaintiff was only entitled to succeed if he proved that the doctors who organised and administered his treatment fell short of the standard of care which a reasonably careful and skilled doctor would have used at the time.

The jury had heard the phrase 'two schools of thought' many times. There was a sincere division of responsible medical opinion, but it was not for the jury to decide which was right. If the defendants' doctors were following an accepted and approved line of medical thought, there was no question of negligence.

It did not assist the plaintiff to say that the record of casualties at Friern was higher than at other hospitals. The number of fractures was a very small proportion and they had heard them described as unpredictable. It was difficult to see how it could be said that the defendants had not taken precautions, and the plaintiff in law and on the facts could not succeed.

Mr Fox-Andrews, for the plaintiff, said that he did not accept that because some doctors thought one thing and others a different thing the jury were bound to say that they could not decide the case because they were not doctors. Their function was to consider the evidence and say whether or not they thought that what was done to the plaintiff was in fact careless or careful.

26 February 1957

Mr Justice McNair, summing up to the jury, said that when the case was opened and they were told the really tragic story of the plaintiff's suffering and experience, they must inevitably have been moved to pity and compassion, but, as counsel had rightly told them, they were entitled to give damages only if the defendants had been proved guilty of negligence.

The case must be looked at in its proper perspective. They had been told by one doctor that he had had one acetabular fracture in 50,000 cases, and it was clear that the particular injury sustained by the plaintiff was one of extreme rarity.

Whereas some years ago when a patient went into a mental institution afflicted with mental illness, which it was agreed was one of the most terrible ills from which humanity suffered, he had very little hope of recovery and could only expect to be carefully and kindly treated until a merciful death released him from his sufferings, today, according to the evidence, the position had changed. Practitioners from leading hospitals had put before them quite staggering figures. Today a man suffering from some particular types of mental disorder had a real chance of recovery. One doctor had said that in his view that was due almost entirely to physical methods of treatment, of which ECT was the most important. In approaching this case, and considering whether negligence was proved against the defendant hospital, they must bear in mind the enormous benefits conferred upon unfortunate men and women by this form of treatment.

The use of ECT had been progressive, and they (the jury) might think that even today there was no standard, settled technique on all points with which all competent doctors would agree. The doctors called as witnesses had mentioned in turn the different techniques they used. Some used restraining sheets, some manual control; but the final question was, whether or not Dr Allfrey, in following the practice which he had learnt and had been shown at Friern, was negligent in failing to use relaxant drugs, in failing to exercise any restraint when he was not using relaxant drugs beyond arranging for the plaintiff's shoulders to be held, his chin supported, and a pillow placed behind his back.

A professional man was not guilty of negligence if he acted in accordance with a practice which was accepted by a competent body of professional men skilled in that particular art, merely because there was a body of opinion which took a contrary view. That did not mean that a medical man could obstinately and pig-headedly carry on some technique if it was proved contrary to substantially the whole body of medical opinion. It was not essential for the jury to decide which of the practices was the better. They must remember also that August 1954 was not February 1957, and they must not look with 1957 spectacles at what had happened in 1954.

As to the allegation that the defendants were negligent in not warning the plaintiff of the risks involved in the treatment, two questions arose: first, did good medical practice require that a warning should be given to a patient before receiving ECT treatment? Secondly, if a warning should have been given, and it was not, what difference would it have made, and were they (the jury) satisfied that the plaintiff, if told of the risks, would have refused to take them? Did the defendants' practice, to say very little and wait for questions, fall below the standard required by competent professional opinion; would it or would it not have been right to warn? They might well think that a doctor, when dealing with a mentally sick man and having a strong belief that his patient's only hope was ECT, should not be criticised if he did not stress the dangers, which he believed to be minimal, involved in that treatment. If they thought that the warning ought to have been given, then the only person who could answer the second question, whether it would have made any difference, was the plaintiff. He (his Lordship) had been waiting for the plaintiff to be asked that question, but it had not been put to him, and it would be mere speculation on their part to decide what his answer might have been. He might well have said that, rather than continue in his condition, he would take the treatment with the risks involved. Unless the plaintiff had satisfied them that he would not have taken the treatment if he had been warned, they might well think that there was nothing in that point.

The defendants said that, balancing what they believed to be a remote risk of fracture against the remote risk of mortality, they decided not to use relaxants except in special cases. Was it open, on the whole of the evidence, to say that the mere failure to give relaxants was negligent? All the witnesses had agreed that there was a firm body of opinion against the use of relaxants as a routine, although one, Dr Randall, preferred to take the risk of relaxants and eliminate the risk of fracture.

As to the use of restraint, there again the defendants said that there were two schools of thought, the one they adhered to being that if a patient was held down the risk of fracture was in fact increased, and they had accordingly since 1951 adopted a new technique of leaving the patient's limbs free. It was interesting, as showing the diversity of practice, that Dr Page at the Three Counties Hospital treated his patients in bed controlled to some extent by the coverings, but it was not right to take that as condemning the practice adopted by the defendants.

Referring in conclusion to the remarks of Lord Justice Denning in *Roe v Minister of Health* [1955] 2 QB 66, his Lordship said that medical science had conferred great benefits on mankind but those benefits were attended by risks and we could not take the benefits without the risks.

The verdict

After a retirement of about half an hour the jury returned a verdict for the defendants but added that they would like to express their sympathy for the plaintiff in his terrible injuries and hoped that some organisation would help to alleviate his position.

(Richard Allfrey is the son of the third defendant in this case.)

Appendices

Appendices

Checklist of records

Checklist of hospital records

Generally

1. Clinical records prepared in outpatient clinics (generally hand-written but very occasionally typed).
2. Clinical records prepared during inpatient admissions.
3. Nursing cardex/notes prepared during admissions.
4. Nursing care plan prepared during admissions.
5. Drug records/chart.
6. Operation notes.
7. Anaesthetist's notes and records.
8. X-rays.
9. Test requests and results (these may relate to visual tests such as X-rays and ultrasounds, blood, urine, faecal, mucous or other bodily sample tests).
10. Charts for temperature, pulse, blood pressure and respiration.
11. Patient consent forms, correspondence.
12. Electroencephalograms (EEG) and reports.
13. Intensive care unit records.

Additionally in obstetric cases

1. Co-operation card (if not retained by mother).
2. Occasionally hard copies of ultrasound scans.
3. X-ray pelvimetry.
4. Birth plan.
5. Booking form.
6. Maternal records of previous pregnancies.
7. Labour notes including initial paediatric records such as baby's condition at birth.
8. Partogram.
9. Midwifery records of labour.
10. Community midwifery records for 10 days post partum.

11. Continuous CTG traces.
12. Special care baby unit records.
13. Photographs.

And additionally in cardiological cases

1. Cardiac cerebral function records.
2. Electrocardiograms (ECG) and reports.
3. Ecocardiagrams and reports.

Checklist of GP records

1. GP appointment cards (usually handwritten).
2. Emergency (24-hour) doctors' records (sometimes inserted separately).
3. Correspondence.
4. Test requests and results.
5. Antenatal co-op card (if not held by mother).

Checklist of dental records

1. Dental card.
2. X-rays.
3. Model/plaster impressions.
4. Photographs.
5. Dental laboratory worksheets.
6. Clinical dental notes.
7. Consent forms.
8. Operation records.
9. Anaesthetic records.
10. Details relating to payment of fees.
11. Correspondence.

These lists are based by permission on similar lists produced by AVMA.

Glossary of medical terms

Common hieroglyphs

✚	much/many
#	fracture
▵	diagnosis
▵▹ ▵▵	differential diagnosis
R$_x$	treatment
o	nil/nothing/no
↑	up, increasing
→	constant, normal or lateral shift (eg of apex of heart)
↓	down, decreasing
⊥	central (of the trachea)
1/7	one day
2/52	two weeks
3/12	three months
T 38.6	temperature 38.6
T−2/40 or 2/52	term (ie date baby due) less 2 weeks
T+1/40 or 1/52	term plus one week
35+4	35 weeks and 4 days
37+3	37 weeks and 3 days
π	period

Common abbreviations

aa	of each (Greek)
AAL	anterior axillary line
ac	before meals
ACTH	adrenocorticotrophic hormone
ad	up to
add	adduction
ADH	antidiuretic hormone

255

ADL	activities of daily living
ad lib	to the desired amount, ad libitum
ADP	adenosine diphosphate
AE	air entry
AFB	acid fast bacillus (TB)
AFP	alpha-fetoprotein maternal serum and occasionally amniotic fluid levels, tested in pregnancy to screen for neural tube defect in foetus
AID	artificial insemination by donor
AIDS	acquired immune deficiency syndrome
AIH	artificial insemination – husband
AJ	ankle jerk (reflex: see also BJ, KJ, SJ, TJ)
alt dieb	every other day
Al S	alimentary system
Anti-D	(This gamma globulin must be given by injection to Rhesus negative mother who delivers/aborts Rhesus positive child/foetus to prevent mother developing antibodies which would damage a subsequent Rhesus positive baby.)
Apgar	Apgar score: means of recording baby's condition at birth by observing and 'scoring' (0, 1 or 2) – five parameters
Applic	applications
aq	water
aq/dest/ster	distilled or sterilised water
aq dest	distilled water
AR	analytical standard of reagent purity
ARC	AIDS related complex (less damage can result in full-blown AIDS)
ARDS	adult respiratory distress syndrome
ARM	artificial rupture of membranes
ASD	atrial septal defect
AST	aspartate aminotransferase
ATP	adenosine triphosphate
aurist	ear drops
A/V	anteverted
bd	both
b.d.	twice a day
BJ	biceps jerk (reflex: see AJ)
blood sugar	Normal 2.5 – 5.5 mmol/l
blood urea	Normal 2.5 – 6.6 mmol/l
BMR	Basal metabolism rate
BNF (plus date)	*British National Formulary* (prescriber's bible, supplied free to all NHS doctors). New edition

each year. You can buy one for about £10.00 from medical bookshops.

BO	bowels open
BP (plus date)	British Pharmacopoeia
BP	Blood pressure
BS	(1) British Standard
	(2) breath sounds
	(3) bowel sounds
	(4) blood sugar
c	with (Latin: cum)
C_2H_5OH	Alcohol
Ca	(1) carcinoma/cancer
	(2) calcium
Caps	capsules
CAT (scan)	computer axial tomograph
cp	compare
CIN	cervical intraepithelial neoplasia (cervical cancer)
CMV	cytomegalovirus
CNS	central nervous system
CO	complaining of
CO_2	carbon dioxide
COETT	cuffed oral endotracheal tube (see COT and ETT)
comp	compounded of
COT	cuffed oral tube (endotracheal tube used for ventilating a patient who cannot breathe unaided)
CPD	cephalo-pelvic disproportion (baby too big to fit through pelvis)
crem	a cream
CSF	cerebro-spinal fluid
CTG	cardiotocograph (trace during labour of baby's heart and mother's contractions)
CVA	cardiovascular accident (stroke)
CVS	Cardiovascular system
Cx	cervix
CXR	chest X-ray
D	diagnosis (GOK – God only knows)
DIC	disseminated intravascular coagulation (a serious complication of many conditions – relates to widespread thrombosis)
dil	dilute
DNA	(1) did not attend
	(2) deoxyribonucleic acid
D & V	diarrhoea and vomiting
DOA	dead on arrival
DOPA	Dopamine

DVT	deep vein thrombosis
D/W	discussed with
Dx	diagnosis
ECG	electrocardiography
ECT	electroconvulsive therapy
EDD	expected date of delivery
emf	electromotive force
EM	electron micrography
EMG	electromogram/graph
emp	emplastrum – a plaster
enem	enemata – enemas
EOG	electro-oculogram
ER	external rotation
ERCP	endoscopic retrograde cholangio-pancreatography/scope
ERPC	evacuation of retained products of conception
ERG	electroretinogram
ESR	erythrocyte sedimentation rate
Ex	extension
FB	finger's breadth
FBC	full blood count
FBS	foetal blood sampling
FH	family history
FHH	foetal heart heard
FHHR	foetal heart heard regular
FHR	foetal heart rate
Flex	flexion
FLK	funny looking kid
FMF	foetal movements felt
FSE	foetal scalp electrode
FSH	(1) family/social history
	(2) follicle-stimulating hormone
GA	general anaesthetic
garg	gargles
glc	gas liquid chromatography
GTT	glucose tolerance test
GFR	glomerular filtration rate
GIT	gastrointestinal tract
GM	Geiger Muller
GUT	genito-urinary tract
Hb	haemoglobin
HCG	human chorionic gonadotrophin
HCO	history of present complaint or HPC
hn	hac nocte – tonight
hs	hora somni – at bed time

HS	heart sounds
HSA	human serum albumin
HVS	high vaginal swab
Hx	history
ICF	intracellular fluid
ICS	intercostal space
IgA, IgB, IgG, IgM	immunoglobulins
IJV	internal jugular vein
IM	intramuscular
implant	implantation
In aq	in water
Inj	injections
IP	intraperitoneal
IR	internal rotation
Irrig	irrigations
IVI	intravenous infusion
K	Potassium
KJ	knee jerk
KPa	kilopascal, approx 7.5 mm Hg
L	litre
LA	local anaesthetic
LATS	long-acting thyroid stimulator
LFT	liver function tests
LH	lutenising hormone
LIH	left inguinal hernia
Linc	linctus
Lin	liniments
Liq	solutions
LMP	last menstrual period
LN	lymph node
LOA	left occipital anterior
LOC	loss of consciousness (or contact, eg on CTG trace)
LOL	left occipital lateral
LOP	left occipital posterior
LSCS	lower segment caesarian section
LSK	liver, spleen, kidneys
m	mix
mane	in the morning
mcg	microgram
MCL	mid clavicular line
mg	milligram
mm Hg	mm of mercury (unit of pressure)
ml	millilitres
mp	melting point

MSH	melanophore stimulating hormone
MSU	midstream specimen of urine
N & V	nausea and vomiting
NAD	nothing abnormal detected
NBM	nil by mouth
Neb	a spray
ng	nanogram
NG	neoplastic growth
NG	nasogastric
NGT	nasogastric tube
NMCS	no malignant cells seen
NOF	neck of femur
N/S	normal size
O	oxygen
Occulent	eye ointment
OA	occipito-anterior
od	daily
OD	outside diameter
OE	on examination
OM	every morning
ON	every evening
OP	occipito-posterior
PR	pulse rate
Pa	pascal
PAS	periodic acid – Schiff reaction
pc	after meals
PCG	phonocardiogram
PCV	packed cell volume
PERLA	pupils are equal and react to light and accommodation
PE	pulmonary embolism
pes	pessaries
PET	pre-eclampsia toxaemia
pH	potential hydrogen (acidity/alkalinity scale)
PH	past history
PID	(1) pelvic inflammatory disease
	(2) prolapsed intravertebral disc
PMH	past medical history
PN(R)	percussion note (resonant)
PNS	peripheral nervous system
PO	per oram – by mouth
PR	per rectum
PRN	as required/as occasion arises
PV	per vaginam
RBC	red blood cells

Rh	Rhesus
rh	relative humidity
RIA	radio immune assay
RIH	right inguinal hernia
ROA	right occipital anterior
ROL	right occipital lateral
ROM	range of movement
RPF	renal plasma flow
RQ	respiratory quotient
RS	respiratory system
RT	reaction time
RTI	respiratory tract infection
S/B	seen by
S/D	systolic/diastolic
SEM	scanning electron microscope
SH	social history
SJ	sole jerk
SOA	swelling of ankles
SOB	shortness of breath
SOS	(1) si opus sit (if necessary)
	(2) see other sheet
SROM	spontaneous rupture of membranes
SVC	superior vena cava
SVD	spontaneous vaginal delivery
TCI 3/52	to come in three weeks time
TGH	to go home
THR	total hip replacement
TID	three times a day
TJ	triceps jerk
TFTs	thyroid function tests
TSH	thyroid stimulating hormone
U & E	urea and electrolytes
UG	urinogenital system
Ung	ointments
URTI	upper respiratory tract infection
VE	vaginal examination
VF	ventrical fibrilation
VT	ventrical tachycardia
V/V	vulva and vagina
WBC	white blood count/corpuscle

The authors are grateful to AVMA for permission to reproduce this list of common abbreviations, set out in their Lawyers' Resource Service Starter Pack.

Case papers: Brown v Barchester Health Authority

Preliminary notes

1 In this appendix the authors have tried to replicate as realistically as possible the central documents which would arise in a real case. This means that there is a considerable volume of documentation, even to reproduce short statements, the principal pleadings, interrogatories, and two medical reports from each side. Space means that we are unable to reproduce the medical records in anything like a realistic form, apart from the cardiotocograph, and so the central obstetric information has been gathered into a digest, which for the purposes of the exercise, is assumed to have been prepared for convenient use. The paediatric information emerges in the course of the reports and pleadings.

2 Interpretation of a CTG trace is exceedingly complex and sometimes controversial. The 'top line' on the trace represents the foetal heart rate and the 'bottom line' is a record of the contracting uterus. It would not be appropriate to offer fuller notes here. Any lawyer dealing with a case involving a CTG trace will require very close advice from an obstetrician on the interpretation of the trace.

3 The authors owe a great debt to a large number of busy professionals who have helped them with this exercise, expressed more fully at the beginning of the book. Since much of the material has necessarily been adapted or changed, any solecisms are their responsibility.

A. Witness statement of Mrs Selina Brown

of 12 Hartford Avenue, Barchester, Barsetshire BR1 9XZ

WHO WILL SAY AS FOLLOWS:

1. I am the mother of John Brown who was born on 17 October 1990.
2. I was born on 25 March 1957 and was aged 33 years at the time of the birth of my son, John, who is my first child. I was booked to

have my baby at St Adomnan's Hospital, Barchester under the care of Mr Rasputin and my antenatal care was shared between Mr Rasputin, my general practitioner, Dr Pink, and my community midwife, Mrs Black. I had hoped to have a normal childbirth and not a caesarian section or a forceps delivery but of course I would have accepted a caesarian section or a forceps delivery if it was necessary for the health of the baby. As well as preparation classes at the hospital I attended classes run by the National Childbirth Trust.

3. I went into labour very early on 17 October 1990 and came to the hospital at just before 4 o'clock in the morning. I had hoped to go into the birth pool but when the midwife, Sister White, performed a tracing of the baby's heart she said that this would not be advisable. She told me that she would need to rupture the membranes and I agreed to this. Thick brown fluid was released when she did so.

4. Sister White told me that the baby was in some distress and that she would ask Mr Rasputin, who was the consultant on call, to come and see me. He arrived some 20 minutes later and examined me. He told me that, although the baby was in some distress, he did not think this was at a dangerous level and, as labour was progressing very fast, he thought I could deliver normally without a caesarian section. I could see that there were very considerable changes in the baby's heart rate recorded on the monitor.

5. At about 5.45 am Sister White encouraged me to push the baby out and I tried to do so in various positions. At around 6.30 Mr Rasputin told me that the baby's heart rate was deteriorating and that he thought he should assist the delivery. I was transferred to another room and Mr Rasputin put a suction cap on the baby's head. As I pushed he pulled and the baby was soon delivered.

6. The baby looked quite ill at birth and did not cry. Mr Rasputin told me that the cord was 5 times around his neck. He was transferred to the Special Care Baby Unit and has since developed cerebral palsy.

7. I have asked my solicitors to investigate whether the birth of my son was managed properly and whether delivery at an earlier stage by caesarian section would have saved the development of cerebral palsy.

SIGNED ....

DATED ....

B. Letter to potential defendant requesting medical records

BLANK, GREEN FORM & COMPANY

SOLICITORS

10 Green Bottle Lane, Muckleborough, Humberside HA1 2HA

DX 123456 Muckleborough . Telephone 4444.555666 . Fax 4444.666555

The Barchester Health Authority
St Adomnan's Hospital
Barchester
Barsetshire

Dear Sirs

John Brown (Date of Birth: 17th October 1990)
and Selina Brown (Date of Birth: 25th March 1957)
Both of 12 Hartford Avenue, Barchester, Barsetshire

We act on behalf of John Brown and are instructed on his behalf to investigate a potential claim for damages for medical negligence arising out of the circumstances of his birth at your hospital, St Adomnan's Hosptial, Barchester.

Mrs Brown's antenatal care was shared between her GP and the obstetric department at St Adomnan's Hospital. The consultant responsible for her obstetric care was Mr Rasputin.

In the early hours of 17th October 1990 Mrs Brown's labour commenced and she was admitted to St Adomnan's Hospital at or about 4.00 am that morning.

On admission she was seen by a midwife. Foetal heart monitoring was commenced. Shortly thereafter the membranes were ruptured. On doing so thick brown meconium was seen.

Mrs Brown was informed by the midwife that the consultant, Mr Rasputin, would have to be called to see her. He arrived about 20 minutes later.

When Mr Rasputin saw Mrs Brown, he advised her that although the baby was in some distress he did not think that this was dangerous and that he thought that she could deliver normally without a caesarian section.

Mrs Brown recalls being encouraged to push at about 5.45 am.

At about 6.30 am Mrs Brown was told by Mr Rasputin that the baby's heart rate was deteriorating. Mrs Brown was then transferred to another room where the baby was delivered by ventouse extraction.

On delivery the baby was transferred to the Special Care Unit.

Subsequently, John Brown has been diagnosed as suffering from cerebral palsy.

If proceedings are issued against your health authority, we anticipate that the allegations will include an allegation that there was a failure to respond appropriately to the signs of foetal distress and that had appropriate response been made our client John Brown would not now suffer from cerebral palsy.

Until we have had sight of all relevant medical records and have had the benefit of independent medical advice on the same it will not be possible for us to advise our client and his family as to whether or not there is a claim to be pursued against your Health Authority. Further, without sight of the records and independent advice on them it will not be possible, in the event of proceedings being issued, for counsel to plead the case properly.

We have set out sufficient particulars to make it clear that this is a case in which Mrs Brown's antenatal and obstetric records and John Brown's paediatric records should be disclosed to us by way of pre-action discovery. We would be grateful if you would confirm within 14 days of the receipt of this letter that pre-action discovery will be given on a voluntary basis and that there will be no need for us to make an application to the court for an order for pre-action discovery. Please also confirm in that letter that the copy records will be disclosed to us within 12 weeks of the receipt of this letter.

We enclose Mrs Brown's signed authority for release of her records and those of her son to this firm. We confirm that we will be responsible for your reasonable copying and administrative charges. We confirm that we will require a continuous copy of the CTG trace and, further, if any permanent images were made of ultrasound examinations, we will require copies of these.

When responding to this request will you please confirm whether there was any internal inquiry into the circumstances of our client's birth. If so, please confirm that the documents relating to that inquiry will be disclosed by way of pre-action discovery.

Please also confirm that pending the resolution of this matter the original documents relating to our client will be preserved in their entirety and that should there be any plan, for example, to microfiche any records we will be given a minimum of one month's notice of this intention so that, if necessary, further copies can be made from the originals.

Should it be necessary for us to make an application for pre-action discovery in this matter we will refer to the contents of this letter both on the substantive application and when the question of costs of that application come to be dealt with.

We look forward to hearing from you.

Yours faithfully,

Blank Green Form & Co

C. Affidavit in support of pre-action discovery

IN THE HIGH COURT OF JUSTICE
QUEEN'S BENCH DIVISION

In the matter of section 33 of the Supreme Court Act 1981; and in the matter of Order 24 rule 7A of the Rules of the Supreme Court 1965

Between

JOHN BROWN

(By his mother and next friend, Selina Brown)   Applicant

- and -

BARCHESTER HEALTH AUTHORITY   Respondent

AFFIRMATION ON BEHALF OF THE APPLICANT

I, Ophelia Dane, partner in the firm of Blank Green Form and Co, solicitors of 10 Green Bottle Lane, Muckleborough, Humberside HA1 2HA do solemnly, sincerely and truly affirm and say as follows:

1. I am instructed on behalf of the Applicant and proposed Plaintiff in this matter and am duly authorised by his mother and next friend, Mrs Selina Brown to make this affirmation in support of an application for pre-action discovery against the Respondent.
2. Save for where it otherwise appears, the contents of this affirmation are based on my knowledge and/or my perusal of documents. The facts to which I depose are true to the best of my knowledge, information and belief.
3. John Brown was born on 17th October 1990 at the respondent's hospital, St Adomnan's Hospital, Barchester. He is the son of Selina Brown.
4. John Brown is severely disabled with cerebral palsy. I am instructed by his mother and next friend to investigate whether this was caused by the care provided to his mother ante-natally and at the time of his birth.
5. In order to be able to investigate the claim I wrote on the (*date*) to the Respondents requesting copies both of Mrs Brown's obstetric records and John Brown's paediatric record. A copy of that letter is now produced and shown to me in the bundle of correspondence marked 'OD1'.
6. In response to that letter I received an initial letter of acknowledgement and then a letter dated (*date*) from the Respondent's solicitor,

Messrs Bentley, Bigge & Blue. That letter is also now produced and shown to me in the bundle of corrxpondence marked 'OD1'. It will be seen from the contents of that letter that it was accompanied by copy records excluding the copy cardiotocograph trace (CTG) which it was said could not be found.

7. I then wrote to Messrs Bentley Bigge and Blue asking them to confirm what searches had been made for the trace and what information there was relating to when it was last available. A copy of that letter is now produced and shown to me in the bundle marked 'OD1'. Since that letter was written 3 months ago there has been no response from Messrs Bentley Bigge and Blue despite repeated requests from me as evidenced in my letters of (*date*), (*date*) and (*date*) which are also now produced and shown to me in the bundle marked 'OD1'.

8. I understand that Mrs Brown was admitted to the respondent's Hospital, St Adomnan's Hospital, on 17th October 1990 in the early stages of labour.

9. Shortly after her admission she was connected to a cardiotocograph monitor. This is a machine which monitors the foetal heart rate. Such machines produce paper traces which provide a permanent visual record of the heart beat.

10. The recording of the baby's heart beat continued up until just before delivery. I understand from instructions given to me by Mrs Brown and from my reading of those records which have been disclosed to me that there was concern about the baby's heart beat and that because of this a decison was made to deliver him urgently. The trace record of the baby's heart beat is, therefore, likely to be central to determining whether or not the obstetric care provided to Mrs Brown was of an appropriate standard and if not, whether the failures in care caused my client's brain damage.

11. In order to be able to advise my client's next friend as to whether or not John Brown suffered brain damage as a consequence of negligent obsteric care it is essential for the medical experts instructed on his behalf to see the CTG trace if it still exists.

12. For the reasons set out above my client is, potentially, a Plaintiff in a claim for compensation for personal injury and loss resulting from negligent medical care against the Respondents.

13. For the reasons set out above the Respondents are likely to be the Defendants to the said claim for compensation for injuries and loss resulting from negligent medical care brought by my client, John Brown.

14. As the Health Authority responsible for Mrs Brown's obstetric care, the Respondents are likely to be in the control of all her obstetric records, including the CTG trace.

15. I humbly request that this court now orders that the Respondents disclose to my firm within fourteen days of the date of the hearing of this application a continuos copy of the said CTG trace, or, if the

said trace cannot be found that they serve an affidavit from the chief
medical records oficer detailing what searches have been made for
the trace and what records there are indicating when it was last seen.

Affirmed at
this   day of   1994

Before me:

....

A Solicitor

D. Digest of case notes: Selina Brown – DOB 25 March 1957

Primigravida aged 33 years, married to a Company Director.
No significant past medical history
LMP – not since stopping oral contraception in September 1989
Ultrasound – 112 May 1990. Single Fetus FHO FL 25 mm = 17 weeks
                        BPD 40 mm, Head circ 148 mm = 17½ weeks
   Posterior Placenta. *EDD – 14 October 1990*

All screening tests satisfactory.   Blood Gp A Pos.   Shared
antenatal care – uneventful.

Labour Notes
Admission – From home   Date – 17.10.90   Time – 03.45
Temps 36.4   Pulse 84   BP 110/70   Urine – Protein trace
Presentation/position – cephalic/LOA   Engaged/Not Engaged (3/5)
FH 140
Contractions 1:3–4   Membranes – Ruptured (ARM) at 0400

Date/ Time	Observations and Examinations	Signature
	Admitted from home i/c history of regular contractions since 01.00 hrs	
04.00	V/E to Assess/ External genitalia + vagina normal Cervix thin, os 4 cms dilated. ARM performed i/c Selina's consent. Thick meconium liquor. FHHR	M White
04.10	FH ▼ 60. Turned onto left side FSE applied. Cx 5 cms dilated	

Date/ Time	Observations and Examinations	Signature
04.20	FH continues to decelerate. Mr Rasputin informed of admission will come and visit. Arrived 04.40.	M White
	Zantac 150 mg given	M White
05.10	Cx 9cm – Head mid to low cavity. Deep early decelerations occurring 1 in 3. Good frequency and baseline variations in between. Some urge to push	MMR
05.40	Fully dilated. ROA – head as before. Start gentle pushing	MMR
05.45	Pushing commenced left lateral. Early decelerations	
06.00	Pushing well, changed to kneel position push not so effective	
06.10	Using birthing cushion	
06.30	S/B Mr Rasputin. pp advancing but decelerations becoming deeper. For transfer to Room 11 for ventouse	
06.47	Ventouse delivery of live male	
06.52	3rd stage	M White

Summary of Labour

	Date	Time	Duration of Labour	Hrs	Mins
Membranes ruptured	17.10.90	04.00	1st stage	4	40
Onset of labour	17.10.90	01.00	2nd Stage	1	07
Fully dilated	17.10.90	05.40	3rd stage		05
Delivery of child	17.10.90	06.47	Total	5	52
Delivery of placenta	17.10.90	06.52	Presentation at delivery Ceph OA		
Placenta + Membranes Complete 700 grams			Blood loss 300 ml		

[cont. p272]

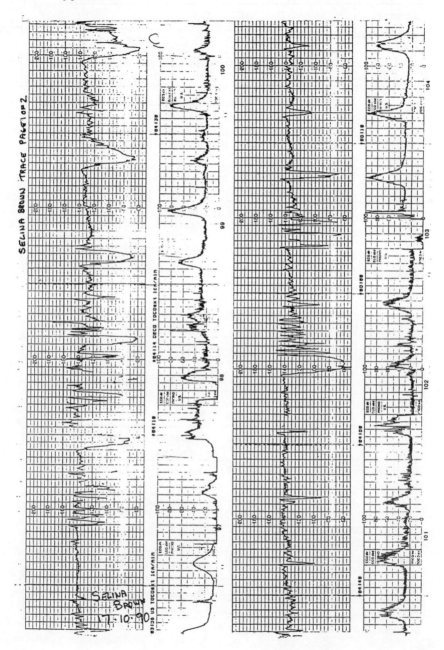

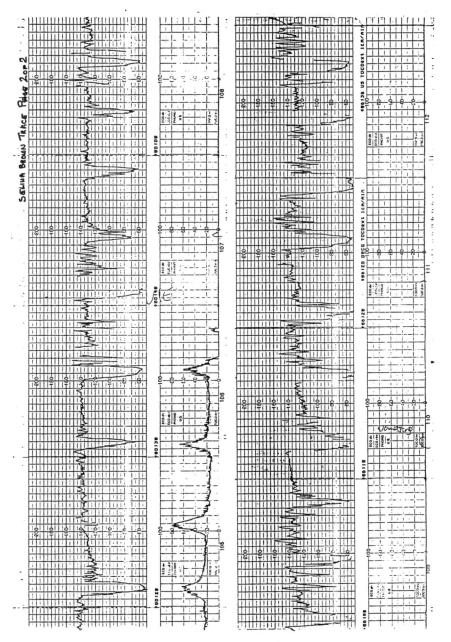

Lacerations.....Perineum.....Episiotomy√
Method of repair: Continuous Vicryl PV√ PR√ Signed: Monk Rasputin
Anaesthetic .... Anaesthetic ....

Summary of delivery *Ventouse Extraction* Delivered by *Rasputin*
Profound early deceleration in first and second stage. Fully dilated Head
LOT ▸ LOA 6 cm silastic Ventouse cap applied. Mediolateral episiot-
omy.
Delivery of head in 4 minutes with 2 contractions.
Live infant – Cord x5 round neck
Placenta delivered by CCT. T-36.7 BP 130/85 P90
Baby – John Gestation T+3   Sex male Wt 3240g Abnormalities...
APGAR SCORE 3/1/6/5/8/10   see paed notes

E. Letter of instruction to plaintiff's obstetric expert

Mr R P Hawk-Monitor
The Wellingfield Healthcare Trust
Rotunda Hospital
Wellingfield
Wellingshire

Dear Mr Hawk-Monitor

John Brown

I write further to our recent telephone conversation when you confirmed
that you would be happy to advise on the quality of obstetric care
provided to my client's mother both antenatally and at the time of my
client's delivery.

Background
As I have explained on the telephone, John Brown was born at St
Adomnan's Hospital in Barchester on 17 October 1990. Since his birth
he has been diagnosed as suffering from cerebral palsy. I am instructed
to investigate whether his cerebral palsy could have been caused by
negligent management of his mother's antenatal care, labour or delivery.

Mrs Brown's antenatal care was shared between her GP and the
hospital. Initially, because the family were based in Southampton, Mrs
Brown was referred to St Axilla's Hospital. There was only one antenatal appointment there.

Documents
To enable you to advise I enclose the following documents:

1. File containing Mrs Brown's antenatal and GP records including records from St Axilla's Hospital, Southampton and her maternity co-op card and continuous copy CTG trace.
2. File containing the neonatal records for John (I am not enclosing subsequent paediatric records at this stage as you will not need to see these in order to be able to advise).
3. File of John's GP records.
4. Statement of Mrs Brown.

When referring to any documents in your report I would be grateful if you could refer to the page numbers which you will see in the bottom right hand corner of all of the copy records.

Your report
As I have explained, I am instructed to investigate whether John's cerebral palsy could have been caused by negligent obstetric care. In order to prove this we will have to satisfy the court on two separate counts. Firstly we will have to prove that the obstetric care was negligent. Secondly, we will have to prove that the identified negligence caused the cerebral palsy. I will be instructing a consultant paediatric neurologist to advise on the causation of the brain damage. In order to do so I obviously need your advice on the question of quality of care.

Your report should summarise the records which relate to the obstetric care and where appropriate comment on the quality of care indicated by these entries. Where you consider care to have been inappropriate, please give an indication of what care should have been provided and *when* it should have been provided.

When referring to the quality of the care, please, where appropriate, refer to those medical texts which you will seek to rely on in support of your opinion. Please attach copies of these texts to your report.

If there is a conflict of evidence between what is recorded in Mrs Brown's statement and what is recorded in the records, please give alternative opinions based on the two separate records of events.

There are some specific points which I am concerned your report should deal with. These are as follows:

1. Mrs Brown's statement and the medical records indicate that there was meconium-stained liquor shortly after Mrs Brown's admission to hospital on 17 October. Was the response to this appropriate? If not, why not and how should the response have differed?
2. The records (and by implication Mrs Brown's statement) refer to the baby's heart beat dropping within the first half hour of the admission to hospital. Was the response to this appropriate? If not, why not and how should it have differed?
3. It appears from Mrs Brown's statement and the records that there was a period of 45 minutes between Mrs Brown being encouraged

to push and the decision to assist delivery. Do you have any comments to make about the length of this period or the care provided during it?

4. Do you consider that John Brown should have been delivered earlier than he in fact was? If so, do you consider it was negligent to fail to deliver him earlier? If so, what time do you consider was the latest acceptable time for his delivery?

5. You have indicated that you expect to be able to provide me with your report within 12 weeks of receipt of these records and instructions. I look forward to receiving it from you.

The law
In assessing whether care provided by doctors has been negligent, the court applies what has become known as the *Bolam* test. Essentially, the test is whether a reasonably competent practitioner in the relevant field at the relevant time faced with the same circumstances would have acted in the same way. If it is possible to show that a reasonable and competent body of medical opinion (albeit a small minority) would have acted in the same way, then the care is not considered negligent

When considering your opinion and preparing your report I would be grateful if you would bear the above in mind and, where appropriate, refer to the test in your report.

Yours sincerely

A Solicitor

F. Letter of instruction to plaintiff's neurological expert

Dr B Wintergarden
Consultant Paediatric Neurologist
Royal Dover Children's NHS Trust
Bluebirds Childrens Hospital
Eatwell Road
Dover

Dear Dr Wintergarden

John Brown
I am grateful to you for agreeing to advise on causation in this case.

Background
As I explained on the telephone my client was born at St Adomnan's Hospital in October 1990. Since then he has been diagnosed as suffering

from cerebral palsy. I am instructed to investigate whether his cerebral palsy has been caused by negligent management of his mother's obstetric care.

I have now received a report from the Consultant Obstetrician whom I have instructed to advise this case, Mr Hawk-Monitor. You will see from his report that he has advised that he considers that John should have been delivered by no later than 5.40. Delivery in fact took place over an hour later at 6.47.

Documents to enable you to advise
I enclose the following documents:

1. File containing Mrs Brown's antenatal and GP records including maternity co-op card and continuous CTG trace.
2. File containing neonatal records for John Brown.
3. File containing paediatric and GP records for John Brown.
4. Statement of Mrs Brown.
5. Report of Mr Hawk-Monitor, consultant obstetrician.

When referring to any documents in your report I would be grateful if you could refer to the page numbers which you will see in the bottom right hand corner of all of the copy records.

Your report
I would be grateful if you would examine my client and having done so and having looked at the medical records please then provide me with a report on the cause of his brain damage. Specifically, I would like your report to deal with the following points:

1. Is it possible to confirm that prior to 5.40 on 17 October 1990 the baby was in a healthy undamaged condition? If so, what is the evidence in the records for this?
2. Is it possible to prove that my client's brain damage occurred during the period 5.40 to 6.47 am on 17 October? If so, what is the evidence of this in the records?
3. Is there any evidence in the records which points to the brain damage having occurred earlier than 5.40? If so, what is this evidence?
4. Is there any evidence to suggest that brain damage occurred after birth? If so, what is this evidence?

The law
In order to pursue successfully a claim on my client's behalf we will have to prove both that the obstetric care provided to him was negligent and that the identified negligence caused his injury. Whilst those advising us on the quality of care provided have to refer to knowledge and information available to obstetricians in October 1990, you, as our

expert on causation, are not tied to information and the state of knowledge available at that time. Thus, if there is any research into the causes of cerebral palsy which has been published since my client's birth you should refer to this where appropriate.

Timetable

I understand that you should be able to see my client some time within the next two months and that you anticipate being able to provide me with your report soon thereafter. As soon as an appointment has been arranged for my client, I would be grateful if you could let me know and if you could then confirm the date on which you anticipate I will receive your report.

I look forward to hearing from you.

Yours sincerely

A Solicitor

G. Report of plaintiff's obstetric expert

Report on the case of Mrs Selina Brown concerning the birth of her son John Brown prepared by R Hawk-Monitor, MA MD FRCOG on the instructions of Ms Ophelia Dane, Solicitor acting on behalf of Selina Brown and John Brown.

1. I, Richard Phipps Hawk-Monitor, qualified as a medical practitioner in 1964. I hold the degree of Doctor of Medicine from the University of London, and have been elected to the Fellowship of the Royal College of Obstetricians and Gynaecologists. I have held consultant posts in Obstetrics and Gynaecology since 1976; until 1983 with Cambridge University and the Cambridge Health District and up to 1992 with the Wellingfield Health District at the Rotunda Hospital. On 1 April 1992 my contract was transferred to the newly formed Wellingfield Healthcare Trust.

   Most of my work as a full time NHS Consultant is in obstetrics, including a special interest in antenatal care and the management of labour.

2. I have received from Ms Ophelia Dane, of Blank, Green Form and Co, Solicitors, a bundle of photocopied notes, papers, correspondence and statements regarding this case. These comprise:

   (a) Statement prepared by Mrs Selina Brown, signed and dated 10 September 1993.

   (b) Statements from Mr Rasputin, the consultant obstetrician and from Sister White, the midwife concerned with the labour.

   (c) Clinical records from St Adomnan's Hospital, Barchester

relating to Mrs Brown's pregnancy and the birth of her son John.

My report is based on the study of these papers. Some of the photocopying of documents is poor and in some documents the handwriting is illegible; when this is the case I will refer to it in my report. I am grateful for the digest of the obstetric notes prepared by the solicitors.

3. Selina Brown was born on 25 March 1957 and was therefore aged 33 years at the time of the birth of her son John. This was her first pregnancy. There was nothing of note in her past medical history. She is a non-smoker and takes only an occasional glass of alcoholic drink. Mrs Brown used to work as a secretary until her marriage to a company director.

4. Mrs Brown stopped taking the oral contraceptive pill in September 1989. She then did not have a menstrual period but only became pregnant in early 1990. An ultrasound scan performed in Southampton, where the family were then based, showed a 4 week pregnancy on 14 February 1990. A second ultrasound scan was carried out on 11 May 1990 when the size of the foetus suggested a gestational age of 17½ weeks (see standard tables of the *British Medical Ultrasound Society*, see Annexe).

   The estimated date of confinement (EDC) as calculated from the first ultrasound scan would have been 26 October 1990. According to the second ultrasound scan the pregnancy was somewhat more advanced, with an EDC of 16 October 1990. The hospital calculated the EDC as 14 October 1990 which is acceptable as based on the second ultrasound scan.

   The discrepancy between the first and second ultrasound scans is 10–12 days and might have been of significance. However, as the actual date of confinement was 17 October 1990, this point would not have been significant in the clinical management.

5. Antenatal care was shared between various care givers. Up to 25 weeks gestation the family were based in Southampton and care was given there. This is recorded on the maternity co-operation card. One visit was made to St Jude's Hospital in Southampton at 17 weeks gestation and then regular care was conducted at St Adomnan's from 29 weeks onwards. This was shared between Mr Rasputin, the consultant gynaecologist, Dr Pink, the general practitioner (GP) and Miss Black, the community midwife.

   Care followed a standard pattern with a total of 20 visits being recorded; there were a large number of visits in the early stage of pregnancy. At all times the foetus appeared to be growing at a standard rate. Mrs Brown's blood pressure was always within normal limits and she never had protein in her urine. During the last two months of pregnancy the baby presented head first, although the foetal head never properly engaged in the maternal pelvis before labour.

6. Mrs Brown was admitted to hospital from home in labour at 0345 on 19 October 1990. At that point it was noted that Mrs Brown's uterus was contracting every 3–4 minutes. The baby was presenting head first (cephalic) and the head was 3/5 palpable in the maternal abdomen.

At 0400 Sister White, the labour ward midwife, performed a vaginal examination. She found the uterine cervix to be 4 centimetres dilated and thin. The foetal membranes were intact and were ruptured artificially. Thick meconium-stained liquor drained.

A cardiotocograph trace was started at 0356 soon after Mrs Brown's admission in labour.

6. As Annexes to this report commentaries are provided on:
   (a) The stages of labour
   (b) Descent of the foetal head
   (c) Effacement and dilatation
   (d) Membrane rupture and meconium-stained liquor
   (e) The interpretation of the cardiotocograph (CTG, foetal heart rate) trace.

[NOTE: The annexes are not reproduced here]

7. At 0410 the note reads

   FH 60
   Turned on left side
   FSE applied
   Cervix 5 cms dilated

   0420 Continues to decelerate

   Mr Rasputin informed of admission
   Will come and visit (arrived 0440)
   Zantac 150 mg given.

Soon after membrane rupture Sister White observed a deceleration in the f0etal heart rate. She responded by turning Mrs Brown on to her left side. She re-examined her and applied a foetal scalp electrode (FSE) to get a more accurate signal. Mrs Brown's cervix was then 5 cms dilated.

At 0420 Sister White noted that the pattern of foetal heart decelerations continued and called for medical help. A consultant obstetrician, Mr Rasputin, arrived 20 minutes later.

7.1 *CTG trace 0356 to 0440, 17 October 1990*

Uterine contractions are recorded as occurring 1 every 3–4 minutes. The foetal heart baseline starts at around 140bpm (beats per minute) and there is reasonable baseline variability. At 0409, probably after a vaginal examination, there is a deep foetal heart deceleration down to 70bpm and lasting just over a minute. Further decelerations occur over the next 5 minutes. These are badly traced but there is a definite deep deceleration down to 60pbm lasting about 40 seconds at 0416. Further deep decelerations occur at 0420, at 0427 and 0435.

The relationship of these decelerations to the uterine contractions is not regular and they are therefore best described as variable decelerations.

8. According to the record Mr Rasputin arrived on the ward at 0440 but he has not made a note until 0510. At this time he re-examined Mrs Brown and wrote

> Cervix 9 cms. Head mid to low cavity.
> Deep early decelerations occurring 1 in 3
> Good frequency and baseline variation in between
> Some urge to push

At 0540 Mr Rasputin made a further note

> Fully dilated ROA (right occipito-anterior)
> – head as before
> Start gentle pushing

8.1 CTG trace 0440 to 0540, 17 October 1990

During this period uterine contractions are occurring approximately 1 every 5 minutes. The foetal heart continues at a baseline rate of around 140bpm. Regular deep and prolonged decelerations occur with some shallower and shorter ones in between. Particularly marked decelerations can be observed at 0455, 0508, 0520, 0530, 0536 and 0540. Again because of the variable nature of these decelerations and their variable relationship with contractions I would class them as variable decelerations.

In between decelerations the foetal heart rate is maintained at around 140bpm and baseline variability is good.

9. The notes continue in Sister White's hand.
0545 Pushing commenced left lateral
    Early decelerations
0600 Pushing well, changed to kneeling position push not so
    effective
0610 Using birthing cushion
0630 Seen by Mr Rasputin. Presenting part advancing but
    decelerations becoming deeper. For transfer to abnormal
    delivery room for ventouse.

Mr Rasputin therefore decided that despite the CTG abnormalities an attempt would be made to achieve a spontaneous vaginal delivery for Mrs Brown. This may have been in deference to her hopes and plans for a non-interventionist birth. It is not clear from the notes whether the consultant remained on the labour ward between 0540 and 0640 or whether he went away and came back.

9.1 CTG *trace 0540 to 0640, 17 October 1990*

Uterine contractions are not recorded during this time. This is probably because the frequent changes in position adopted by Mrs Brown in an attempt to find the best and most effective position for delivery made consistent monitoring impossible.

The foetal heart rate starts at around 135bpm. Regular deep and long decelerations occur; it is impossible to relate these to uterine contractions as these were not recorded. At 0511 there is a particularly deep deceleration down to 55bpm with slow recovery; at 0515 and 0521 decelerations seem to reach 50bpm. Following this long and very deep decelerations occur until the trace finishes at 0540. In between contractions the foetal heart rate is good and there is usually normal baseline variability. However on occasions this may be exaggerated.

John Brown was born by ventouse extraction at 0647 on 17 October 1990. A 6 cm Silastic cup was attached by suction to his head and delivery was achieved over a 4 minute period with two contractions. The umbilical cord was noted to be 5 times round his neck.

John Brown weighed 3.24 kg and was in poor condition at birth. On the Apgar score which measures the condition of the newborn on a scale of 0-10 the readings were 3 at 1 minutes, 6 at 5 minutes and 8 at 10 minutes. A paediatrician was present for resuscitation. Sadly John Brown has gone on to develop cerebral palsy.

11. My instructing solicitor has requested that I advise her on the management of Mrs Brown's pregnancy, labour and delivery and as to whether or not this management was satisfactory and carried out to a sufficiently high standard. In order to do this I will discuss separately Mrs Brown's pregnancy and early labour
    (a) Up to the time of her admission to hospital at 0345 on 17 October 1990.
    (b) From 0345 to 0540 on 17 October 1990.
    (c) From 0540 to delivery at 0647 on 17 October 1990.

12. *Mrs Brown's pregnancy and early labour up to the time of her admission to hospital at 0345 on 17 October 1990.*
    No significant criticism can be made of the management of Mrs Brown's pregnancy. The disagreement between the two ultrasound scans concerning the gestational age of the baby and the EDC should have been further investigated but the subsequent events do not indicate that this would have led to alternative management being indicated or adopted. It seems that Mrs Brown was given the usual advice on admission to hospital at the start of labour and admitted herself fairly promptly when this occurred.

13. *0345 to 0540, 17 October 1990*

    This period of time covers Mrs Brown's first stage of labour, that is up to full dilatation of the uterine cervix. The admission procedures were carried out promptly and by 0420 Sister White had decided that signs of foetal distress were present. These were

    (a) Thick meconium-stained liquor.

    (b) Deep variable foetal heart decelerations.

    The combination of these two signs suggest the possibility of foetal hypoxia (oxygen lack) being present; of themselves variable foetal heart decelerations often correlate with obstruction of the placental circulation and oxygenation by the tightening of the umbilical cord round the foetal neck.

    Sister White correctly requested medical help and Mr Rasputin was present on the labour ward some 20 minutes later. This response time is somewhat greater than is desirable.

    After assessing the situation Mr Rasputin should have realised that there was a significant chance that foetal hypoxia was present. He then would have had one of two options open to him. These would be:

    (a) Carrying out a foetal scalp sample. Foetal scalp samples may be used to test the acidity of foetal blood and hence indirectly the degree of oxygenation of the baby.

       It may be that foetal scalp sampling was not available in that unit (it is available in under 50% of units in the United Kingdom).

    (b) Making immediate plans for delivery by caesarian section. If such plans were implemented with due haste, caesarian section should have been performed to result in the delivery of the baby at the most 30 minutes later, that is, by 0540.

    It may well have been that once Mrs Brown had been transferred to the operation theatre the uterine cervix would have been found to be fully dilated. Under those circumstances attempted assisted vaginal delivery might have been acceptable as an alternative to caesarean section.

14. *0450 to 0647, 17 October 1990*

    Rather than implement the above management, Mr Rasputin adopted a 'wait and see' policy. He noted that full dilatation of the uterine cervix occurred at or just before 0540 on 17 October 1990. At this point vaginal delivery would have been possible, the foetal head would have passed through the fully dilated cervix and was already in mid to low cavity. As assisted vaginal delivery would have been comparatively easy to achieve with the ventouse or the obstetric forceps, there was no longer the indication to perform foetal scalp sampling; delivery should have been accomplished using the ventouse or obstetric forceps as soon as possible. Using instrument-assisted vaginal delivery at this point could have been accomplished by 0550 at the latest.

The indication to perform an urgent assisted vaginal delivery was present throughout the remainder of the labour.

15. *Was alternative management indicated in this case and if so, would such alternative management have led to John Brown being born in better condition and not developing cerebral palsy?*

No alternative management was indicated up to the time of admission in labour and the discovery of signs of foetal distress by Sister White at 0410 on 17 October 1990.

As has been outlined in section 13, foetal scalp sampling or immediate caesarean section was indicated on account of the foetal distress which should have been diagnosed presumptively from the CTG trace. If foetal scalp sampling had been undertaken, it is likely that a pH value of below 7.20 would have been recorded, and this would have indicated the need for immediate delivery.

Whichever course of action was followed, delivery by caesarean section should have been accomplished by 0540 at the latest. If Mrs Brown had been found to be fully dilated when she was being prepared for caesarean section then assisted vaginal delivery would have resulted in the birth of the child by about the same time.

Even with the 'wait and see' policy adopted by the consultant in this case urgent delivery was required once full dilatation of the uterine cervix had been reached at 0540. This could have been by the ventouse or obstetric forceps and would have resulted in John Brown being born in better condition.

The relationship between John Brown's condition at birth and his subsequent development of cerebral palsy must be determined from the reports of experts in neonatal paediatrics and paediatric neurology. Nevertheless it seems likely that if John Brown had been born in better condition the risk of his developing cerebral palsy would have been reduced.

16. In summary, therefore, it is my opinion that in the case of Mrs Selina Brown and her son John Brown:

16.1 Mrs Selina Brown's pregnancy was uneventful and managed adequately. No criticism of her management can be made up to the time of her admission to hospital at 0345 on 17 October 1990.

16.2 Soon after admission to hospital signs of foetal distress (meconium liquor and abnormal CTG tracing) were noted and Mrs Brown's cervix was only 5 cms dilated. At that point a doctor should have been asked to attend who should have performed a foetal scalp sample to confirm the presence of foetal distress. It is likely that this diagnosis would have been confirmed at this time. If foetal distress was confirmed by scalp sampling or, if foetal scalp sampling was not to be undertaken, arrangements should have resulted in the birth of the baby by 0540 at the latest.

16.3 Instead of this a 'wait and see' policy was followed. However at full dilatation of the uterine cervix at 0540 am on 17 October 1990 signs of foetal distress were still present. Immediately assisted vaginal delivery was indicated at this point using the ventouse or the obstetric forceps.

16.4 If the management recommended above had been followed John Brown would have been born earlier and in better condition and it appears to me likely that he would have been at a lesser risk of developing cerebral palsy.

RICHARD HAWK-MONITOR

H. Report of plaintiff's neurological expert

Medical report on causation of disabilities on behalf of the plaintiff John Brown (DOB 17.10.90) prepared by Dr B Wintergarden, MB FRCP DCH, Consultant Paediatric Neurologist, Royal Dover Children's NHS Trust, Bluebirds Children's Hospital, Eatwell Road, Dover, 3 September 1993.

From my perspective as a paediatric neurologist I am asked on behalf of the plaintiff to describe the disabilities of John Brown and give my views in respect of their causation.

Prior to the preparation of this report I examined John in August 1993 and I have reviewed the relevant case notes. I have also read the report on the case prepared by Mr Richard Hawk-Monitor FRCS, consultant obstetrician advising the plaintiff. I have also read witness statements in the case made by Mrs Brown, Mrs White, the midwife concerned with labour, and Mr M M Rasputin, the obstetrician in charge of labour.

Relevant clinical information
He is a first child and there is no family history of neurological disorder or handicapping conditions.

Following a normal pregnancy mother went into labour at term plus three days. She was admitted in labour at 03.45 on October 17, 1990. Artificial rupture of membranes performed at 04.00 produced thick meconium in the liquor.

At 04.10 the cervix was 5 cm dilated and the CTG showed a deceleration to 60. Further decelerations are identified in the report of Mr Hawk-Monitor, which he believes to indicate foetal distress.

Full cervical dilatation was achieved at 05.40 but following the commencement of the active second stage of labour at 05.45 further periodic decelerations were noted on the CTG and these increased in severity compatible with a picture of increasing fetal distress.

Ultimately John was delivered by ventouse at 06.47.

He was asphyxiated at birth and Apgar scores are given as 3 at one minute, 6 at five minutes and 8 at ten minutes. Following suction with some meconium being aspirated from below the vocal cords he was intubated at three minutes.

It was possible to extubate him at nine minutes, at which time he was transferred to the special care baby unit.

Birth weight was 3240 g and head circumference on the 10th centile at 33 cm. Cord blood pH was 7.08 with base excess of −12.

In the special care baby unit he was noted to have some dysmorphic features including a small anterior fontanelle, wide spaced eyes and an accessory nipple.

In the early hours he had grunting and tachypnoea and chest X-ray showed bilateral shadowing. PO2 was satisfactory and it was decided not to re-ventilate him.

Within two hours of birth neurological abnormalities were noted initially in the form of stiffness and irritability. Six brief generalised convulsions occurred in the course of the first thirty-six hours in spite of treatment with Phenobarbitone and the empirical use of steroids.

Ultrasound scan performed at age eight hours showed small ventricles consistent with some degree of cerebral oedema.

After thirty-six hours there were no further fits but the child remained irritable and floppy, possibly as a consequence of Phenobarbitone medication. He was tube-fed for four days but then bottle feeding was slowly established.

At the time that he was allowed home at thirteen days he had regained his birth weight, head circumference was 33.5 cm but he was still noted to be irritable and to have some general decrease in muscle tone.

Initially he was thought to be making satisfactory progress and was thought to have smiled at six weeks. However as time has gone on it has become apparent that at the age of almost three years there are significant developmental problems.

Thus he is a small and slight child with length and weight on the 10th centile and head circumference on the 3rd centile. He has mild dysmorphic characteristics which are not diagnostic of any particular syndrome (neurogenetics database − See reference x). He has mild generalised four limb spasticity which is symmetrical and is accompanied by significant motor developmental delay. Thus he is only just able to stand with support. Psychosocial development is less delayed but is at a two year level. There are no contractures or fixed deformities.

His head is good but he had one convulsion in association with a febrile illness at age eight months.

Chromosome analysis is normal as also is aminoacid chromatogram. No brain imaging has hitherto been performed.

Opinion on prognosis
This child will almost certainly have long-term dependence needs. He is unlikely to be able to look after himself even as an adult. He will have a fair insight into his disabilities. It is too early to estimate his life expectation. Life expectancy in such patients has historically been reduced to a varying degree, but with improvements in care, that historical picture may not be reliable as a guide to the future.

Opinion on causation
I must recognise from the beginning that there is at least one feature of this case which in general might point to other causes for the plaintiff's disability than perinatal asphyxia. I refer to his non-specific dysmorphic features. However I emphasise that the features are not diagnostic of any known medical syndrome and there is no compelling link between such features and internal abnormality in any given individual.

I believe there are more convincing reasons for linking the disability to perinatal events. The irritability shown by the plaintiff shortly after birth is consistent with hypoxic ischaemic encephalopathy (HIE), although I must concede here that the Apgar scores are better than one normally expects to find with the HIE baby. The fact that meconium was aspirated from below the vocal cords is a definite indicator of distress in labour, indicating that the foetus has been attempting to breathe *in utero*. The disproportionately small head present now contrasts with the normal sized head in the 17 week scan and the proportionately sized head at birth, indicating a failure of the head to grow from around the time of birth. It is recognised that the infant skull grows in response to a 'demand' for room from the growing brain, and that a failure of the brain to grow normally will lead to microcephaly.

I have read the account in the history suggesting that the plaintiff smiled at 6 weeks of age. If this were so, it would be a very strong pointer against the brain damage being caused by perinatal asphyxia. However, I fear that it is very frequently the case that parents interpret a merely reflex rictus as a smile, particularly where there has been any reason for anxiety about the condition of a baby, and a natural desire to discern positive signs as to development.

The general spread and nature of the plaintiff's disabilities is consistent with a perinatal asphyxial causation. The precise pattern of brain damage might be more clearly mapped if the plaintiff were to undergo magnetic resonance imaging, and it may be that a report of a paediatric neuro-radiologist would assist the thinking in the case.

On balance, I am able to say that I believe this boy's damage resulted from HIE, which in turn arose from his perinatal asphyxia.

I now turn to the further key question of whether he would have been spared his damage given the care which Mr Hawk-Monitor states was the acceptable minimum on the facts of the case. As I read his report, John should have been delivered by 05.40/05.50 at the latest. He was actually delivered at 06.47, and thus if his obstetric care had been handled as Mr Hawk-Monitor suggests, he would have been spared the last hour of perinatal asphyxia.

To my inexpert eye, the CTG trace is at its worst during this period, and I believe that is what Mr Hawk-Monitor is indicating in his report. If that is correct, it follows that John would have been spared the worst hour of his intra-uterine asphyxia, and on that basis one would expect on a balance of probabilities that he would have avoided the significant brain damage from which he suffers. I believe that he would probably have been born neurologically intact and normal if delivered at 05.40 to 05.50 instead of an hour later.

DR B WINTERGARDEN
Consultant Paediatric Neurologist

I. Endorsement on High Court writ

The Plaintiff's claim is for damages for injury and loss sustained as a result of the negligence of the Defendants, their servants or agents, in their treatment of him at St Adomnan's Hospital, London Road, Barchester, at or about the time of his birth on 17th October 1990 and, further, for interest upon such damages at such rate and for such period as the Court thinks fit pursuant to section 35A of the Supreme Court Act 1981.

This Writ includes a claim for personal injury, but may be commenced in the High Court because the value of the action for the purposes of article 5 of the High Court and County Courts Jurisdiction Order 1991 exceeds £50,000.

J. Plaintiff's statement of claim

IN THE HIGH COURT OF JUSTICE   1993 B No.
QUEEN'S BENCH DIVISION
BETWEEN :

JOHN BROWN
(a minor) suing by his mother and
Next Friend, MRS SELINA BROWN   Plaintiff

– and –

BARCHESTER HEALTH AUTHORITY   Defendant

– and –

STATEMENT OF CLAIM

---

1. At all material times set out below, the Plaintiff and his mother were patients of St Adomnan's Hospital, Barchester, Barsetshire and the Plaintiff was owed a duty of care by all medical, surgical and nursing staff in the said hospital, namely to treat him with reasonable professional care and skill. The said duty was owed to the Plaintiff both before and after his birth. The said staff had the care of the Plaintiff pursuant to their contracts of engagement or employment with the Defendants, and accordingly the Defendants are liable to the Plaintiff in respect of any breach of duty on their part.
2. The Plaintiff's mother Mrs Selina Brown was born on 23.iii.57 and was aged 32 years when she became pregnant with the Plaintiff. This was the Plaintiff's mother's first pregnancy. Her last menstrual period (LMP) was in September 1989, but the expected date of delivery (EDD) was recorded in the notes disclosed by the Defendants as being 14.x.90
3. Pregnancy care followed an accepted pattern, and was uneventful. Care was shared between the hospital staff, the General Practitioner and the Community Midwife, with the hospital staff being responsible for more of the visits towards the end of the pregnancy. The consultant responsible for her care in the said hospital was Mr M M Rasputin FRCS.
4. The Plaintiff's mother was admitted in labour to the said hospital at 3.45 am on 17.x.90. She was examined and assessed by Sister White, a midwife, following admission. A cardiotocograph (CTG)

trace was made of the contractions and of the foetal heart, a copy of which has been disclosed. This trace was commenced at about 3.55 am and after 04.09 demonstrates decelerations in the foetal heart, with deep decelerations at 04.09, 04.16, 04.20, 04.27 and 04.35. They are best described as variable decelerations.

5. A vaginal examination was performed at about 04.00 am and part of the note reads:
   'V/E [vaginal examination] to assess . . . cervix thin, os dilated ARM [artificial rupture of the membranes or foetal sac] performed . . . thick meconium stained liquor, foetal heart beat: regular'

6. The combination of thick meconium stained liquor and marked deep and wide foetal heart decelerations indicates that the foetus was undergoing significant stress. These signs combine to indicate that (a) there were significant adverse features to the labour and (b) the labour required urgent review by an experienced obstetrician as soon as it became clear that the pattern of foetal decelerations were persisting.

7. The organisation of obstetric services in the said hospital is such that midwifery staff should have direct access to consultant level obstetric staff. In this case, attention was required from the duty consultant, who was Mr Rasputin, and he required to be summoned from his home. In those circumstances, Sister White should have contacted Mr Rasputin and asked him to attend within a few minutes after 04.00 am.

8. The labour note suggests that Sister White informed Mr Rasputin of the admission at 04.20 am, and that he agreed to come into the hospital to visit the Plaintiff's mother. It appears that no member of the medical staff within the said hospital was informed or attended the Plaintiff's mother. It was thus at about 04.40 am when the progress of the labour and the condition of the foetus was first assessed by any doctor.

9. As set out above, the CTG between 04.10 am and 04.40 am (when Mr Rasputin arrived in the hospital and saw the Plaintiff's mother) shows a number of variable but deep and wide decelerations of the foetal heart, which should have given rise to real concern for the condition of the foetus, and that there was a significant chance of foetal hypoxia. A broadly similar but very gradually deteriorating pattern is demonstrated on the CTG until at about 05.40 am. During this period the foetal heart was able to recover sufficiently between decelerations to indicate that, while the foetus was stressed, it was probably not compromised.

10. Provided that foetal blood sampling was available in the said hospital, the signs set out above, as they appeared from approximately 04.00 am and thereafter, should have led the said sister and/or Mr Rasputin to institute one or more foetal blood

samples, so as to establish whether and to what degree the foetus was suffering from acidosis [an elevated acidity of the blood] which is a consequence of hypoxia. No such sample was taken throughout the labour.

11. When a sample of blood was taken from the umbilical cord immediately after the birth, the result confirmed that the baby was significantly acidotic. Had such a sample or samples been taken by or before 05.40 am, the foetus would probably have been revealed to be acidotic, to a gradually increasing degree over that period, and thus in need of the speediest possible delivery.

12. The variable pattern of decelerations recorded on the CTG trace could be interpreted as a consequence of the effect on the foetal heart produced by compression of the umbilical cord. Mr Rasputin made that interpretation, concluded that the decelerations were innocuous, and made no intervention in the labour until about 6.30 am, as set out below.

13. The combination of signs set out above should have led Mr Rasputin to perform a foetal blood sample [FBS] by 05.10 at the very latest, provided foetal blood sampling was available. If the sample was taken before 05.10 and was borderline [pH of 7.20/7.25] or worse, or by 05.10 in any event given the pattern of decelerations, then the decision should have been taken immediately to move to deliver by Caesarean section.

14. Once the cervix reached full dilatation, [at 05.40 am] then Mr Rasputin should immediately have commenced to assist delivery with a Ventouse [a device by which a cup is firmly applied to the foetal head by suction, enabling direct traction to assist delivery]. If the Plaintiff had not been delivered easily vaginally within a few minutes of commencing any attempt at Ventouse extraction, Mr Rasputin should have instituted an immediate Caesarean section delivery of the Plaintiff, and should have been in a state of preparedness to achieve that within a few minutes. In any event, the foetus should have been delivered by about 05.40 to 05.50am.

15. The second stage of labour commenced at 05.40 am. The Plaintiff's mother began to push by at least 05.45 am and Mr Rasputin noted early decelerations in the foetal heart. The CTG trace confirms that the foetal heart deteriorated throughout the period from 05.45 am until the Plaintiff was delivered at 06.47 am. The Plaintiff's mother was permitted to attempt to push without assistance or intervention until 06.30 am, when she was transferred to an operative delivery room. Thereafter, a Ventouse cap was applied and the Plaintiff was delivered.

16. The said medical and/or midwifery staff were negligent and in breach of their duty of care.

PARTICULARS OF NEGLIGENCE

The said staff were negligent in that:

A Sister White failed to call for a doctor to attend the Plaintiff's mother and assess the condition of the foetus at 04.00 am or within a few minutes thereafter.

B They caused or permitted no doctor to attend the Plaintiff's mother until 04.40 am.

C They failed to take a foetal blood sample by at least 04.30 am, or at all thereafter.

D Mr Rasputin failed to deliver the foetus by 05.50 at the latest.

17. The Plaintiff was asphyxiated at birth and his Apgar scores [a standardised measure of condition at and immediately after birth] were 3 at one minute, 6 at five minutes and 8 at ten minutes, indicating that the Plaintiff was in poor condition. Meconium was aspirated from below the vocal cords, indicating that there had been intra-uterine hypoxia. He was significantly acidotic at birth, with a cord blood pH of 7.08 and base excess of -12. He suffered fits within the early hours of life. He sustained a hypoxic ischaemic encephalopathy as a result of asphyxia during labour. He now suffers from cerebral palsy.

18. By reason of the said negligence, the Plaintiff has suffered injury, loss and damage. His very severe brain damage has been pleaded above. A medical report setting out the particulars of the Plaintiff's condition and prognosis is served herewith. An initial schedule of loss and damage is served herewith.

19. Further the Plaintiff claims interest on any damages he may be awarded pursuant to section 35A of the Supreme Court Act 1981 at such rate and for such period as this Honourable Court shall think fit.

AND the Plaintiff claims:

(1) DAMAGES
(2) INTEREST
(3) COSTS

KNOX COVENANTER

SERVED by Blank Green Form & Co, 10 Green Bottle Lane, Muckleborough, Humberside HA1 2HA, Solicitors for the Plaintiff.

K. Initial schedule of special damages

IN THE HIGH COURT OF JUSTICE   1993.B.NO.
QUEEN'S BENCH DIVISION
BETWEEN:

JOHN BROWN
(an infant) suing by his mother and
Next Friend, SELINA BROWN   Plaintiff

– and –

BARCHESTER HEALTH AUTHORITY   Defendant

INITIAL SCHEDULE OF SPECIAL DAMAGES

The Plaintiff was born on 17.x.90. He suffers from severe spastic quadriplegic cerebral palsy.

SPECIAL DAMAGES
Expenses incurred by family to date

Additional transport costs associated with medical appointments and other appointments attributable to the Plaintiff's disabilities. Estimated at	£350.00
Additional laundry costs estimated at an average of £240 per annum from birth to date £240 x 3 years =	£720.00
Extra heating costs estimated at an average cost of £1.00 per day since discharge from hospital 23 November 1990 to date £1.00 x 1042 =	£1042.00
Extra car seat	£85.00
Cost of care provided by family to date	to be quantified

FUTURE LOSSES AND EXPENSES

These will include:

Cost of future care and equipment

Cost of future therapies including physiotherapy and speechtherapy

Cost of purchasing suitable accomodation and adapting the same

Cost of transport

Loss of earnings

served by Messrs. Blank Green Form & Co., 10 Green Bottle Lane, Muckleborough, Humberside HA1 2HA

L. Defendants' witness statements

(A) Obstetrician

NAME: M Monk Rasputin, Consultant Obstetrician
ADDRESS: St Adomnan's Hospital, Barchester

1. I have been a consultant obstetrician for seventeen years, the last six of which have been spent at St Adomnan's Hospital. Mrs Selina Brown was under my care. The course of her pregnancy was uneventful and care was shared between the community midwife, the general practitioner and me.
2. Mrs Brown was admitted in labour in the early hours of 17 October 1990. On admission Sister White, who was an experienced midwife, performed a CTG trace. She was unhappy with the result of this because the trace showed deep decelerations of the foetal heart and because of this she telephoned me and asked me to come immediately to review the case.
3. I arrived in the hospital at or soon after 4.40. When I reviewed the CTG trace there certainly were decelerations, although immediately after my arrival these seemed to be improving. I therefore decided the labour should be allowed to progress for the time being, but I would stay on the labour ward to keep a close watch on progress. The trace did not deteriorate in its characteristics and at around 05.40 Mrs Brown's cervix was found to be fully dilated. My interpretation of the CTG trace was that it was most likely to be due to the umbilical cord being around the baby's neck but that the condition of the baby was not deteriorating.
4. Mrs Brown attempted to push the baby out for about three quarters of an hour, making progress. However at 06.30 I reviewed the case again and decided that as the foetal heart decelerations continued and progress was slow I should expedite delivery. This I did using the ventouse and Mrs Brown delivered her son at 06.47. The baby was born in poor condition: he initially seemed to respond well to resuscitation but has since gone on to develop cerebral palsy.

SIGNED...........................
DATED............................

(B) Midwife

NAME: Mrs Mary White, Midwifery State Registered Nurse
ADDRESS: St Adomnan's Hospital, Barchester

1. I am a G Grade Midwife employed at St Adomnan's Hospital. I have been employed there for the past 7 years. In all I have been practising as a midwife for the past 15 years and hold the Advanced Diploma in Midwifery as well as my basic qualifications. I am often the senior midwife in charge of the Labour Ward.

2. I was on night duty on 17 October 1990 and the labour ward was quiet. I took Mrs Brown as a case when she was admitted to hospital at 03.45. I followed my normal practice which was to perform a CTG tracing soon after admission when Mrs Brown was in established labour. Mrs Brown had hoped to have her baby naturally with minimal intervention.

3. On assessing the CTG trace I found that marked foetal heart decelerations were occurring. I therefore ruptured Mrs Brown's membranes, finding her cervix to be 4 centimetres dilated and released thick meconium stained liquor. I therefore called in the duty consultant, Mr Rasputin, who was also Mrs Brown's consultant.

4. Mr Rasputin arrived promptly and assessed the situation. He told Mrs Brown in my presence that he considered that the signs of foetal distress shown by the baby did not warrant immediately Caesarean section but that she could try for normal delivery. Following membrane rupture Mrs Brown did progress very quickly indeed, becoming fully dilated at 05.40. I then encouraged her to attempt to push the baby out. Progress was fairly slow and the signs of foetal distress worsened. At 06.30 Mr Rasputin decided he should deliver the baby as a matter of urgency and did so with the Ventouse. A paediatrician was present at the birth to resuscitate the baby. I noticed that the umbilical cord was wound 5 times around the baby's neck.

SIGNED.........................
DATED.........................

M. Report of defendants' obstetric expert

Medical report relating to the case of Mrs Selina Brown and her male infant, John Brown. This report has been prepared for Mr F Bruneau, Bentley Bigge and Blue, 19 Lavender Hill, London W11 4JL, Defendant's Solicitor. This report has been prepared by:
Mr Owain Glyndwyr MD(Lond), FRCOG, Obstetrician & Gynaecol-

ogist/Clinical Director, Department of Maternity & Gynaecology, The Magwich Hospital, Magwich, Dorset MW4 5PD, Telephone: Secretary (Direct Line) 0999 783 010. Address for communication: 49 Huil Road, Magwich, Dorset MW1 3QF

The following documents have been used in the preparation of this report:

(a) The case notes of Selina Brown
(b) The CTG trace relating to the labour of Selina Brown (not a continuous copy however)
(c) The statement by the defending obstetrician – Mr Monk Rasputin
(d) The statement prepared by Midwife Sister M White
(e) The report prepared by the neurologist Sir James Snoddie.

Mrs Selina Brown, the wife of a company director, was 33 years of age when she attended the booking clinic at St Adomnan's Hospital on 11 May 1990. Judging by an ultrasound examination which had been carried out on 14.2.90, she was 16½ weeks pregnant. The date of the booking clinic is given in one place as 11.6.90 but this is assumed to be an error.

This was her first pregnancy. She had experienced no menstrual loss since stopping oral contraception in September 1989. The EDD (expected date of delivery) was therefore calculated from ultrasound measurements which, on the day of booking, were equivalent to 17½ weeks, suggesting an EDD of 14.10.90 plus/minus one week.

There were no adverse features in her past medical history and there were no apparent abnormalities of the routine blood tests taken in earlier pregnancy or of the triple screen taken on booking.

Her antenatal care was shared between the hospital and the GP. She was seen four times by the Defendant including the booking appointment and at examination two days prior to the due date. The notes suggest that weight gain was static in the last two weeks. However, there were no obvious abnormalities or foetal movement.

At the onset of labour which was spontaneous, there were no known adverse factors. She presented to the hospital at 03.45 on 17.10.90 at an estimated term plus 3 days. Contractions had been occurring regularly since the onset of labour at 01.00 hours. The presentation was cephalic or 'by the head' and the position of the head was anterior (meaning occipito-anterior which is the usual and normal). The head was fixed in the pelvis but not engaged. The level of the foetal head at the time of the first pelvic examination is not recorded.

The first examination was carried out at 04.00 hours when the cervix was noted to be thin and 4 cms dilated. The examining midwife was Sister M White. She obtained Selina Brown's permission to rupture the membranes artificially according to hospital policy I presume. Thick meconium stained liquor was seen. Prior to the examination, a cardiotocographic recording showed a normal foetal heart rate with narrowed baseline variation. The reaction to a contraction at 03.56 showed what is known as 'saltatory variation'. This wide-swinging of the foetal heart about the mean rate is a normal response in mid-labour.

At 04.10 a deceleration of foetal heart rate to 60 beats per minute was noted by both the midwife and the monitor. The cervix was then 5 cms dilated but it is not clear whether the vaginal examination was a repeat or a continuation of the first. The patient was turned to her left side in case the change of FHR was due to her position. Two further decelerations were noted within the next ten minutes and the consultant, Mr Rasputin, was called.

The consultant, Mr Rasputin, arrived at 04.40 by which time there had been a total of five deep decelerations and nine regular contractions occurring approximately once every three minutes.

It is apparent that the possibility of an operative delivery with a general anaesthetic was considered, as Zantac (Ranitidine – a hydrogen ion blocker and therefore a suppressor of stomach acidity) was given. However, it is apparent from the witness statement of both attendants that the signs of fetal distress were not sufficiently severe or progressive to warrant Caesarean section and that it was reasonable to go for a vaginal delivery, which was what Mrs Brown was hoping for.

Between 04.40 and 04.55 the heart rate was normal, the baseline variation only slightly narrowed and the response to contractions normal in the form of narrow spikes of deceleration.

At 04.55 there occurred a deep deceleration to 60 beats per minute; this appears to have recovered by the end of the contraction except for saltation which persisted through until the next contraction to which the FHR responded again with a spike. Saltation occurred again between 05.03 and 05.05 where the contraction record is temporarily deficient. Again, at 05.07 there was a narrow but deep deceleration, the type of deceleration often seen in association with cord compression.

The notes then refer to another vaginal examination at 05.10, this time by Mr Rasputin who recorded deep early decelerations occurring 1 in 3 with good frequency and baseline variation in between. The cervix was 9 cms dilated and the head was in the lower half of the pelvic cavity. Progress had therefore been rapid, going from 4 cms to 9 cms in 70 minutes with simultaneous descent of the head occurring.

There was some urge to push but full dilation was not confirmed until 05.40, some thirty minutes later. This is normal progress.

The pattern of not invariable, deep, cord-compression type decelerations persisted over the next half-an-hour. Recovery from each deceleration was rapid and complete by the end of the contraction. Contractions were occurring every 4 – 5 minutes. At 05.40 the patient was fully dilated and ready to push but it is not clear whether this was determined by vaginal examination or by external observations. At this point the tocographic element of the CTG was discontinued. The cardiograph, however, was continued. It showed a normal baseline rate with all degrees of baseline variation between 'silence' (at 05.46 and at 06.10) and 'saltation' (at 05.42 and at 06.40). Accelerations were a constant feature throughout the second stage but they were consistent in pattern, being precipitous at onset and, in all but one instance, being quick to return to normal baseline.

A decision to expedite delivery was taken by Mr Rasputin at 06.30 when it was apparent that the decelerations were becoming deeper and wider. Mrs Brown was transferred to Room 11, presumed to be an operative delivery area, and an uneventful ventouse delivery was carried out by Mr Rasputin at 06.47. Two pulls were required over four minutes, using a 6 centimetre Silastic cup and a mediolateral episiotomy.

A live male, John, was born. The Apgar score was recorded as 3 at one minute, 6 at 5 minutes and 8 at ten minutes. The birth weight was 3240 grams which is well within the normal range at term. The cord was noted, both by Sister White and by Mr Rasputin to be wound around the baby's neck five times.

A paediatrician was present at the delivery and the paediatric report refers to an initial reasonable response to resuscitation. Intubation was required at three minutes. Examination is said to have shown some dysmorphic features. The paediatricians tested blood from the cord at an unspecified time. The pH of the blood was 7.08 and the base excess -12.

The delivery of the placenta and membranes took place without event and there are no recorded placental abnormalities.

Regrettably, the infant suffers from cerebral palsy of a quadriplegic nature, despite an apparently good initial response and despite a good report at 8 weeks of age.

Opinion

I have been asked to give my opinion on this case as an expert witness in my capacity as a practising obstetrician in a district general hospital both now and at the time of John Brown's birth. I have also been asked to report in view of my thesis on the use of cardiotocography which was accepted by London University in 1978.

Selina Brown's pregnancy was conceived, according to reliable and consistent ultrasound evidence, sometime in the latter half of January 1990, at least four months after cessation of oral contraception. This is an important observation for two reasons:

1. There is a reported raised risk of non-specific foetal abnormality in pregnancies conceived within three months of the cessation of oral contraception.
2. There is an increase in the chance of a foetus passing meconium in post-maturity (more than 42 weeks).

There were no notable features in Mrs Brown's antenatal period except for the need to assess the expected date of confinement (EDD) from ultrasound measurements and observations. Antenatal care was provided correctly throughout, despite a move from one district to another in the mid-trimester. There are several references to foetal mobility and to breech presentation but these were made at a stage in pregnancy when such observations would be entirely normal. The presentation appears to have been stable from 32 weeks gestation as one would expect in an *entirely normal pregnancy.*

The specific reference is made to the *static weight* in the last two to three weeks of pregnancy. There is a significant body of obstetric opinion against the use of maternal weight as a useful observation. Whilst I do not subscribe to that body, I would accept static weight in the last two to three weeks as being entirely normal provided there were no abnormal patterns of foetal movement. The records contain a column for foetal movement observations and this has been completed appropriately, suggesting that they were discussed.

Two conflicting observations regarding *engagement* of the foetal head are seen in the notes (8.10.90 and 12.10.90). This suggests to me that either the head was bouncing in and out of the pelvis, which would be most unusual in a primigravid patient of normal stature, or, more likely, that the head was fixed in the pelvis with either two or three fifths of the head above the pelvic brim. Sister White refers to 3/5ths in her initial observations in labour.

Sister White refers to her usual *good practice of carrying out a CTG* (cardiotocographic tracing) in all patients soon after admission in established labour. The decelerations which she observed would have surprised her. It is possible that artificial rupture of the membranes (ARM) is a routine practice in Barchester once the active phase of the first stage of labour is confirmed; whether or not this is the case, it was *quite correct* for her to obtain further information about the liquor by performing *ARM at this stage* and having determined the presence of meconium, to apply a *scalp electrode* to facilitate more accurate and easier heart rate monitoring. Again, she was quite correct to reposition the patient and to then summon obstetric help.

Ironically the CTG trace had returned to an acceptably normal pattern for mid-labour by the time the obstetrician arrived twenty minutes later, at 04.40. The trace remained within normal limits for a further 40 minutes apart from one isolated, deep early onset of decelerations at 04.55. During this time, at 05.10, Mr Rasputin recorded signs which suggested continued, rapid progress – 9cm dilatation, head in low cavity, urge to push etc. The deep early decelerations to which he refers *at that time* are an entirely normal finding at near full dilatation. By 05.40, some of these decelerations had appeared wider and deeper but Mr Rasputin correctly states that his interpretation of the trace was that it 'was most likely to be due to the umbilical cord around the baby's neck'. The *decision to commence pushing at 05.40 seems to have been a perfectly reasonable one*. The labour had been efficient, perhaps too much so, there had been variable response to the contractions, and the foetal heart had been normal between contractions.

It is important to remember that this decision was taken by an *experienced consultant obstetrician who was in attendance* – he had stayed on the labour ward 'to keep a close watch on progress'. Had there been any doubt in his mind, then, on the fact of it, a foetal blood sample (FBS) would have been indicated. Not all units have this facility. Where it is available its use in this case might be avoided for any one of five reasons.

1. *Progress had been rapid* and an experienced observer would have anticipated a quick second stage, say, of half an hour.
2. In the event of poor progress in the second stage a *vacuum extraction* would be anticipated in which case an FBS would present the small risk of a bleed from the foetal scalp.
3. The presence of *meconium* can make the determination of the foetal pH both difficult and unreliable.
4. According to Sister White's statement, Mrs Brown had hoped to have her baby naturally with *minimal intervention*, although there is no reference to this in the appropriate box in the notes.
5. Certainty of diagnosis from the CTG trace based on considerable experience in the use of CTGs.

Had an FBS been carried out the points at which it may have been considered are at 04.40, the time of Mr Rasputin's arrival, at 05.00 just after an isolated deep deceleration or in the second stage at 06.00 to 06.10 when it became apparent that progress had slowed. The first two occasions were followed by 15 to 30 minutes of CTG normality and on the third occasion a decision to expedite delivery would have been more appropriate. This is an objective, practical view and I would contend that any opposing view would be expressed with too much dependence on the 'retrospectoscope.'

It might be argued that a *decision to expedite delivery* should have been taken at 06.10 when the foetal heart was slower to recover than before but I note that the patient was vomiting at that time and subsequent decelerations were, again, quick to recover. Unfortunately there is no *tocograph* (recording of contractions) so that it is no longer safe to assume that the decelerations were early in onset although one suspects that they were, simply because of their shape.

There will, inevitably, be debate over the 37 minutes which elapsed between 06.10 and the time of delivery at 06.47 and whether or not the 'poor condition' referred to in Sister White's statement could have been predicted. In 1972 evidence was presented to suggest that the perinatal condition was predictable to a degree by the 'area under the curve' and in that respect, a low Apgar score might have been predicted. However, that measurement has never been adopted as a realistic 'on-line' measurement and instead an obstetrician will look for other signs of hypoxia in addition to decelerations. In this case, in the last 37 minutes of labour there were no such signs – the rate was normal, the baseline variability was acceptable, there were no rebound accelerations and to the best of our knowledge, there was no delay in onset of deceleration. To the expert eye, these decelerations were likely to be associated with cord compression, usually nuchal (around the neck). Nuchal cord occurs in 30 per cent of deliveries.

I would contend therefore that, although a decision at 06.10 to deliver by intervention might have been wiser, *there is nothing in the subsequent trace to suggest that the foetus might be asphyxiated.*

The decision to deliver was taken at 06.30. Obstetricians in the UK are divided about the *use of the vacuum extractor,* particularly when the indication for delivery is one of so-called 'foetal distress'. The subject is reviewed well in the textbooks which refer to inconsistent opinion in the 1960s. However, more recently authors have found that extractions completed with no more than four pulls were not causative of hypoxia and that easy extraction is not associated with 'depressed' (low Apgar) infants in a causative manner. Results with the modern Silastic cups, as used in this delivery, are even better.

Reference is made above to *nuchal cord.* Usually, when this occurs, it is just one loop, rarely tight. Five turns is exceptionally rare and must imply either an abnormally long cord or a very tight cord or both. Both long and tight cords will present a greater resistance to blood flow which, in turn, will produce *haemodynamic and autonomic* changes. If the turns around the neck are reasonably loose, the changes will only *become manifest during contractions* when there is increased pressure on the cord from without (amniotic pressure), and greater resistance within owing to a tightening of the cord consequent upon the head descending further away from the point of cord insertion into the placenta.

In addition to the above effects of a significant nuchal cord, there is the effect of strangulation. This possibility must be considered in the light of an occasional autopsy finding of ridges and depressions caused by a tight nuchal cord in an otherwise unexplained perinatal death. Such pressure on the neck will reduce cerebral blood flow both by direct pressure on the carotid blood vessels and also by stimulating the carotid body which produces bradycardia (slowing of the heart).

I am not in an expert position to comment on the aetiology of spastic quadriplegia. I am led to believe that it is in this group of cerebral palsy that the greatest heterogeneity of factors exists. I note that cerebral scanning has been confined to early ultrasound examinations.

In conclusion and in answer to Mrs Selina Brown's request for information I am of the opinion that her antenatal care and her labour were managed in a manner which is acceptable to a significant proportion of both midwifery and obstetric specialists. In areas of potential dispute I have shown reasons for dispute and arguments which support the management which was adopted. Whilst acknowledging the presence of decelerations which might be labelled 'foetal distress' I have explained why these were not necessarily signs of foetal asphyxia. Subsequent cord blood analysis showed a degree of perinatal asphyxia (pH 7.08 and base excess −12) but the cord was shown to be nuchal times five. I have shown how this cord complication could affect the foetus particularly at the very end of labour; under these circumstances the pH can fall at 0.1 every two minutes. The base excess was only slightly outside normal limits for the time of delivery.

For a caesarean section to have been carried out in response to the changes seen in this labour, a very low threshold of interference would have been necessary with a consequentially high section rate.

Even allowing that a degree of foetal asphyxia was shown and without proof that a multiple nuchal cord was responsible for rapid changes in the foetal acid-base balance at the very end of labour, there is no way of showing that the cerebral palsy is attributable to foetal asphyxia. It is thought that in 90 per cent of cases of spastic quadriplegia, the cause is something other than asphyxia. The dysmorphic features noted by the paediatricians must raise the likelihood of a prenatal cause.

signed

Owain Glyndwyr MD (Lond) FRCOG

References supplied.

N. Report of defendants' neurological expert

Medical report in the case of John Brown, an infant. This report has been prepared for Mr F Bruneau, Bentley Bigge and Blue, 19 Lavender Hill, London W11 4JL. This report has been prepared by Sir James Snoddie, FRCP, Consultant Neurologist, 199b Harley Street, London W1, Telephone 071 233 5000.

1. I have been asked to give a neurological report in this case where it is alleged that poor obstetric care has led to brain damage in the infant Plaintiff, who sues by his mother and 'Next Friend'.
2. I have had the benefit of reading all the medical notes on the case

from St Adomnan's Hospital, Barchester. I have also seen the general practitioner notes on mother and child up to late 1992. I have seen a factual statement from Mr Rasputin, the obstetrician concerned and from his midwife sister, Mrs White. I have seen a short statement from the mother.

3. I have had the very great benefit of reading the full and helpful report into the obstetric care provided given by Mr Owain Glyndwyr FRCS MD of Magwich District General Hospital. I am able to dispense with any narrative in this report given the clarity of Mr Glyndwyr's account of events and the full and accurate instructions from the solicitors who have favoured me with these instructions. I will confine myself to comment and my conclusions upon the case.

4. It is the burden of Mr Glyndwyr's report that there has been no obstetric negligence in this case. Intrinsic to that view is the conclusion that the depressions in heartbeat to be observed on the cardiotocograph trace are not sinister but are either temporary effects of pressure on the umbilical cord or are 'saltatory' dips. I am naturally not expert in the reading of cardiotocographs, and I would defer to Mr Glyndwyr on this topic. However, it is worth noting that I have some experience of cardiotocographs since their introduction into the United Kingdom took place in Guy's Hospital, in 1973, whilst I was a consultant neurologist with a paediatric interest in that hospital. I have observed them many times since as a diagnostic aid. I am in agreement with Mr Glyndwyr's views on this trace.

5. Therefore my view would be there is no evidence from the cardiotocograph here that the foetus was suffering from distress during labour. There is evidence from the presence of meconium in the liquor at the time of artificial rupture of membranes, that the foetus had suffered from some *previous* distress. Meconium can often be present in liquor when the baby is born pink, screaming and fit. It can however be a sign of intrauterine distress. Either the meconium here means nothing or it indicates that the baby was in distress at some time before the membranes were ruptured. I am not in a position to say which it is. Neither is helpful to the Plaintiff's case.

6. This little boy was born with a number of dysmorphic features. Our understanding of congenital and indeed genetic abnormality is still very limited, despite the enormous strides which are being made by geneticists at present. We do know that dysmorphic features are associated with a much greater than normal incidence of brain abnormality. That is the case even where no specific 'syndrome' can be identified as the cause of the unusual appearance of the child. [Reference 1 below]. The presence of dysmorphic features here can be regarded as indicative (although not conclusive) of a pre-natal cause of the observed brain abnormality.

7. The presentation of this baby at birth was far from typical of the child with hypoxic ischaemic encephalopathy. Usually, the child is very 'flat' indeed at birth. Indeed, very often such a baby is effectively dead when born and is only revived after sustained efforts at resuscitation. The Apgar scores indicate that this baby was very far from such a condition at birth. This is not wholly inconsistent with the child having suffered from hypoxic ischaemic encephalopathy, but in my view it is wholly inconsistent with an episode of intra-uterine asphyxia just before the birth. If this foetus had been severely starved of oxygen during the half-hour or hour before birth, then I believe it would have been quite incapable of relatively rapid recovery demonstrated by the Apgar scores.

8. Another strong indicator in the case is the lack of any report of hypoxic damage to other organs in the body than the brain. It is established that the brain is the most sensitive organ to oxygen lack. Thus it is *possible* for the brain to be damaged by asphyxia and yet for no other organ to show signs of similar damage. Usually, however, in the baby whose body has been generally deprived of oxygen during the last stages of labour, some sign or signs of damage to other organs will occur during the hours and days after birth. Frequently this effect will be manifested as transient kidney damage. The effect may be relatively subtle, but there are a range of ways in which the effect may be observed. My understanding of this case is that no such effect was noted at any point in the immediate period after the birth. I believe this to be persuasive that there was no hypoxic ischaemic encephalopathy, at least at the end of labour.

9. The child has now demonstrated microcephaly, his head size being on the 3rd centile. This may well be advanced as a sign of brain damage at the time of birth, since the previous indicators (such as they are) tend to show normal head growth and size. I believe this sign is of very little value in deciding the precise cause of damage here. There is no doubt of brain compromise after birth. This makes it likely that the head would fail to grow normally, *whatever the cause of the brain compromise*. The last measurement before birth was a scan at 17 weeks or thereabouts, and the head size was normal then. The head size at the time of birth appears unaccountably absent from the notes I have seen. The first measurement I have discovered is some four weeks after the birth. By that time, there was definite reduction in head size. This merely establishes that the damage was probably present by then. That body of evidence is consistent with an event or events compromising the brain (and thus head growth) weeks before birth, days or hours before the birth, or immediately before delivery. It is of no help in determining causation here.

10. However, the diminution in head size within four weeks of the

delivery does mean that we can discount the suggested 'smiling' or responsiveness of the child at 6 weeks. I do not believe this can be reliable evidence.

11. Studies over 20 years in Australia, the United States of America and more recently in this country have demonstrated that only some 8% to 10% of children suffering from cerebral palsy have received their brain injury as a consequence of perinatal asphyxia (see references 2 to 22 appended to this report). This is in marked contrast to the previously orthodox view that all such injuries were occasioned in that way. Naturally, only a small proportion of that minority sustained their asphyxia in association with any form of sub-standard obstetric care.

12. I do not believe this child falls into that restricted category. It is entirely likely that his brain injury was determined by a genetic fault which also gave rise to his dysmorphic features, and might well also have left him more vulnerable to the normal stresses of labour, thus giving rise to the cardiotocograph appearances observed.

13. Equally, it is entirely possible that he did have an episode of asphyxia or of some other significant stress inside the uterus, which gave rise to his brain damage. We will never be sure. If, however, he did have such an episode perinatally, it is likely to have been before the artificial rupture of the membranes, so as to explain the meconium found in the liquor at that time. In those circumstances, the damage would not have been avoided whatever obstetric care was given to his mother after her admission to hospital on 17 October 1990.

James Snoddie

O. Defence

IN THE HIGH COURT OF JUSTICE   1993 B No.
QUEEN'S BENCH DIVISION
BETWEEN:

JOHN BROWN
(an infant suing by his mother
and Next Friend SELINA BROWN)   Plaintiff

– and –

BARCHESTER HEALTH AUTHORITY   Defendant

DEFENCE

---

1. Paragraph 1 of the Statement of Claim is admitted.
2. The Defendant admits and avers that:
   (1) Selina Brown was born on the 25th March 1957.
   (2) Conception occurred in the pregnant woman the subject matter of this litigation in the latter half of January 1990.
   (3) Selina Brown had not had a menstrual cycle since September 1989. She had taken the oral contraceptive pill, but had stopped in July 1989.
   (4) She was a primigravida.
   (5) Her estimated date of delivery calculated from an ultrasound scan taken on her booking visit (1.5.90) was the 14th October 1990. Within the limits of scan dating, the EDD is within plus or minus one week.
3. Save as is admitted and averred in paragraph 2 herein, paragraph 2 of the Statement of Claim is denied.
4. Paragraph 3 of the Statement of Claim is admitted.
5. With respect to the care afforded to Selina Brown and to her baby on Wednesday the 17th October 1990, the Defendant's case is as follows:
   (1) At 03.35 am Selina Brown was admitted to St Adomnan's Hospital from home with a history of regular contractions since 1 am.
   (2) She was placed under the care of Sister White – a Senior Midwife who was responsible for the Labour Ward.
   (3) At 03.55 am Sister White commenced the cardiotocographic trace. Prior to 04.00 am the trace showed a normal foetal heart

rate with narrowed baseline variation. At 03.56 am there was a saltatory variation. This is a normal response in mid-labour.

(4) At 04.00 am Sister White carried out a vaginal examination in order to assess progress. Dilation was 4 cms and the cervix was thin. Upon artificial rupture of the membranes, the liquor was noted to be thick and meconium stained. However, the foetal heart rate was heard and was regular.

(5) At 4.10 am the foetal heart rate decelerated to 60 beats per minute. Dilation was 5 cms. Selina Brown was turned onto her left side. A foetal scalp electrode was applied.

(6) Between 04.10 am and 04.20 am two further decelerations occurred and at 04.20 am the Consultant Obstetrician, Mr Monk Rasputin was informed. There had been no requirement or imperative to inform him earlier. The arrangement at St Adomnan's was for midwives to have direct access for obstetric opinion to the Consultant.

(7) At 04.40 am (some 55 minutes after Selina Brown's admission) she was attended by Mr Rasputin – a Consultant of 17 years standing – and thereafter the management of the delivery was under his care.

(8) Between 04.10 am and 04.40 am the CTG trace revealed a total of 5 decelerations and 9 regular contractions (occurring once in every 3 minutes).

(9) Between 04.40 am and 05.10 am the CTG trace remained within normal limits, save for one isolated deep early onset deceleration at 04.55 am.

(10) At 05.10 am Mr Rasputin recorded signs which suggested continued rapid progress. Deep early decelerations were present, but were considered to be an entirely normal finding at nearly full dilation.

(11) Between 05.10 am and 05.40 am the CTG trace was within normal limits.

(12) At 05.40 am there was full dilation. The progress of labour into the second stage had been normal.

(13) From 05.40 am onwards the topographic element of the CTG was discontinued. The cardiograph showed a normal baseline varying with a consistent pattern of decelerations which were quick to return to the normal baseline.

(14) at 06.30 am the decelerations on the cardiograph were becoming deeper and wider. Mr Rasputin determined to expedite delivery at 06.30 am, and Selina Brown was transferred to Room 11 and an uneventful Ventouse delivery was carried out by Mr Rasputin with the Plaintiff being born at 06.47 am.

6. Save as is set out in paragraph 5 herein the Plaintiff's case as

contained in paragraphs 4 to 15 inclusive of the Statement of Claim is denied. For the avoidance of doubt, it is denied that:

(1) The expressions of opinion and timings relating to the interpretation of the CTG trace are correct;

(2) The suppositions and assertions made as to what level of foetal acidosis would have been revealed by samples taken at or before 05.40 am or at any other time, are correct.

7. It is denied that the Defendant or its servants or agents were guilty of any negligence as alleged in paragraph 16 of the Statement of Claim. Without prejudice to any evidence and/or argument that may be adduced at trial the Defendant pleads to the four particulars of negligence as follows, adopting the Plaintiff's lettering:

A. At 04.00am there was no imperative for Sister White to immediately summon obstetric help. The CTG was indicating normal responses in mid-labour. Meconium is not necessarily indicative of foetal distress. The foetal heart was actually heard at this time and was regular.

B. The first occasion upon which a responsible midwife would have summoned obstetric assistance was at 04.20 am – which is precisely what Sister White did. A Consultant Obstetrician of 7 years' standing was with the mother within 20 minutes of this request and within 55 minutes of her admission to hospital. Such a response – both in time and in level of expertise when mother and baby are considered to be in no danger – was entirely proper and appropriate.

C. There was no requirement or imperative for a foetal blood sample to be taken before 04.30 am. From 04.40 am onwards, Mr Rasputin, the Consultant Obstetrician was in attendance. In the light of the rapid progress, the possibility of an assisted delivery, the fact that meconium would make determination of foetal pH both unreliable and difficult and the continuous trace interpreted by an experienced consultant, it was a reasonable decision not to require foetal blood samples.

D. There was no 'combination of signs' prior to 04.30 am which made the taking of foetal blood samples mandatory and nothing to suggest with any certainty what such samples would have revealed, nor that they would have been reliable. The CTG was within normal limits and there was no mandatory requirement for hourly foetal blood samples and no indications that immediately assisted delivery was required at 05.40 am, nor an emergency Caesarean required immediately thereafter.

8. Save that the Apgar scores were 3 at 1 minutes: 6 at 5 minutes and 8 at 10 minutes, no admissions are made as to the first sentence of paragraph 17 of the Statement of Claim. The second and third

sentences thereof are not admitted. The fourth sentence thereof is denied. The fifth sentence is admitted.

9. No admissions are made as to any injury, loss and damage as pleaded in paragraph 18 of the Statement of Claim. The causation thereof is denied. The Defendant's case is that on the balance of probabilities:
    (1) The Plaintiff's cerebral palsy was not caused by any asphyxia during labour.
    (2) The presence of dysmorphic features indicates that the more likely cause is pre-natal.
10. Save as is hereinbefore expressly admitted or otherwise pleaded to, the Defendant denies each and every allegation contained in the Statement of Claim as though the same were hereinafter set out and traversed seriatim.

Portia Ford

Served this . . . day of . . . 1993 by Bentley Bigge and Blue of 19 Lavender Hill, London W11 4JL. Solicitors for the Defendants.

P. High Court Summons for directions

IN THE HIGH COURT OF JUSTICE   1993 – C – NO.
QUEEN'S BENCH DIVISION
BETWEEN:

Plaintiff

– and –

Defendant

SUMMONS FOR DIRECTIONS

LET ALL PARTIES attend the Master in Chambers in Room Number   , Royal Courts of Justice, Strand, London WC2 on day the day of 1993 at o'clock in the noon on a hearing of an application by the Plaintiff for directions in this action:

1. The Plaintiff within 28 days serve on the Defendants and the Defendants within 28 days serve on the Plaintiff a List of Documents stating what documents are or have been in its possession

custody or power relevant to issues arising in this action. Inspection of documents within 7 days thereafter.

2. Pursuant to RSC Order 38 Rule 2A as amended the parties do simultaneously exchange by way of signed and dated written statements the substance of the evidence of all witnesses as to facts on issues of liability that they intend to rely upon at trial within 3 months from the date of this order. Such statements to be agreed if possible. Where a party fails to comply with this direction he shall not be entitled to adduce evidence to which this direction relates without the leave of the Court.

3. (a) The parties do mutually simultaneously exchange the substance in writing of all medical expert evidence on liability and causation issues that they propose to rely upon at trial within 3 months from the exchange of the witness evidence referred to in para 2 above.

   (b) Reports on the Plaintiff's condition and prognosis to be served by the parties by way of mutual and simultaneous exchange within 6 months of the date of this order;

   (c) Any consequential supplementary reports on liability and causation or supplementary reports as to the present condition, prognosis and needs of the Plaintiff from the experts whose evidence has already been disclosed to be disclosed not less than 56 days before the date fixed for trial.

   (d) Medical reports to be agreed if possible. Leave to call expert medical witnesses at trial to give opinion evidence limited to those witnesses the substance of whose evidence has been so disclosed, and to (number) expert medical witnesses for each party.

4. The Plaintiff serve on the Defendant within six months from the date of this order a Schedule of Special Damages, such Schedule to specify the amount claimed for each item and the period for which it is claimed, and to be accompanied by copies of all documents and Reports relied upon in support of any item mentioned in the said Schedule.

5. The Defendants serve on the Plaintiff within 3 months of service of the Plaintiff's Schedule a Counter-Schedule setting out which items are conceded and which are disputed, giving reasons where there is a dispute, such Counter-Schedule to be accompanied by copies of all documents and reports relied upon in support of any contention advanced on behalf of the Defendants.

6. Each party be at liberty to call to give expert evidence those experts whose Reports have been disclosed in accordance with para 3 above and limited to (number) of non-medical experts per party.

7. If any expert witness proposes to rely on any textbook, article, or other literature a first list and photocopies be served by mutual

exchange on the other party at the time at which the report relying on that literature is served.

8. Set down for trial within 56 days at London, non jury, category . Estimated length of trial   days.
9. Liberty to restore.
10. Costs in cause.

This Summons was issued the   day of   1994 by Messrs
              of   *Solicitors for the Plaintiff*

TO: The Defendants and to their Solicitors

Q. Answers to interrogatories

(A) Sister Mary White

IN THE HIGH COURT OF JUSTICE   1993 B No.
QUEEN'S BENCH DIVISION
BETWEEN:

JOHN BROWN
(a minor suing by his mother and
Next Friend, MRS SELINA BROWN)   Plaintiff

– and –

BARCHESTER HEALTH AUTHORITY   Defendant

ANSWERS TO INTERROGATORIES

THE ANSWERS of MARY WHITE to Interrogatories numbered 1 to 6 inclusive of the Interrogatories served on behalf of the Plaintiff on . . . 1994 are as follows:

1. To the first interrogatory, namely 'At what time did you rupture Mrs Brown's membranes?' the answer is shortly after 4.00am on 17.x.90.
2. To the second interrogatory, namely, 'Did you regard the "marked foetal heart decelerations" described in your witness statement dated . . . at paragraph 3 as deep variable foetal heart decelerations?', the answer is that the decelerations were both deep and variable.

3. To the third interrogatory, namely, 'Did you regard the combination of marked foetal heart decelerations and thick meconium stained liquor at about 4.00am as clear signs of possible fetal hypoxia?' my answer is yes.

4. To the fourth interrogatory, namely, 'If the answer to the third interrogatory is in the affirmative, did you consider that a possible cause of foetal hypoxia was tightening of the umbilical cord around the fetal neck?' my answer is yes.

5. To the fifth interrogatory, namely, 'At what time did Mr Rasputin arrive on the labour ward?' my answer is he arrived at about 4.40am and I made a note accordingly on the record of delivery form.

6. To the sixth interrogatory, namely, 'What was your understanding on 17.x.90, from your experience of working in St Adomnan's Hospital, as to the length of time it would normally take from the decision to deliver a baby by emergency Caesarean section to the completion of delivery?' my answer is that I would expect the overall time to be between 20 and 30 minutes, although it could be shorter or longer depending on the particular circumstances.

SWORN etc   MARY WHITE

(B) M. Monk Rasputin

IN THE HIGH COURT OF JUSTICE   1993 B No.
QUEEN'S BENCH DIVISION
BETWEEN:

JOHN BROWN
(a minor suing by his mother and
Next Friend, MRS SELINA BROWN)   Plaintiff

– and –

BARCHESTER HEALTH AUTHORITY   Defendant

ANSWES TO INTERROGATORIES

THE ANSWERS of M. MONK RASPUTIN to Interrogatories numbered 7 to 10 inclusive of the Interrogatories served on behalf of the Plaintiff on 13 January 1994 are as follows:

1. To the 7th interrogatory, namely 'Did you regard the combination of marked foetal heart decelerations and thick meconium stained

liquor at about 4.00am as clear signs of possible fetal hypoxia?' my answer is that I regarded the signs referred to and the overall progress of labour by the time of my arrival at the hospital as ambiguous signs, which might be consistent with foetal hypoxia but might have other causes. Accordingly, I maintained a careful monitoring of the progress of labour from my arrival onwards.

2. To the 8th interrogatory, namely 'If the answer to the 7th interrogatory is in the affirmative, did you recognise that a possible cause of foetal hypoxia might be the tightening of the umbilical cord around the neck of the foetus?' my answer is that I recognise this as one of a number of possible causes of foetal hypoxia. In view of the improvement shown in the foetal heart trace very soon after my arrival, careful monitoring of the progress of labour was called for rather than any intervention such as a decision to move to delivery by Caesarean section.

3. In answer to the 9th interrogatory, namely, 'Is it your normal practice to obtain a foetal scalp blood sample in order to assess the acidity of the blood and the degree of oxygenation present?' my answer is that I do not regard a foetal blood sample as essential in monitoring the progress of labour. Foetal blood sampling can be helpful but it can also be a diversion from care and from a full clinical assessment of the condition of mother and baby. The procedure itself may cause foetal distress and the results can sometimes be misleading. It was my judgment that foetal blood sampling during the course of this labour was not necessary.

4. In answer to the 10th interrogatory, namely 'Do you now accept that a Caesarean section could have been carried out achieving delivery of the baby by 05.40?' my answer is that I do accept that delivery could have been achieved by 05.40. I do not accept however that at the time a decision to move to delivery by Caesarean section was obligatory or even appropriate.

SWORN etc   M. MONK RASPUTIN

Affidavit on limitation

IN THE BARCHESTER COUNTY COURT   CASE NO.
BETWEEN:

EUGENIA JONES   Plaintiff

– and –

BARCHESTER DISTRICT HEALTH
AUTHORITY   Defendant

AFFIDAVIT OF THE PLAINTIFF

I, EUGENIA JONES of 114 Marblethorpe House, Enderly, Barsetshire, hereby make oath and say as follows:

1. I am the Plaintiff in this action and I make this Affidavit in support of my claim for medical negligence in respect of the treatment I received at Barsetshire District General Hospital in about July 1990. The facts and matters set out below are true to the best of my knowledge and belief.

2. I was born on 14th July 1929. I went to school from the age of 5 until I was 13. I have no educational or other qualifications. Just before my 14th birthday I started work for Deeping & Co who were manufacturing parachutes. I helped in the packing department. In late 1945 I became pregnant and married Arthur Jones on 3rd April 1946. My first child Tom was born in September 1946. My second child, Adrian was born in August 1947 and my youngest child, Sally in September 1948.

3. After Sally was born I became extremely depressed and spent about 3 months in a psychiatric hospital in Appleton. Over the next 25 years I was readmitted to hospital on about 10 occasions and

diagnosed as schizophrenic. My husband divorced me in 1967 and I have lived alone ever since. I see my daughter Sally quite often but only see my sons at Christmas time. I do not work. I receive income support and mobility allowance (now mobility component of disabled living allowance).

4. My last admission to psychiatric hospital was in about 1970. Since then I have been prescribed various drugs which have helped me and I have not needed to return to hospital. My current prescription for drugs is set out in the report of Dr Bolam, Consultant Psychiatrist which is exhibited at 'ExEJ1'. Although the drugs I take are helpful, they do make me sleepy and forgetful and sometimes I forget to take them. When this happens I get frightened and believe that I am hearing voices. I am unable to leave the house. I have no telephone and have to rely on neighbours to call the doctor for me.

5. In July 1990 I was admitted to Barsetshire Hospital for the removal of a cyst in my left leg just behind the knee. I was in hospital for about a week and after being discharged I went home. I attended outpatients on one occasion. My knee was swollen for about a month after the operation but gradually got better. I was left with a slight limp because I could not straighten my leg. It was as if there was a tightness around my knee. I went to see my GP, Dr Kapur, about this but he said it would probably improve and said that if it didn't he would send me to a physiotherapist.

6. At first my knee did not cause me much trouble but about a year after the operation I found it more and more difficult to walk. I stayed in a lot and got very depressed. In the winter of 1991/92 I must have missed taking my medication and I began to hear voices a lot. My daughter Sally was worried about me and called the doctor. I was admitted to Appleton Hospital for a few weeks and came home in the Spring of 1992. My knee was no better but by that time I just regarded it as a part of life.

7. By early 1994 I was finding it more and more difficult to walk and was depressed about this. Sally said I should get a mobility allowance if I couldn't walk. She got the forms and filled them in for me. The mobility people sent me to a Consultant for a medical report and the doctor told me that something had gone wrong during the operation in 1990. He didn't say it was negligent – just that something had gone wrong.

8. In March 1994 Sally took me to see Mrs Smith at Tupplestone Wade and Whatnot. Mrs Smith obtained the hospital records and told me that the operation at Barsetshire Hospital might be negligent. She sent the papers to Mr Carnegie, a Consultant Surgeon, and we got his report in November 1994. I understand that the case was started in December 1994.

9. The medical records are included at exhibit 'EJ2'. I have been

shown the entries at pages 48 and 53 and I understand that a nerve was damaged when I was in hospital in 1990. I don't remember anyone at the hospital telling me about nerve damage. They just said that my knee was stiff because of the operation and that it would get better in time. The first I knew that they might have done something wrong was in about February 1994 when I saw the mobility doctor.

10. I am almost unable to walk at all now, even with a walking stick. My leg is very painful and even if I just sit in an armchair it swells up and hurts.

SWORN ETC   EUGENIA JONES

Major case damages checklist

GENERAL DAMAGES – [A] Pain and suffering, loss of amenity
              [B] Smith v Manchester
              [C] Shock/PTSD
              [D] Distress/inconvenience (legal negligence cases)

Interest on general damages

HISTORIC LOSS

Past expenditure –
- [A] Equipment
- [B] Heating and lighting
- [C] Private medical care/prescriptions
- [D] Extra/special food
- [E] Transport costs
- [F] Holidays
- [G] Clothing/laundry
- [H] Building/alteration costs
- [I] Wear and tear on house/furnishings
- [J] Counselling

Loss of earnings
Past care
Interest on historic care expenditure

FUTURE LOSS

Future expenditure –
- [A] Equipment
- [B] Heating and lighting
- [C] Private medical care/prescriptions
- [D] Extra/special food
- [E] Transport costs
- [F] Holidays
- [G] Laundry
- [H] Counselling

315

Future care cost
Physiotherapy
Speech/language therapy
Occupational therapy
Computers
Housing/building cost
Plaintiff's future loss of earnings
Relative/carer's future loss of earnings
Pension loss
Loss of expectation of life
Court of Protection/Financial advice

STRUCTURE?

Schedule of loss: Smith v Barchester Health Authority

Preliminary notes

1. In compiling this schedule we have followed the approach which we recommend. As a generality, we suggest that the Schedule should be able to stand alone, without need to return to the formal pleadings for important information. We suggest that the text can be fairly full, so as to be persuasive on first reading. We suggest that detailed mathematical information can be hived off into sub-schedules or appendices, leaving the principal calculations to be placed into the main schedule. Hence, in this example, past expenditure, life tables, compound interest, the 4% money tables and calculations of apportionment of multipliers between various periods have all been devolved into appendices. We have not reproduced these as they are either widely available or so specific to the individual case as not to be helpful.

2. An index to a big schedule and to the documents which support it is essential. This will mean that the schedule itself can refer to the relevant pagination in sub-schedule or supporting report, and also that the reader can find his or her way around.

IN THE HIGH COURT OF JUSTICE   1993 B No
QUEEN'S BENCH DIVISION
BETWEEN:

GARY SMITH
(an infant suing by his father and
Next Friend MR FREDERICK SMITH)   Plaintiff

– and –

BARCHESTER HEALTH AUTHORITY   Defendant

SCHEDULE OF LOSS

PREAMBLE

1   The Plaintiff was born on 27.v.87, and suffers from severe cerebral
    palsy, due to perinatal hypoxia and consequent hypoxic ischaemic
    encephalopathy. The Statement of Claim was served on 1.vi.93 and
    a Defence was entered on 4.xi.93. Liability was admitted on
    22.iii.94. Any award will be under the control of the Court of
    Protection and the Plaintiff's father as Receiver.

2   The Plaintiff's father (the Next Friend) owns and runs his own
    greengrocer's shop. The Plaintiff's mother is a graduate pharmacist
    who had risen to be a pharmacy manager, until giving up work just
    before the Plaintiff's birth. The Plaintiff has a younger brother
    named Douglas, born on 10.v.90.

3   The care of the Plaintiff has fallen entirely upon the immediate
    family. The Plaintiff needs constant attention whilst awake and
    often during the night. Mrs Smith has been unable to return to
    work as she would have done. Mr Smith has been unable to expand
    his business, as he believes he would have been able to do.

4   The family house is unsuitable for the Plaintiff in many respects,
    and a major priority for the family since the admission of liability
    has been to seek for a more suitable house, a process which is
    nearing completion at the date hereof.

5   In summary, the Plaintiff has spastic quadriplegia, with the left side
    more seriously impaired than the right. His spasticity is worse in
    the legs than in the arms. He has relatively good control of his trunk
    and head. He does not have curvature of the spine and he is not
    particularly prone to chest infection. He has not had urinary tract
    infections. He has no epilepsy presently. If looked after well, his

expectation of life is near-normal. Advances in medical care will tend to expand that life expectancy.

6 The Plaintiff has a severe learning difficulty. He recognises members of his family and will react to the presence of others. He presently has eight vocalisations which are distinguishable and meaningful to his immediate family, and can use some more signs and signals. He is affectionate and can be very demanding of attention. He dribbles a great deal. He can grasp some objects with his right hand, but still tends to cast them. Much of his movement is purposeless. He likes music. He can lie and roll on the floor, and can sometimes sit propped on his right hand. Otherwise, he needs support when still and help for movements.

7 The Plaintiff is conscious of his own disability, particularly focusing on the abilities and activity of his younger brother. He will never progress so as to achieve any meaningful intellectual satisfaction, or any independence. He will never marry or work. He will remain totally dependent on others for daily life. It is the intention of the family that they will be actively involved until Gary attains his majority, and they hope that he will always be able to live in a family context, with professional care.

GENERAL DAMAGES

8 The appropriate level of damages for pain, suffering and loss of amenity for this Plaintiff is at the very maximum of awards. The Plaintiff would submit the award should be   £130,000
Interest on general damages to 31.vii.94
(Writ issued 27.v.93) at 2%pa [2.35%]   £3,055
Credit will be given for any interim payment made.

HISTORIC LOSS – PAST EXPENDITURE

9 Past expenses have been set down in a sub-schedule, marked Annex 1. They total   £15,986.41

LOST EARNINGS

10 The report of Henry Lumberjack and Associates sets out the loss of earnings sustained by Mrs Smith. Averaging the figures on page 5 of the report, she had a gross loss of earnings of £139,707. Making allowance for tax and National Insurance at 25%, her nett loss was £104,780. It is recognised that there would have been child care cost to enable Mrs Smith to work full-time. No precise costing of the child care can be made, since it is likely it would have been made up of different methods and strategies of child care. The average cost over those years is most unlikely to have exceeded £5,000 per annum, making a gross cost of £35,000. This gives a nett loss of earnings to Mrs Smith of £69,780. In addition to this loss Mrs

Smith lost the benefit of her annual bonuses and shopping discount. These are estimated at £500.00 pa net. This, therefore gives a total net loss of £73,280.00.

It is noted that this figure is far in excess of the valuation of the care provided by Mrs Smith, detailed in paragraph 11 hereof. However, the computation of the valuation of the care offered by Mrs Smith is offered for completeness. If contrary to the Plaintiff's case, the value of Mrs Smith's earnings is not recovered or recovered in full, the claim should not under any circumstances fail to enable the Plaintiff to repay to his mother damages in line with her care as valued below.

The Plaintiff gives credit for:

Attendance allowance in the sum of	£5,688.10
High rate care element of disability living allowance in the sum of	£5,613.85
sub-total	£11,301.95
making a nett claim of	£61,978.05

LOSS OF PENSION

11   Mrs Smith's employer contributed to a pension scheme for her, which scheme has ceased. There may, therefore, be a loss of pension benefits. This is yet to be quantified.

PAST CARE

12   As stated above, this claim is in the alternative to the loss of earnings claim set out above. Reference is made to the report of Mrs Marie Rambert of July 1994. Gross rates to residential workers providing such care, where the benefit of accommodation is taken into account and without additions for holiday pay, relief help and sickness cover, would have been:

Period 1	
Hospital discharge to 26.v.89	£5,387.76
Period 2	
26.v.89 to 26.v.90	£4,170.88
Period 3	
27.v.90 to 26.v.91	£4,963.40
Period 4	
27.v.91 to 26.v.93	£12,914.82
Period 5	
27.v.93 to 31.vii.93	£10,408.32
sub-total	£37,845.18

The Plaintiff would give credit for

[1] 25% of £37,456.11 in respect of notional tax and National Insurance	£(9,364.03)

[2] Benefits as above   £(11,301.95)

       subtotal of deductions   £(20,665.98)

           nett total   **£17,179.20**

INTEREST ON HISTORIC LOSSES

13 The total of historic loss, including expenditure and lost earnings, is £77,964.46. Interest at half the special account rate from (for convenience) 1.vi.87 to 31.vii.94 is 40.23%. Thus the interest due on the claim is   £31,365.10

14 In the light of *Hunt v Severs* [1993] QB 815 and [1994] 2 WLR 602, the Plaintiff submits:

 (a) there should be a discount rate of 4%, reflecting the current and predicted financial climate

 (b) life expectancy is thought to be normal or very nearly normal in the case, and is likely to be extended by improved medical techniques. The average expectation of life for a boy of the Plaintiff's age is not less than 66.81, which on a 4% return on capital, would require a multiplier of 23.15 (see consolidated compound table Annex 2). Allowing for a reduction in that multiplier to reflect the contingencies of life, but adopting actuarial figures as a check, the Plaintiff submits that the proper full-life multiplier for future loss is 21 years.

 (c) recurring replacement costs should be calculated by reference to the 4% present value table and the extrapolation from that table annexed hereto marked Annex 3 in which initial purchases are omitted and cumulative multipliers are in bold type.

 (d) a 4% discount factor should be employed in computing the cost of extra requirements for accommodation.

 (e) the overall judicial multiplier for future cost and loss is apportioned with the 4% actuarial figures as a reference point. The multipliers are thus:

present to age 10 [26.v.97] 2.5

age 10 to 14 [26.v.2001] 3.0

age 14 to 16 [26.v.2003] 1.25

age 16 to 19 [26.v.2006] 1.75

             SUB-TOTAL   8.5

19 onwards   12.5

full life   21.0

FUTURE CARE

15 Carers as set out in the report of Mrs Rambert

until age 19 – 8.5 x £20,577.71   £174,910.53

School worker – 8.5 x £9,146.64   £77,746.44

Parental care:

present to 10 years – 2.5 x £677.63   £1,694.08

10 years to 14 years – 3.0 x £1680.52	£5,041.56
14 years to 16 years – 1.25 x £3,903.13	£4,878.91
16 years to 19 years – 1.75 x £3,903.13	£6,830.48
Professional care from 19 on:	
12.5 x £46,702.11	£583,776.37
Total future care cost	£854,878.37

Please note: It is intended that much of this care may be given by carers who are also trained in giving conductive education, but this will not alter the costs.

16 THERAPY COSTS

A **Occupational therapy**
The report of Mrs Rambert of February 1994 refers at paragraph 5.2.6.

present until age 9 – £900.00 x 1.75	£1,575.00
age 9 until age 14 – £500.00 x 3.75	£1,875.00
age 14 for life – £300.00 x 14.5	£4,350.00
sub-total	£7,800.00

B **Speech therapy**
The report of Nellie Melba refers.

initial programme	£713.00
present until 19 – £279 x 12 x 8.5	£28,458.00
adult life – £248 x 12.5	£3,100.00
sub-total	£32,271.00

C **Physiotherapy**
The report of Lucia Popp refers.

present until 12 – £600 x 4	£2,400.00
12 until 19 – £420 x 4.5	£1,890.00
as an adult – £420 x 12.5	£5,250.00
sub-total	£9,540.00
Total therapy costs	£49,611.00

AIDS AND APPLIANCES

17 See the reports of Mrs Rambert, Maria Callas, Nellie Melba and Lucia Popp, summarised at Annex 4 hereto. The total aids and appliances cost claimed is **£93,904.00**

TRANSPORT

18 The report of Mrs Rambert refers.

Volkswagen Caravelle until circa age 20	
£3,439.50 x 9	£30,957.00
Volkswagen Caravelle from circa age 20	
less credit for ordinary car	
£1708.50 x 12	£20,502.00
sub-total	£51,459.00

Credit will be given for the mobility

allowance element in disabled living allowance
£31.40 x 52 x 21   −(34,288.80)
                                            Total   £17,170.20

ACCOMMODATION

19 See the reports from Mr F Lloyd Wright and Capability Brown and
Co, and the note from Messrs Conveyancing Solicitors & Co
[1] Alterations   £61,570.81
    less increased value   £12,500.00
              sub-total   £49,070.81
[2] Hydrotherapy pool £54,700.00 plus VAT at 17.5%
    (£9,572.50)   £64,272.50
[3] Additional expenditure on purchase   £4,600.71
[4] Additional maintenance cost (see Lloyd Wright
    p10) £1,088.45 pa − £800.37 pa = £288.08 pa
    £288.08 x 21 =   £6,049.68
[5] Additional insurance cost (Lloyd Wright p11)
    £136.55 x 21 =   £2,867.55
[6] Conveyancing fees on purchase of house
    for £275,000, say   £1,000.00
[7] Stamp duty on purchase   £302.50
[8] Land registry fees   £350.00
[9] Price of new house less proceeds of old
    £302,500 − £90,000 = £212,500
    £212,500 x 4% x 21 =   £178,500.00
              Total accommodation costs   £307,013.75

PLAINTIFF'S FUTURE LOSS OF EARNINGS

20 The report of Messrs Lumberjack refers. The Plaintiff's family, both
maternal and paternal, demonstrates considerable advance in educational achievement in his parents' generation over the previous
generation, and it is likely that the same tendency will be repeated in
his generation within the family. He is likely to have graduated and
taken up a successful professional career of some kind.

The Plaintiff is unemployable. Uninjured, the probability is that
his income would have been:
[1] from 22 to 24 would have been £11,954 gross, and £8,965.50
    nett
[2] from 24 to 26 would have been £16,632 gross and £12,474 nett
[3] from 26 to 31 would have been £22,357 gross and £16,767.75
    nett
[4] from 31 to 39 would have been £28,933 gross and £21,699.75
    nett
[5] from 39 to 65 would have been £44,480 gross and £29,356.80
    nett
The Plaintiff submits that the overall multiplier for the period

from 22 to retirement should be 11.5. This should be apportioned as follows:

[1] 1.09 [2] 1.01 [3] 2.12 [4] 2.73 [5] 4.55

The calculation for the apportionment of these multipliers is set out in a separate sub-schedule served herewith as Annex 5. The future losses of earnings are thus:

[1] £8,965.50 x 1.09 = £9,772.83
[2] £12,474.00 x 1.01 = £12,598.74
[3] £16,767.75 x 2.12 = £35,547.63
[4] £21,699.75 x 2.73 = £59,240.32
[5] £29,356.80 x 4.55 = £133,573.44
Total = £250,732.96   say £250,000.00

FUTURE LOSS OF EARNINGS – MRS SMITH

21   The report of Messrs Lumberjack refers. If Mrs Smith returns to work in the year 1994/5, her annual gross earnings is likely to be (£18,179 + £18,487) ÷ 2 = £18,333. (See Lumberjack paragraph 3.0). Her salary would have been in the region of £23,569, a gross loss of £5,236. Deducting 30% for tax and National Insurance, there is an annual nett loss of £3,665.20. If she re-enters work as a salaried pharmacist, she will never be likely to regain the level of salary she would have commanded without a long career break. In addition, the figures above do not reflect the loss of setting up a pharmacy or group of pharmacies, which Mr and Mrs Smith would own and for which Mrs Smith would be the responsible professional.

Mrs Smith is now 36 years of age. The Plaintiff adopts the arguments set out in paragraph 12 as to the appropriateness of assuming a 4% return on money, and as to its effects on the proper multiplier for the purposes of this action. The 4% replacement cost to be found in Annex 3 over the 23 years remaining in Mrs Smith's working life is 14.857. The Plaintiff submits that the proper multiplier for Mrs Smith's loss of earnings is 12.5.

The Plaintiff submits that the multiplicand should reflect the loss of income which would have been derived from setting up a business. Thus a multiplicand of £5,000.00 is put forward as reasonable. The claim under this head is for   £62,500.00

EXTRA COSTS

22   The report of Mrs Rambert refers.

Extra laundry cost	£445.88 x 21 = £9,363.48
Extra heating cost	£365.00 x 21 = £7,665.00
Extra telephone cost	£100.00 x 21 = £2,100.00
Extra holiday cost	£1,680.00 x 21 = £35,280.00
	total £54,408.48

COURT OF PROTECTION CHARGES
23 An award in the sum claimed will attract charges from the Court of
    Protection as follows:

Fixed costs for the first year	(£257.00 plus VAT)	£301.98
Commencement fee		£50.00
Transaction fee on conveyance:		
0.25% of purchase price of house		£687.50
Administration fee:		
£850 x 21		£17,850
5% of clear income exceeding		
£15,000 pa: £1,750 x 21		£36,750
	Total	£55,639.48

SUMMARY OF CLAIM

General damages	£130,000.00
Interest on general damages	£3,055.00
Past expenditure	£15,986.41
Past loss of earnings	£61,978.05
Interest on historic loss	£31,365.10
Future care cost	£854,878.37
Therapy cost	£49,611.00
Aids and appliances	£93,904.00
Transport	£17,170.20
Accommodation cost	£307,013.75
Plaintiff's loss of earnings	£250,000.00
Mrs Smith's loss of earnings	£62,500.00
Miscellaneous extra cost	£54,408.48
Court of Protection charges	£55,639.48
Total	**£1,987,509.60**

KNOX COVENANTER

Counsel for the Plaintiff

Calculation of apportionment of multiplier for future loss

IN THE HIGH COURT OF JUSTICE   1993 B No
QUEENS BENCH DIVISION
BETWEEN:

GARY SMITH
(an infant suing by his father and
Next Friend MR FREDERICK SMITH)   Plaintiff

– and –

BARCHESTER HEALTH AUTHORITY   Defendant

ANNEX 5   CALCULATION OF APPORTIONMENT OF
MULTIPLIER FOR FUTURE LOSS OF EARNINGS

Period	Mean year	4% figure	Value of period
[1] 2 years (2)	1	0.962	1.924
[2] 2 years (4)	3	0.889	1.778
[3] 5 years (9)	7.5	0.746	3.730
[4] 8 years (17)	13	0.601	4.808
[5] 26 years (43)	30	0.308	8.008
			Total 20.248

SPLIT OF MULTIPLIER

[1] [11.5 ÷ 20.248] =0.5679 x 1.924 = 1.09
[2]   0.5679 x 1.778 = 1.01
[3]   0.5679 x 3.730 = 2.12
[4]   0.5679 x 4.808 = 2.73
[5]   0.5679 x 8.008 = 4.55

Schedule of financial loss

IN THE HIGH COURT OF JUSTICE   1990 –B
QUEEN'S BENCH DIVISION
BETWEEN

JANE GREEN   Plaintiff

– and –

BARCHESTER HEALTH AUTHORITY   Defendant

SCHEDULE OF FINANCIAL LOSS

PREAMBLE

The Plaintiff will be 28 at the time of trial. She is a married woman with two children aged 6 and 8. At the time of her admission to hospital she was working part-time as a clerk. This work enabled her to take her children to school and to collect them at the end of the school day.

As a consequence of the Defendant's negligence the Plaintiff's admission to hospital lasted 8 days instead of the anticipated 2 days. On her discharge from hospital she required almost total bed rest for the first fortnight and was unable to take part in any household activities. A consequence of this was that a considerable burden of care fell upon her husband. A child-minder had to be employed to take her children to school, collect them at the end of the day and look after them until the Plaintiff's husband could collect them on his return from work. This arrangement was necessary for a total of 7 weeks including the additional unplanned period in hospital.

During the first fortnight of the Plaintiff's convalescence her husband took two weeks off work in order to look after his wife. He had previously planned only to take the day of her discharge off work.   327

Although the Plaintiff works as a clerk, a considerable amount of her work involves lifting heavy boxes of stationary. As a consequence of the negligently caused injury she was unable to lift any weights (including shopping) for three months and for the following three months found carrying and lifting difficult. She was, therefore, not fit enough to return to work until four months after her discharge from hospital.

As a consequence of the negligence the Plaintiff has a unsightly scar which requires plastic surgery.

Past expenditure

Taxi fares attributable to the Plaintiff's inability to drive for the first six weeks after her discharge from hospital estimated at £5.00 per week for six weeks		£30.00
Additional food costs due to the need to purchase convenience food because of the Plaintiff's inability to prepare the family meals estimated at an average of £20.00 per week for 6 weeks		£120.00
Additional laundry costs attributable to the need for frequent washing of the Plaintiff's nightdresses and bed linen due to the surgical wound weeping for the first fortnight after her discharge home, estimated at £5.00 per week for two weeks		£10.00

Additional clothing purchased as a consequence of the lengthy stay in hospital and lengthy period of bed rest and the need for loose clothing due to the Plaintiff's scarring:

4 nightdresses at £21.99 each	£87.96	
2 track suits at £39.99 each	<u>79.98</u>	£167.94

Additional expenditure on newspapers, magazines and books at an estimated £7.50 per week for 12 weeks		£90.00
Child minder fees at £3.50 per hour for 4 hours per day, 5 days per week for 6 weeks − £3.50 × 120 hrs		£420.00

Plaintiff's loss of earnings

The Plaintiff's net income after tax was £120.00 per week. During the first

4 weeks of her absence from work she was
paid full pay. For the next 4 weeks she
received half pay and thereafter she
received no pay at all. Thus her loss of
earnings was £120.00 per week × 20 weeks =
£2,400 less £720.00 sick pay. Net loss =   £1,680.00

Plaintiff's husband's loss of earnings due
to having to take two weeks' holiday   £420.00

Plaintiff's husband's travelling expenses
to hospital at £1.60 per day for 8 days   £12.80
                    Total past loss and expenditure   £2,950.74

Interest on special damages   to be calculated

Future losses and expenses
The Plaintiff will have to undergo
plastic surgery on her scar. This will
be done privately. The costs associated
with the private admission including the
surgeon and anaesthetist's fees will
be   £4,000.00

During the admission to hospital and
during the anticipated 10 day admission
to hospital the Plaintiff will require
child care support from a child minder.
She will require 5 hours per day for the
5 day admission to hospital and thereafter
4 hours per day for the anticipated 10 day
convalescent period. It is anticipated,
therefore, that future child care costs
will be £3.50 per hr × 65 hrs =   £227.50

Psychotherapy/counselling: 52 sessions
at £75.00 per session   £3,900.00

                    Anticipated total future expenditure £8,127.50

Served by Messrs_____, Solicitors for the Plaintiff

Practice Direction (Structured Settlements)

[1992] 1 All ER 862, QBD

Damages – Personal injury – Structured settlement – Approval of court – Procedure – Listing of applications – Documents to be lodged – Transfer of Admiralty and Commercial Registry matters to Central Office – Plaintiff under mental disability.

1. This practice note applies not only to proceedings in the Central Office and the Admiralty and Commercial Registry of the High Court. It concerns settlements of claims in respect of personal injury or death where approval of the court is required and which include a structured element. The practice set out below, adapted as indicated, is appropriate whether or not the Court of Protection is involved. It will apply, on an experimental basis, until further notice. If the plaintiff is under mental disability then the additional steps set out in paras 6(viii) and 8 of this practice note should be taken.

2. By this practice note it is intended to establish a practice to overcome the present administrative difficulty caused by the short period over which life offices keep open offers of annuities at a given price. It has proved difficult for plaintiff's solicitors to do all that is necessary to obtain the approval of the court within the period during which the annuity offer remains open.

3. As from 30 March 1992 all applications for approval in structured settlement cases will be listed for hearing on Friday mornings during term time.

4. After setting down, applications for the fixing of dates for these purposes should be made to the Clerk of the Lists in room 547.

5. Once a hearing date has been obtained, documents should be lodged in room 547 not later than noon on the Thursday immediately before the Friday for which the hearing is fixed.

6. The following are the classes of document which should be lodged in accordance with para 5 above: (i) copies of originating process or pleadings, if any; (ii) an opinion of counsel assessing the value of the claim on a conventional basis (unless approval has already been given) and, if practicable, the opinion of counsel on the structured settlement

proposed; (iii) a report of forensic accountants setting out the advantages and disadvantages, if any, of structuring bearing in mind the plaintiff's life expectancy and the anticipated costs of future care; (iv) a draft of the proposed agreement as approved by the Inland Revenue (and by the Treasury where the defendant or other paying party is a health authority); (v) sufficient material to satisfy the court that enough capital is available free of the structure to meet anticipated future capital needs. Particular reference to accommodation and transport needs will usually be helpful in this context; (vi) sufficient material to satisfy the court that the structure is secure and backed by responsible insurers; (vii) evidence of other assets available to the plaintiff beyond the award the subject of the application; (viii) in cases where the plaintiff is under mental disability the consent of the Court of Protection.

The classes of document required to be lodged should be separately bundled and clearly marked so that the presence of the appropriate classes of document (but not the adequacy of their content) may be checked by the clerks in room 547.

7. If the proceedings are in the Admiralty and Commercial Registry application should be made to the Admiralty Registrar in good time for the transfer of the proceedings to the Central Office for the purpose of the application for approval only.

8. In cases where the plaintiff is under mental disability, the documents set out in para 6(i) to (vii) (inclusive) should be lodged in the Enquiries and Acceptances Branch of the Public Trust Office, Stewart House, 24 Kingsway, London WC2B 6JH not later than noon on the Monday immediately before the Friday for which the hearing is fixed. Unless an application has already been made for the appointment of a receiver, there must also be lodged an application for the appointment of a receiver (form CP1) (in duplicate), a certificate of family and property (form CP5) and a medical certificate (form CP3). (Blank forms are available from the same address.) The Court of Protection's approval, if granted, will be available by 10.30am on the Thursday immediately before the Friday fixed for the hearing.

9. This practice note is issued with the approval of the Deputy Chief Justice, the judge in charge of the non-jury list, the Admiralty Judge and the Master of the Court of Protection.

KEITH TOPLEY
Senior Master,
Queen's Bench Division.

12 February 1992

APPENDIX 10
Structure adjournment order

Dated the   day of   199
IN THE HIGH COURT OF JUSTICE
QUEEN'S BENCH DIVISION
Before the Honourable Mr Justice Bullingham
BETWEEN:

ANN SMALL
(an infant suing by her mother and
Next Friend MARY SMALL)   Plaintiff

– and –

BARCHESTER HEALTH AUTHORITY   Defendant

UPON HEARING Mrs Jane Jones one of Her Majesty's Counsel and Mr J. Blue of Counsel on behalf of the Plaintiff and Mr B. Knight one of Her Majesty's Counsel on behalf of the Defendants;

AND UPON the Defendants having by Counsel made an Undertaking to keep open an offer of the sum of £1,100,000.00 (One Million One Hundred Thousand Pounds) in full and final settlement of the Plaintiff's claim herein and agreeing to pay interest from the date hereof at the Judgement rate from time to time on costs and at the Special Account rate from time to time on any lump sum hereafter ordered to be paid, interest accruing on the sums in court on the Special Investment Account to be credited against this obligation.

AND UPON the Plaintiff's solicitors undertaking to notify the Defendant's solicitors not less than seven days before instructing any accountant or actuary to advise upon a Structured Settlement;

AND UPON the Plaintiff and the Defendants having agreed to the terms set forth in the orders hereinafter and approved by the Court:

BY CONSENT

IT IS ORDERED that this action do stand adjourned to a date to be fixed in the absence of the agreement of both parties for further directions to include a provision for costs relating to implementation of this Order and any proposal for a Structured Settlement.

IT IS FURTHER ORDERED that of the sum of £950,000 (Nine Hundred and fifty Thousand Pounds) now in Court standing to the credit of this action the sum of £20,000.00 (Twenty Thousand Pounds) be paid out forthwith to the Plaintiff's solicitors for the benefit of the Plaintiff.

IT IS FURTHER ORDERED that the Defendants do within 7 days of the date hereof pay the sum of £150,000.00 (One Hundred and Fifty Thousand Pounds) into Court the said sum of £150,000.00 (One Hundred and Fifty Thousand Pounds) be placed together with the sum of £930,000.00 (Nine Hundred and Thirty Thousand Pounds) being the balance of the monies remaining in Court and the total sum being £1,080,000.00 (One Million And Eighty Thousand Pounds) (bearing a first charge under section 16(6) of the Legal Aid Act 1988) to be transferred to a Special Investment Account to be invested and accumulated with interest to accrue thereon to the credit of the Minor Ann Small pending further order.

IT IS FURTHER ORDERED that any interest accrued on the total sums in Court up to the date hereof be paid out to the Defendants' solicitor.

IT IS FURTHER ORDERED that the Defendants do pay to the Plaintiff's solicitors their costs to the date hereof to be taxed forthwith if not agreed, the Plaintiff's solicitors waiving entitlement to any further costs.

IT IS FURTHER ORDERED that the costs of the Plaintiff be taxed in accordance with Regulation 107 of the Civil Legal Aid (General) Regulations 1989.

AND IT IS FURTHER ORDERED that the parties be at liberty to apply generally.

Letter of instruction to forensic accountant

Dear Mr Accountant,

Ann Small

I write further to our telephone conversation when you confirmed that you could advise on the relative merits of a structured settlement as against a lump sum and your letter estimating your fees for doing so.

We have now been granted authority by the Legal Aid Board to obtain a forensic accountant's report on the merits of a structured settlement to include a conference with leading and/or junior counsel at a fee not exceeding £6,000.00 plus VAT and expenses.

I would now like to instruct your firm to advise us in this case. To enable you to do so I am enclosing a file containing the following documents:

Documents

1. Schedule of loss served on behalf of Ann
2. Report on care and equipment needs
3. Reports on physiotherapy and speech therapy needs
4. Report of clinical psychologist
5. Report of on computer and technology needs
6. Report of architect on housing needs
7. Report of employment expert on Ann and her parents' loss of earnings claims
8. Report of paediatric neurologist
9. Order
10. Leading counsel's analysis of the settlement on a lump sum basis
11. Copy guidelines on investment from Court of Protection.

Background
As I have explained, I act for this little girl who has cerebral palsy as a consequence of the negligent management of her mother's antenatal and obstetric care.

Last month Mr Justice X indicated that if he was asked to approve a lump sum award he would approve an award in the sum of £1.1 million which was the amount offered in settlemen⸗ of the claim and paid into court by the Defendants.

The case has now been adjourned to enable us to investigate whether it would benefit my client for her award to be structured rather than to be paid in the form of a lump sum settlement.

Ann lives in North London with her parents. She suffers from athetoid cerebral palsy. What this means is that she is severely physically disabled. She is able to walk around her home with some difficulty. Outside the house her mobility is wheelchair-based. She is an intelligent little girl and it is hoped she will move into mainstream secondary school and will then go on to some form of tertiary education.

As a consequence of her cerebral palsy Ann is unable to speak. She, therefore, has to communicate through a computerised touch talker. Although she is unlikely ever to be able to find employment to support herself financially, it is probable that she will rapidly become frustrated and depressed if, in adulthood, she is placed in the sort of day centres that are available for people with disabilities such as her own. For these reasons, her parents anticipate that in her adulthood she may well wish to use some of her compensation to enable her to set up some sort of non-profit-making organisation.

Because of Ann's level of intelligence her affairs will never come under the jurisdiction of the Court of Protection. Thus, during her minority any capital award will have to be administered by a trust. At the age of 21 she will then be entitled to manage her own affairs.

It has been agreed with the defendants that we will instruct accountants to advise whether or not structuring the award will be more beneficial to Ann than if she receives her compensation by way of a lump sum and, if so, what structure offer would have to be made to ensure that the structure is more beneficial.

Structured settlement

Since the defendants in this case are a health authority, any structured settlement is likely to be self-funded.

As already indicated, Ann's award will be adminstered by a trust rather than by the Court of Protection because she is intellectually unimpaired.

Clearly, if this award is to be structured we need to look at whether it is possible to find a form of structure which will both ensure that Ann's annual care and equipment needs can be met and that there is sufficient flexibility to ensure that any unexpected contingencies can be covered and/or the potential that Ann's desire to have some control over her financial affairs in her adulthood can be facilitated.

It is clearly going to be important to ensure that any structure maximises the general benefits of a structure, namely:

a) the fact that it will continue to pay for as long as the individual lives; and
b) the tax break.

With these points in mind I highlight below particular points to be considered and/or on which we require your advice.

Discount
What justification is there for *any* discount?

Guarantee period
As Ann is currently so healthy, I think that we should assume no guarantee period for the structure.

Annual needs
In considering what annual payments would be required to cover Ann's needs, reference obviously needs to be made both to the plaintiff's schedule and reports served in support of the Schedule and the analysis of the settlement.

Comparison of structure against lump sum

In relation to a lump sum award

1. What will be the net first year return on the award?
2. Assuming life expectancies of 58, 68 and 78 years what identical sum per annum would be required over the years to exhaust the capital in each of 58, 68 and 78 years?
3. When will the lump sum be exhausted if the care and equipment needs are as envisaged in the plaintiff's schedule?
4. When will the lump sum be exhausted if the care and equipment needs are as envisaged in the analysis of the settlement?
5. How will the answers to 1 – 4 be changed by £100,000 of the award being used in one block by Ann when she is aged 22 or when she is aged 30?
6. It has been said that care costs rise by 2% per annum over RPI. How would such an assumption affect the answers to the previous questions?
7. What difference would be made by direct tax increases to say 27% and 40%?

8. How much below the established multiplicands can actually be saved in the early years?

In relation to a structured settlement

1. Assuming the care and equipment needs are as envisaged in the plaintiff's schedule:
   a) what periodic payments will have to be made under a structure to provide for these?
   b) how much would the contingency element be?
   c) how much net income would be generated from a contingency fund of this size?
   d) assuming life expectancies of 58, 68 and 78 years, what identical additional sum per annum would be required to exhaust the contingency fund?
2. Assuming the care and equipment needs are as envisaged in the analysis of the settlement:
   a) what periodic payments will have to be made under a structure to provide for these?
   b) how much would the contingency element be?
   c) how much net income would be generated from a contingency fund of this size?
   d) assuming life expectancies of 58, 68 and 78 years, what identical additional sum per annum would be required to exhaust the contingency fund?
3. Assuming the need to ensure maximum flexibility for the future by increasing the contingency element by £100,000 in each of the examples above, how will the answers to 1(a)–(d) and 2(a)–(d) be changed?
4. It has been said that care costs rise by 2% per annum over RPI. How would such an assumption affect the answers to the previous questions?
5. What difference would be made by direct tax increases to (say) 27% and 40%?
6. How much below the established multiplicands can actually be saved in the early years?

In advising on the net return on the lump sum and contingency fund, please bear in mind the current investment advice from the Court of Protection and, in particular, please illustrate the effect of investments in the following splits: 70% equity/30% gilts; and 100% gilts. If other investment splits are considered, please indicate why these might be appropriate.

Please let me know if you consider that for your advice to be based on the most realistic assessment of this particular Plaintiff's needs and likely long term plans it is essential for there to be a meeting between a representative of your firm and her parents.

If you have any queries arising out of the contents of this letter, please do not hesitate to contact me.

Yours sincerely

A Solicitor

APPENDIX 12
Health circulars

A. Insurance arrangements from April 1991 (EL(90) 195)
B. Clinical negligence funding scheme (EL(91) 19)
C. Medical negligence claims against NHS hospital medical staff (HC(89) 34)

A. **Department of Health Guidance (Ref EL(90) 195)**

INSURANCE ARRANGEMENTS FROM APRIL 1991

1. The general principle to be applied to insurance is that the public sector should generally carry its own risks unless greater value for money is obtained by alternative arrangements. Authorities should not enter into commercial insurance arrangements in respect of any of their insurable risks unless Departmental approval has been granted (and this requires Treasury agreement). At present approval has been given only for income generation activities and for a very limited number of specific schemes for the business use of Crown Cars. This letter gives a more general approval in respect of NHS Trusts; and sets out the arrangements to be used for certain specific risks, in particular clinical negligence.

NHS Trusts

2. NHS Trusts will not be able to spread all risks widely in the way that health authorities can. Furthermore their funding arrangements differ significantly from those of other NHS bodies. NHS Trusts will therefore be free to make insurance arrangements which they consider to be cost effective for most risks. This is expected to be a combination of self-insurance and commercial insurance. Guidance on some specific risks is given below, and further guidance will be issued as appropriate.

3. Trusts will not bear the costs of meeting any claim relating to events prior to the date that they are operational, even if that date is after 31 March 1991. These will be met by Regional Health Authorities and handled as the Regional Health Authority considers appropriate.

Clinical Negligence Losses for Acts performed before 1 April 1991

4. Losses arising out of pre-April 1991 clinical negligence claims should be met by health authorities as at present. Most Regional Health Authorities have already established financial arrangements for dealing with such losses. Access to the reserve established from existing medical defence organisation funds (as set out in HC(89) 34/HC(FP) (89)22 and Appendix 4 of EL(89)P208) will be restricted to pre-April 1991 clinical negligence.

Clinical Negligence Losses for Acts Performed from 1 April 1991

5. Thereafter, for losses arising out of clinical negligence, common principles will apply to both NHS Trusts and directly managed units so that the costs are borne by the units concerned and reflected in their costs for the purposes of financial reporting and pricing. In respect of losses arising from negligent (or alleged negligent) acts performed after 31 March 1991 (other than those dealt with in paragraph 3):

a. units will have to bear in the year of cash settlement the costs of any claims arising up to a specified amount;

b. costs in excess of the amount in (a) will be borne by the unit through an advance which will be repaid, together with an amount equal to interest, by the unit concerned over a period of years. In the case of directly managed units this will take the form of a cash limit addition made by the Regional Health Authority to the appropriate District Health Authority; no additional funding will be available to Regions to cover these adjustments. For NHS Trusts the sums will be advanced by the Secretary of State within External Financing Limits; and

c. the accounting cost to be recognised by units, including NHS Trusts, in any one year will be equal to the sum of amounts borne under (a) and the amounts plus interest repaid under (b).

The details of this scheme are being developed by a working group convened by the NHS Management Executive Finance Directorate. Further guidance will be issued.

6. These arrangements are unlikely to have a significant immediate financial impact on units. Litigation in respect of clinical negligence typically takes several years to settle and alleged negligent acts arising after 31 March 1991 are unlikely to result in significant financial cost before 1993/94. The scheme will be kept under review and will be modified as appropriate in the light of experience of clinical negligence claims settlement.

Business interrruption

7. For their non-NHS business, NHS Trusts will be free to take out business interruption insurance if they wish to do so. For NHS work, it would not be appropriate for either NHS Trusts or DMUs to take commercial insurance. The postion should rather be covered by contract arrangements, and by local cooperation in the event of any major incident.

8. When an incident occurs which causes all or part of a provider unit to cease operating, it is unlikely that the unit will be able to continue to fully meet all its obligations under its contract(s), in particular for block contracts and cost-and-volume contracts with significant minimum volumes specified. In such cases there will need to be urgent discussion between the provider unit and their purchasing authorities, with a view to establishing

    a. the immediate arrangements to provide for patients who would have been treated in the facilities not in use, and whether adjustment of contracts for facilities (and local priorities) is needed;

    b. the longer term position – over what time period the unit can be made fully operational; whether significant capital spending is required and, if so, whether and where proposals for reprovision should be made;

    c. the interim financial arrangements to be made. It would generally be appropriate for purchasing authorities, where a significant NHS provider unit is seriously affected, to ensure that the essential costs of the provider can continue to be met until normal services resume (or for long enough to ensure an orderly run down if this is the decision). This will be a natural and proper call on their resources, along with the costs of providing services elsewhere.

Discussions on contracts will need to reflect this approach. However, DHAs and providers should not make excessive provision against the possibility of business interruption; the emphasis, as above, is on the need for the NHS to co-operate to minimise damage to patient care in the event of any event causing significant loss of facilities.

Third Party Liability

9. Significant third party liability claims will be rare. One particular case which may arise is product liability claims, in particular where a unit is manufacturing or processing pharmaceuticals. NHS Trusts may insure for third party risks if they wish to do so. DMUs will be required to pay these claims as they arise.

Pooling arrangements

10. Many RHAs at present have some form of pooling arrangement within their Region to spread the cost of larger claims falling on an individual DHA. In the past these have principally been medical negligence claims, which will now be handled through the arrangements for

advances described above (paragraph 6). For the future, all Regions will need to review these arrangements, but may want to continue some pooling or other arrangements so that individual units do not face unrealistically high demands in any one year from any sort of eventuality.

11. Ministers have taken powers in Section 21 of the National Health Service and Community Care Act 1990 to operate a scheme for meeting all classes of liability falling on health authorities and NHS Trusts. The NHS Management Executive will consider the desirability of implementation of such a scheme at a later stage.

B. **Department of Health Guidance (Ref EL(91) 195)**

CLINICAL NEGLIGENCE FUNDING SCHEME

1. In EL(90) 195 dated 2 October 1990 the basic principles of a scheme to assist DMUs and Trusts with the costs of future clinical negligence claims were outlined, and a working group established to consider the details of such a scheme. The note attached to this letter sets out the detailed arrangements arising from the work of the group. Regional Directors of Finance have been consulted.

2. The schme will operate to cover all cases of clinical negligence arising from incidents which occur from 1 April 1991.

3. Enquiries should be addressed to: Mr M D Horah, Room 638, Friars House, 157–168 Blackfriars Road, London SE1 8EU, telephone 071–972 3024.

Clinical Negligence Funding Scheme

1. This note sets out the details of a funding scheme to apply to payments in respect of claims for clinical negligence.

2. From 1 April 1991 all *new* claims for clinical negligence (as defined in paragraph 2 below) will be met within the framework of the scheme described here. For the purpose of this scheme a new claim is one which relates to clinical negligence committed on or after 1 April 1991. (Clinical negligence committed prior to then remains the responsibility of health authorities under existing arrangements.) The scheme does not include Special Health Authorities who have different arrangements.

Definition of Clinical Negligence

3. For the purposes of this scheme *clinical* negligence is defined as follows:

'Clinical negligence is a breach of a duty of care by members of the health care professions (including medical and dental practitioners, nurses and midwives, professions allied to medicine, ambulance personnel, laboratory staff and relevant technicians) or by others consequent on decisions or judgements made by members of those professions acting in their professional capacity on relevant work, and which are admitted as negligent by the employer or are determined as such through the legal process.'

In this, 'breach of a duty of care' has its legal meaning: health authorities will need to take legal advice in individual cases, but the general position will be that the following must all apply before liability for negligence exists:

a) There must have been a duty of care owed to the patient by the relevant professional(s);

b) The standard of care appropriate to such duty must not have been attained and therefore the duty breached, whether by action or inaction, advice given or failure to advise;

c) Such a breach must be demonstrated to have caused the injury and therefore the resulting loss complained about by the patient;

d) Any loss sustained as a result of the injury and complained about by the patient must be of a kind that the Courts recognise and allow compensation for; and

e) The injury and resulting loss complained about by the patient must have been reasonably foreseeable.

Liability for Clinical Negligence

4. From 1 April 1991 NHS Trusts will be liable for acts of clinical negligence by their staff legally and financially. Health Authorities will continue to be liable for acts of clinical negligence by staff in DMUs, but the financial consequences will be met by DMUs through the operation of the scheme described below. It will remain necessary for appropriate apportionment to be determined between DMUs and Trusts where more than one NHS employer is involved and with the MDOs for GPs, and to ensure that the NHS Indemnity and the financial cover provided through this scheme is only given to NHS staff in the course of their NHS employment.

Basic Principles

5. The basic principles of the scheme are that units both Trusts and DMUs should bear the costs of clinical negligence, reflecting those costs in their financial accounts and in prices. Assistance to spread the costs of clinical negligence is provided in the form of repayable advances for DMUs from their Regional Health Authority via the District Health Authority; and, for Trusts, loans from the Secretary of State within External Financing Limits. Advances and loans are subject to interest. In setting prices, it should be the aim that costs arising from this scheme should as far as is feasible be borne in the prices of the relevant clinical activity and not treated as a general overhead.

Structure of the Scheme

6. All units, whether Trusts or DMUs, will be able to obtain a repayable advance or loan for aggregate 'new' payments made in respect of clinical negligence in a given year, in excess of half of one percent of the unit's forecast revenue income for that year. This will be known as the 'percentage threshold'. Expenditure that qualifies for triggering the percentage threshold and for advances excludes repayments of past advances but includes damages, plaintiffs' legal costs and fees, defence legal costs and fees, and any other costs incurred by HAs attributable to clinical negligence on behalf of units and thus recharged to the unit (see paragraph 11 below). For Trusts, loans will be within their EFL agreed with the DoH before the start of the financial year. Trusts should be

able to predict the incidence of major claims allowing them to plan in advance and bid for any loans required to meet them.

7. In practice, for DMUs, the DHA (or RHA) will pay the costs and damages in a case and will be recharging the unit(s) concerned the relevant costs. DHAs should of course discuss the case with the unit before payment is made, so that the unit is aware of the recharge. A loan will be available if a payment places the unit over their percentage threshold or if their threshold has already been exceeded. Relatively small cash excesses over this threshold can be excluded on de minimis grounds. Trusts will need to pay damages and costs directly and obtain loans when their percentage threshold has been triggered.

Type of Loan

8. For Trusts, loans from the Department for this purpose will be handled in the same way as other loans within the EFL. They will normally be of the annual repayment type, which will be repayable on a fixed repayment basis and with fixed rates of interest, payable half yearly. As with other loans under EFL multiples of £100K will be used and interest will be payable six months from when the loan is taken. Advances to DMUs will be repayable in annual instalments, and will be at a common rate of interest fixed at the end of the financial year during which advances were obtained. This rate will be set by the Department and will be the rate of interest, set by Treasury, that would apply to a Trust taking a loan at that time for the relevent period of repayment (the rate of interest varies with the period of repayment). This rate will be applied to the aggregate of advances made for that year. For Trusts the rate of interest will be as determined under the EFL arrangements.

Period of Repayment

9. The repayment periods vary according to the size of the loan:

Size of Loan or Advance	Repayment Period
£100,000 or less	1 year
£100,001–£300,000	1–3 years
£300,001–£500,000	3–5 years
£500,001–£700,000	5–7 years
£700,001–£900,000	7–9 years
£900,001 or more	10 years

Trusts and DMUs may, with the agreement of the DHA/Department, opt for the shorter repayment periods above, which will be kept under review.

348 *Appendices*

Determination of Clinical Negligence Costs

10. In many cases the total cost of a successful claim cannot be determined until after the settlement or court judgement. In most cases the plaintiff's legal costs are not settled until some time after damages have been paid, as are defence costs. These separate costs may have to be treated as new advances, possibly subject to different terms for example if the payments straddle different financial years. A successful claim should not be excluded from the calculation of aggregate expenditure pending agreement on costs if damages have actually been paid. Payments into court should fall outside the loans scheme until they are drawn on to meet awards or legal costs when a claim is finalised. Interim payments may qualify.

11. For the purpose of assessing the quantum of costs and damages, other costs incurred by Health Authorities i.e. internal legal advisers and administration, should be included unless separate arrangements have been made for their reimbursement, for example fixed price retainer contacts for HA legal services covering a variety of legal liabilities and services. 'Structured settlements', where an annual payment is made to a plaintiff rather than a capital sum, may become more common in future and annual payments after the year in which the arrangement is set up should be excluded from these arrangements.

NHS Management Executive
Finance Directorate A2

February 1991

C. HEALTH CIRCULAR HC(89)34
HC(FP)(89)22

DEPARTMENT OF HEALTH

To:
Regional Health Authorities
District Health Authorities
Special Health Authorities

Family Practitioner Committees
Community Health Councils } for information

December 1989

CLAIMS OF MEDICAL NEGLIGENCE AGAINST NHS HOSPITAL
AND COMMUNITY DOCTORS AND DENTISTS

This circular will be cancelled and deleted from the current communications index on 1 December 1993 unless notified separately.

SUMMARY

This circular describes the arrangements to apply from 1 January 1990
to the handling of claims of negligence against medical and dental staff
employed in the hospital and community health services. General
practitioners are not directly affected by these new arrangements,
unless they have a contract of employment (for example, as a hospital
practitioner) with a health authority.

ACTION REQUIRED

Health authorities are asked, with effect from 1 January 1990, to:
i)   assume responsibility for new and existing claims of medical
     negligence;
ii) ensure a named officer has sufficient authority to make decisions on
     the conduct of cases on the Authority's behalf;
iii) cease to require their medical and dental staff to subscribe to a
     recognised professional defence organisation and cease to reimburse
     two-thirds of medical defence subscriptions;
iv) encourage their medical and dental staff to ensure they have ade-
     quate defence cover as appropriate;
v)   distribute urgently to all their medical and dental staff, including
     those with honorary NHS contracts, copies of a leaflet explaining
     the new arrangements (which will be sent separately).

HANDLING CLAIMS OF MEDICAL NEGLIGENCE

Claims lodged on or after 1 January 1990

1. Health authorities, as corporate bodies, are legally liable for the negligent acts of their employees in the course of their NHS employment. From 1 January 1990 health authorities will also be formally responsible for the handling and financing of claims of negligence against their medical and dental staff. With regard to claims lodged on or after 1 January 1990, it is for each health authority to determine how it wishes claims against its medical or dental staff to be handled. Health authorities may wish to make use of the services of the medical defence organisations (at rates to be agreed), but they may also put the work out to other advisers or deal with it in-house, provided they have the necessary expertise.

Claims notified to an MDO before 1 January 1990

2. Subject to final agreement with the medical defence organisations (MDOs) on the detailed financial arrangements, health authorities will take over financial responsibility for cases outstanding at 1 January 1990. The medical defence organisations have been asked to inform health authorities of the cases in which they may have a substantial liability.

3. Health authorities are entitled to take over the management of any cases outstanding, since they will become liable for the costs and damages arising. However, they are strongly advised to employ the MDOs to continue to handle such claims, in consultation with them and on their behalf, until completion. This is essential not only because of the amount of work in progress, but mainly because the re-insurance cover of the MDOs for claims initiated before 1990 would remain valid only if the MDO currently handling the case continued to do so. If required, health authorities should co-operate with an MDO's re-insurers in the conduct of a claim. Since some of the cover is on an aggregate basis the advice in this paragraph applies to both large and small claims. Health authorities are asked to give prior notice to the Department (finance contact point at paragraph 17) where they wish to adopt a different approach in the handling of claims notified before 1 January 1990.

General handling principles

4. Health authorities should take the essential decisions on the handling of claims of medical negligence against their staff, using MDOs or other bodies as their agents and advisers. Authorities should particularly ensure that authority is appropriately delegated to enable decisions to

be made promptly, especially where representatives are negotiating a settlement, and are asked to give such authority to a named officer.

5. . . . They should also have clear regard to:

(i) any point of principle or of wider application raised by the case; and

(ii) the costs involved.

6. Where a case involves both a health authority and a general medical practitioner (or any other medical or dental practitioner in relation to work for which a health authority is not responsible), the health authority should consult with the practitioner(s) cited or their representative to seek agreement on how the claim should be handled. Where a health authority (or its employees) alone is cited, but there is reason to believe that the action or inaction of a practitioner outside the health authority's responsibility was a material factor in the negligence concerned, the health authority should similarly consult with a view to obtaining a contribution to the eventual costs and damages. Conversely, in cases where such a practitioner alone is cited, there may be circumstances in which an MDO asks the health authority to make a similar contribution, as if it were a defendant. In any such circumstances, health authorities should co-operate fully in the formulation of the defence and should seek to reach agreement out of court on the proportion in which any costs and damages awarded to the plaintiff should be borne. . . . .

COVERAGE OF THE SCHEME AND PRACTICAL ARRANGEMENTS

8. The Health Departments' views on some of the questions that have arisen about the coverage and practical operation of the new arrangements are at Annex A. The indemnity scheme applies to all staff in the course of their HCHS employment, including those engaged through private agencies. The Annex is to be reproduced as a leaflet, which the Health Departments will shortly be making available to health authorities who should distribute them to all their medical and dental staff, including those with honorary NHS contracts.

9. Since authorities will be taking financial responsibility in cases of medical negligence it will no longer be necessary for them to require employed staff to subscribe to a recognised professional defence organisation, for example, as in the recommended form of consultant contract at Annex D of PM(79)11. Authorities should inform their

medical and dental staff that the provision no longer applies, but they should encourage such staff to ensure that they have adequate defence cover as appropriate.

FINANCIAL ARRANGEMENTS

Pooling arrangements for major settlements

10. Where they have not already done so RHAs are strongly recommended to introduce arrangements (for both medical and non-medical negligence) so as to share with Districts the legal costs and damages of individual large settlements or awards, whose incidence can be quite random. The Department will be making arrangements for Authorities without an RHA, for example the London SHAs, to limit the financial effects on them of substantial settlements.

Funding of claims

11. Subject to final agreement with the MDOs, the public sector will have access to a share of the MDOs' reserves in respect of the hospital and community health services. It is expected that the MDOs will each establish a fund to be drawn on according to criteria set by the Health Departments. The Health Departments will be introducing a transitional scheme under which these reserves will be made available to assist health authorities to meet the costs of particularly large settlements. These will usually, but not necessarily, be cases which arose from incidents before 1 January 1990. The Departments propose to set a threshold, initially £300,000 in England and Wales; 80 per cent of the costs of a settlement above this threshold, including the legal costs, would be met from this source, until the identified funds are exhausted. Detailed information on the means of access to the funds will be given in the December 1989 edition of 'Financial Matters'.

NHS TRUSTS

12. NHS Trusts will be responsible for claims of negligence against their medical and dental staff. The Departments are considering what arrangements will apply to NHS Trusts and further guidance will be issued in due course.

MONITORING RESOURCE CONSEQUENCES

13. To enable the Department of Health to assess the resource consequences of these changes, health authorities will be required to submit a return (in the form set out at Annex B) shortly after the end of each financial year, starting with the period 1 January – 31 March 1990 in order to obtain an early indication of the costs of the scheme.

REVIEW

14. The Health Department plan to review the operation of these arrangements in 1992, including the effects on individual practitioners.

CANCELLATION OF EXISTING GUIDANCE

15. Circulars HM(54)32 and HM(54)43 will be cancelled from 1 January 1990. Paragraph 4 (iii) of Annex 1 of EL(89)P/148 (Hospital medical and dental staff: Locum tenens engaged through private agencies) will be cancelled from 1 January 1990.

16. Paragraph 310 of the Terms and Conditions of Service for Hospital Medical and Dental Staff, and paragraph 289 of the Terms and Conditions of Service for Doctors in Community Medicine and the Community Health Service, (the two-thirds reimbursement scheme) shall not have effect after 31 December 1989.

17. Enquiries which cannot be dealt with by RHAs should be addressed as follows:

General
Mr A Doole
FPS1A2
Room 426 Portland Court
158–176 Great Portland Street
London W1N 5TB

Tel: 01–872–9302
Ext. 48306

Finance
Mr M Horah
FA2
Room 629 Friars House
157–168 Blackfriars Road
London SE1 8EU

Tel: 01–972–2000
Ext 23024

From:
Family Practitioner Services Division 1A
Portland Court
158–176 Great Portland Street
London W1N 5TB

Further copies of this Circular may be obtained from DHSS Store, Health Publications Unit, No 2 Site, Manchester Road, Heywood, Lancs OL10 2PZ quoting code and serial number appearing at top right-hand corner.

ANNEX A
(BC(89)34)

MEDICAL NEGLIGENCE: NEW NHS ARRANGEMENTS

Introduction
1. New arrangements for dealing with medical negligence claims in the hospital and community health services are being introduced from 1 January 1990. Subject to final agreement with the medical defence organisations on the financial arrangements, health authorities will take direct financial responsibility for cases initiated before that date, as well as for new claims. In future, medical and dental staff employed by health authorities (health boards in Scotland and Northern Ireland) will no longer be required under the terms of their contracts to subscribe to a medical defence organisation. However, the health authority indemnity will cover only health authority responsibilities. The Health Departments advise practitioners to maintain their defence body membership in order to ensure they are covered for any work which does not fall within the scope of the indemnity scheme.

Set out below are the Health Departments' replies to some of the questions most commonly asked about the operation of the new arrangements.

2. Why is this change necessary?
Medical defence subscriptions rose rapidly in the 1980s, because of growth both in the number of medical negligence cases and in the size of the awards made by the courts. Subscriptions tripled between 1986 and 1988, and the Doctors' and Dentists' Review Body concluded that to take account of the increase in subscriptions through practitioners' pay would lead to distortions in pay and pensions. The pressure to relate subscription rates to the practitioner's speciality underlined the difficulty of maintaining the system. The Health Departments issued in March 1989 a proposal for a health authority indemnity. The new arrangements follow discussions with the medical defence organisations, the medical profession, health authority management and other interested bodies.

Coverage
3. Who is covered by the health authority indemnity scheme?
Health authorities as employers are liable at law for the negligence (acts or omissions) of their staff in the course of their NHS employment. The legal position is the same for medical and dental staff as for other NHS employees, but for many years doctors and dentists have themselves taken out medical defence cover through the three medical defence

organisations (MDOs). Under the indemnity scheme, health authorities will take direct responsibility for costs and damages arising from medical negligence where they (as employers) are vicariously liable for the acts and omissions of their medical and dental staff.

4. *Does this include clinical academics and research workers?*
Health authorities are vicariously liable for the work done by university medical staff and other research workers under their honorary contracts in the course of their NHS duties, but not for pre-clinical or other work in the university.

5. *Is private work in NHS hospitals covered by the indemnity scheme?*
Health authorities will not be responsible for a consultant's private practice, even in an NHS hospital. However, where junior medical staff are involved in the care of private patients in NHS hospitals, they would normally be doing so as part of their contract with the health authority. It remains advisable that any junior doctor who might be involved in any work outside the scope of his or her employment should have medical defence (or insurance) cover.

6. *Is Category 2 work covered?*
Category 2 work (eg reports for insurance companies) is by definition not undertaken for the employing health authority, and will therefore not be covered by the indemnity scheme; medical defence cover would be appropriate.

7. *Are GMC disciplnary proceedings covered?*
Health authorities should not be financially responsible for the defence of medical staff involved in the GMC disciplinary proceedings. It is the responsibility of the practitioner concerned to take out medical defence cover against such an eventuality.

8. *Is a hospital doctor doing a GP locum covered?*
This would not be the reponsibility of the health authority, since it would be general practice. The hospital doctor and the general practitioners concerned should ensure that there is appropriate medical defence cover.

9. *Is a GP seeing his own patient in hospital covered?*
A GP providing medical care to patients in hospital under a contractual arrangement, eg where the GP was employed as a clinical assistant, will be covered by the health authority indemnity. On the other hand, if the health authority is essentially providing only hotel services and the patient(s) remain in the care of the GP, the GP would be responsible and medical defence cover would be appropriate.

10. *Are GP trainees working in general practice covered?*
In general practice the responsibility for training and for paying the
salary of a GP trainee rests with the trainer (with funds from the FPC).
Where the trainee's medical defence subscription is higher than the
subscription of an SHO in the hospital service, he or she may apply
through the trainer for the difference in subscription to be reimbursed.
While the trainee is receiving a salary in general practice it is advisable
that both the trainee and the trainer, and indeed other members of the
practice, should have medical defence cover.

11. Are clinical trials covered?

The new arrangements do not alter the current legal position. If the
health authority was responsible for a clinical trial authorised under the
Medicines Act 1968 or its subordinate legislation and that trial was
carried out by or on behalf of a doctor involving NHS patients of his,
such a doctor would be covered by the indemnity scheme. Similarly, for
a trial not involving medicines, the health authority would take financial
responsibility unless the trial were covered by such other indemnity as
may have been agreed between the health authority and those responsible for the trial. In any case, health authorities should take steps to
make sure that they are informed of clinical trials in which their staff are
taking part in their NHS employment and that these trials have the
required Research Ethics Committee approval.

12. *Would a doctor be covered if he was working other than in
accordance with the duties of his post?*
Such a doctor would be covered by the health authority indemnity for
actions in the course of NHS employment, and this should be interpreted liberally. For work not covered in this way the doctor may have a
civil, or even in extreme circumstances criminal, liability for his actions.

13. *Are doctors attending accident victims ('Good Samaritan' acts)
covered?*
By definition, 'Good Samaritan' acts are not part of the doctor's work
for the employing authority. Medical defence organisations are willing
to provide low-cost cover against the (unusual) event of a doctor
performing such an act being sued for negligence.

14. *Are doctors in public health medicine or in community health
services doing work for local authorities covered? Are occupational
physicians covered?*
Doctors in public health medicine, or clinical medical officers, carrying
out local authority functions under their health authority contract
would be acting in the course of their NHS employment. They will
therefore be covered by the health authority indemnity. The same

principle applies to occupational physicians employed by health authorities.

15. *Will NHS hospital doctors working for other agencies, eg the Prison Service, be covered?*
In general, health authorities will not be financially responsible for the acts of NHS staff when they are working on a contractual basis for other agencies. (Conversely, they will be responsible where, for example, a Ministry of Defence doctor works in an NHS hospital.) Either the agency commissioning the work would be responsible, or the doctor should have medical defence cover. However, health authorities' indemnity should cover work for which they pay a fee, such as domiciliary visits and family planning services.

16. *Are retired doctors covered?*
The health authority indemnity will apply to acts or omissions in the course of NHS employment, regardless of when the claim was notified. Health authorities will thus cover doctors who have subsequently left the Service, but they may seek their co-operation in statements in the defence of a case.

17. *Are doctors offering services to voluntary bodies such as the Red Cross or hospices covered?*
The health authority would be responsible for the doctor's actions only if the health authority were responsible for the medical staffing of the voluntary body. If not, the doctors concerned may wish to ensure that they have medical defence cover, as they do at present.

18. *Will a health authority provide cover for a locum hospital doctor?*
A health authority will take financial responsibility for the acts and omissions of a locum doctor, whether 'internal' or provided by an external agency.

19. *Are private sector rotations for hospital staff covered?*
The medical staff of independent hospitals are responsible for their own medical defence cover, subject to the requirements of the hospital managers. If NHS staff in the training grades work in independent hospitals as part of their NHS training, they would be covered by the health authority indemnity, provided that such work was covered by an NHS contract.

20. *Will academic General Practice be covered?*
The Health Departments have no plans to extend the health authority indemnity to academic departments of general practice. In respect of general medical services FPCs will be making payments by fees and

allowances which include an element for expenses, of which medical defence subscriptions are a part.

Practical arrangements
21. *On what basis will medical defence organisations handle claims for health authorities?*
MDOs, in advising on claims for health authorities, will act as their agents; the charging arrangements for such services are for agreement between the MDO and the Authority concerned.

22. *Will doctors be reimbursed by MDOs for the 'unexpired' portion of their subscriptions?*
This is a matter between each MDO and its members.

23. *Will membership of a medical defence organisation continue to be a contractual obligation?*
On an individual basis doctors and dentists may wish to continue their membership in order to receive the cover referred to in paragraphs 5–20 above, as well as the other legal and advisory services provided by the MDOs. The Health Departments are advising health authorities that they should no longer require their medical and dental staff to subscribe to an MDO, but a health authority could require a doctor to be a member of an MDO if the doctor were to be carrying out private work on NHS premises. The two thirds reimbursement of subscriptions will cease at the end of 1989.

24. *Will medical defence subscriptions be tax-allowable in future?*
The Health Departments understand that medical defence subscriptions will continue to be allowable under income tax rules.

25. *What happens if a doctor wishes to contest a claim which the health authority would prefer to settle out of court, eg where a point of principle or a doctor's reputation is at stake?*
While the final decision in a case rests with the health authority since it will bear the financial consequences, it should take careful note of the practitioner's view. Health authorities may seek the advice of the relevant MDO on whether a case should be contested, and they should not settle cases without good cause.

26. *If a doctor wishes to have separate representation in a case, what would be the extent of his liability?*
Since it is the health authority which is sued for the medical negligence of its staff and which will in future be solely financially liable, then it must have the ultimate right to decide how the defence of a case is to be handled. Subject to this, a health authority may welcome a practitioner

being separately advised in a case without cost to the health authority. However, if a practitioner claims that his interests in any case are distinct from those of the health authority and wishes to be separately represented in the proceedings, he will need the agreement of the plaintiff, the health authority and the court. If liability is established, he would have to pay not only his own legal expenses but also any further costs incurred as a result of his being separately represented. The health authority would remain liable for the full award of damages to the plaintiff.

27. *Will health authorities put restrictions on the clinical autonomy of doctors?*
Health authorities have a responsibility to organise services in a manner which is in the best interests of patients. In the past, medical defence organisations have advised doctors and dentists on patterns of practice carrying unacceptable dangers to patients. However, there is no question of health authorities barring certain services which carry risks but are a high priority for patients.

28. *Will health authorities be able to secure statements from doctors for the defence of a case of medical negligence?*
Health authorities will need co-operation from medical and dental staff if they are to defend cases. As part of this, practitioners should supply such statements or documents as the health authority or its solicitors may reasonably require in investigating or defending any claim. A doctor's refusal without good reason to provide a statement could result in the health authority being unable to defend itself properly and so incurring additional costs.

29. *Will health authorities be able to trace doctors who formerly worked for them?*
It is accepted that health authorities may have difficulty in tracing the doctors responsible, especially if they were junior medical staff at the time, and in securing statements from them; they may find the MDOs helpful in this respect. Often, however, good medical records kept at the time will be of more value than statements made some years after the event.

30. *Will the new arrangements apply to NHS Trust hospitals (self-governing units)?*
As employers, NHS Trusts will be vicariously liable for the acts of their employed medical and dental staff, and will take the financial responsibility for negligence. Further guidance will be issued in due course.

Financial effects
31. *How can District Health Authorities meet damages which could be as much as £1m for a single case?*
RHAs have been asked to make arrangements under which they will provide an element of cost-sharing with Districts for medical negligence costs above a certain level, as most RHAs do for non-medical negligence actions at present. And for a transitional period health authorities will have access (under certain criteria) to some of the reserves of the MDOs.

32. *The incidence of medical negligence damages may be uneven as between Regions; how will that be met?*
It is quite likely that some Regions will have to pay out more under the new arrangements then they would in reimbursing two-thirds of medical defence subscriptions. The funds from the MDO will be of some help in the short term, but in the longer run the incidence of medical negligence costs and damages will fall on the Regions where they arise.

UK Health Departments
December 1989

ANNEX B
(HC(89)34)

INFORMATION TO BE RETURNED ANNUALLY, NO LATER
THAN 31 MAY (STARTING 31/5/90)

1. The following information should be supplied for the previous
financial year:

i.   The number of claims of medical negligence against the health
     authority and/or its employees, including the number of cases
     brought forward from an earlier period;
ii. The number of such cases settled during the period with the health
     authority's costs, including damages payable, in the following cost
     bands:

Number of cases	£	£
(a)		0–100,000
(b)		100,000–200,000
(c)		200,000–300,000
(d)		over £300,000

iii. The total cost of the settlements reached or awards made;
     distinguishing

   a) the Authority's costs from the payment of the plaintiff's costs
      and damages; and
   b) an estimate of costs and damages attributable to medical
      negligence, as distinct from negligence of other staff.

2. Returns to be sent to: FPSIA2
                          Room 426 Portland Court
                          158–176 Great Portland Street
                          London W1N 5TB

Useful organisations

(The authors are grateful to AVMA for providing their list of useful organisations, upon which this is based).

Afterwards
380–384 Harrow Road
London W9 2HU
Tel: 0171-266 2300 (support line)

Baby Life Support Systems (BLISS)
17–32 Emerald Street
London WC1N 3QL
Tel: 0171-831 9393/8996

National Back Pain Association
16 Elmtree Road
Teddington
Middlesex TW11 8ST
Tel: 0181-977 5474

Birth Trauma Support Group
27 Harrow Road
Armthorpe
Doncaster DN3 3HU
Tel: 01302 831040

Royal National Institute for the Blind (RNIB)
224 Great Portland Street
London W1N 6AA
Tel: 0171-388 1266

The National Association for Children with Lower Limb Abnormalities
(STEPS)
15 Statham Close
Lymm
Cheshire WA13 9NN
Tel: 01925 757525

The Compassionate Friends (counselling for bereaved parents)
National Office
53 North Street
Bristol BS3 1EN
Tel: 0117-953 9639 (helpline)
    0117-966 5202 (admin)

BACUP (helping people live with cancer)
3 Bath Place
Rivington Street
London EC2A 3JR
Tel: 0800 181199 (outside London)
0171 613 2121 (inside London)
0171 696 9000 (counselling service)

Child Bereavement Trust
1 Millside
Riversdale
Bourne End
Buckinghamshire SL8 5EB

The British Digestive Foundation
3 St Andrew's Place
London NW1 4LB
Tel: 0171-486 0341

United Response (offering community-based residential services and
support for people in their own homes)
162/164 Upper Richmond Road
Putney
London SW15 2SL
Tel: 0181-780 9686

Disability Law Service (free advice for the disabled on legal matters,
benefits and grants)
16 Princeton Street
London WC1R 4BB
Tel: 0171-831 8031

Disabled Living Foundation
380–384 Harrow Road
London W9 2HU
Tel: 0171-289 6111

The National Endometriosis Society
35 Belgrave Square
London SW1X 8QB
Tel: 0171-235 4137 (crisis support line 7pm – 10pm)

British Epilepsy Association
Anstey House
40 Hanover Square
Leeds LS3 1BE
Tel: 0113-243 9494

International Glaucoma Association
King's College Hospital
Denmark Hill
London SE5 9RS
Tel: 0171 737 3265

Headway
National Head Injuries Association
200 Mansfield Road
Nottingham NG1 3XH
Tel: 0115-962 2382

The IRIS Fund
York House, Ground Floor
199 Westminster Bridge Road
London SE1 7UT
Tel: 0171 928 7743/7919

National Kidney Federation
6 Stanley Street
Worksop
Notts. S81 7HU
Tel: 01909 487 794

The British Lung Foundation
8 Peterborough Mews
London SW6 3BL
Tel: 0171 371 7704

Lupus UK
Queen's Court
9 – 17 Eastern Road
Romford
Essex RM1 3NG
Tel: 01708 731251

The National Meningitis Trust
Fern House
Bath Road
Stroud
Glos. LG5 3TJ
Tel: 01453 755049 (welfare helpline)

National Association for Mental Health (MIND)
22 Harley Street
London W1N 2ED
Tel: 0171 637 0741

Motor Neurone Disease Association (MNDA)
PO Box 246
Northampton NN1 2PR
Tel: 01604 250505 or 01604 22269 (24-hour service)

Muscular Dystrophy Group
7–11 Prescott Place
London SW4 6BS
Tel: 0171-720 8055

The Myalgic Encephalomyelitis (ME) Association
Stanhope House
High Street
Stanford-le-Hope
Essex SS17 0HA
Tel: 01375 642466

The Narcolepsy Association (UK)
South Hall
High Street
Barmingham
Kent DA4 0DE
Tel: 01322 863056

The Association for Post-Natal Illness
25 Jerdan Place
Fulham
London SW6 1BE
Tel: 0171-386 0868 (10-5 Monday – Friday)

Reynaud's and Scleroderma Association
112 Crewe Road
Alsager
Cheshire ST7 2JA
Tel: 01270 872776

Scope (formerly the Spastics Society)
12 Park Crescent
London W1N 4EQ
Tel: 0800 626216 (1–7 pm daily)

Stillbirth Neonatal Death Society (SANDS)
28 Portland Place
London W1N 4DE
Tel: 0171-436 5881

Index

372 *Index*

general practitioner, 193
health authority, 193–194
NHS trust, 194
potential defendants, obtaining
  records from, 51
Natural causes
  medical inquest verdict, 227
Negligence
  formulating allegations of, 88
  meaning, 20
  See also Medical negligence
Negotiation, *See* Settlement
Nervous shock
  compensatory damages, 149
No-fault liability, 238
Non-defendant
  obtaining records from, before
    proceedings commence, 54
Notes. *See* Records
Numbers of expert witnesses,
  124–125
Nursing staff
  contractual duty of care, 12–13

Occupational therapy
  future losses and expenses, 168
Ogden tables, 156–157
Order
  pre-action discovery, relating to,
    53
  witness evidence, exchange of,
    132–133
Organisations, useful, 362–366
Organising records, 59

Pain and suffering
  compensatory damages, 146–147
Paramedical staff
  contractual duty of care owed by,
    12–13
Patient
  medical practitioner, relationship
    with, 2
  private, duty of care owed to,
    11–12
  questions of, answers for, 23
  true nature of illness concealed
    from, 63
Patient-held records, 54–55
Payment into court

negotiation of settlement,
  195–196
Payments on account
  Legal aid, 31
Peace of mind
  compensatory damages, 149–150
Pensioner
  Legal aid, financial eligibility
    for, 30
Person under disability. *See* Disability,
  person under
Physiotherapy
  future losses and expenses, 168
Place of trial, 126
Plaintiff
  discovery of, 123
  earnings, past loss of, 163
  limitation, effect of action on, 102
  service of schedule of, 124
  structured settlement, advantages
    and disadvantages of,
    201–202
Pleading
  approach, 106–107
  conclusion, 119
  full, 109–115
  further and better particulars,
    generally, 115–116
    giving, 117–118
    requesting, 116–117
  interrogatories, 118–119
  multipliers, 158–159
  See also Statement of claim
Post mortem examination, 219
Prayer
  statement of claim, structure of,
    115
Pre-action discovery
  application for, 52
  costs, 53
  order, 53
  right to, 50
  service of summons, 52–53
  voluntary, 50–51
  See also Records
Pre-exchange conference
  conduct of, 139–140
  counsel's preparation for, 139
  experts, with, organisation of,
    136–137